GODLAND

VOLUME FOUR
AMPLIFIED NOW

CO-CREATORS
JOE CASEY
TOM SCIOLI

COLORS
NICK FILARDI

LETTERS
RUS WOOTON

DESIGN
DREW GILL

COVER DESIGN
RICHARD STARKINGS & COMICRAFT

IMAGE COMICS, INC.

Robert Kirkman - Chief Operating Officer
Erik Larsen - Chief Financial Officer
Todd McFarlane - President
Marc Silvestri - Chief Executive Officer
Jim Valentino - Vice-President
ericstephenson - Publisher
Joe Keatinge - PR & Marketing Coordinator

Branwyn Bigglestone - Accounts Manager
Tyler Shainline - Administrative Assistant
Traci Hui - Traffic Manager
Allen Hui - Production Manager
Drew Gill - Production Artist
Jonathan Chan - Production
Monica Howard - Production

TML

www.imagecomics.com

THOSE WE'VE MET BEFORE

ADAM ARCHER

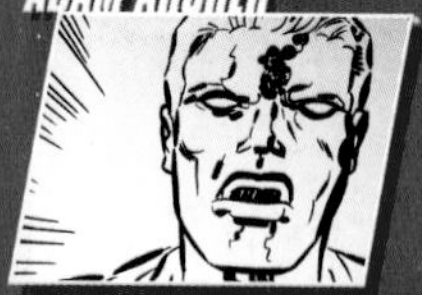

NEELA ARCHER

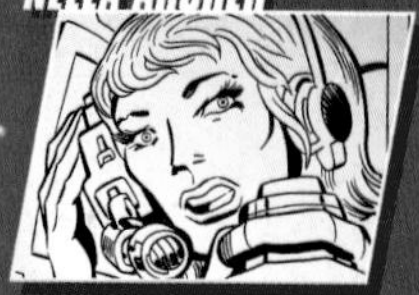

ANGIE ARCHER

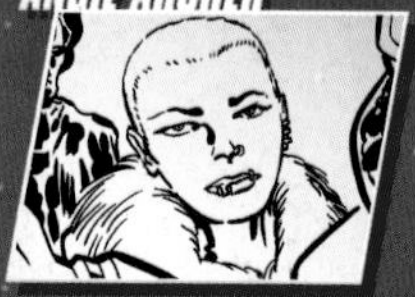

STELLA ARCHER

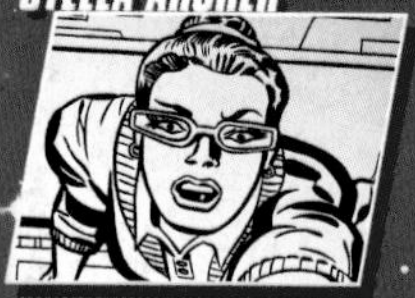

MAXIM

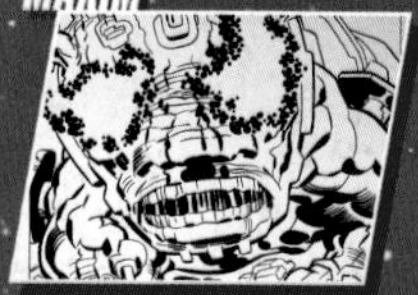

CRASHMAN

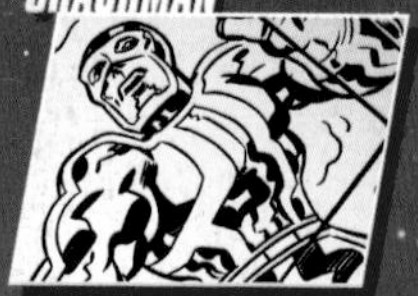

BASIL DISCORDIA

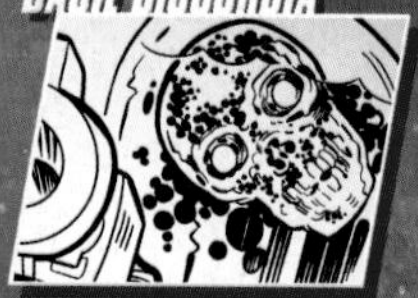

THE TORMENTOR

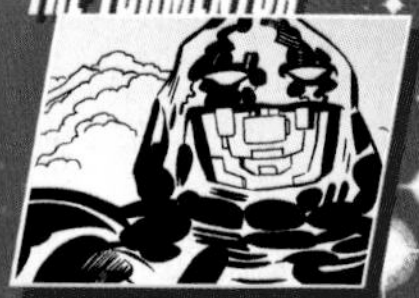

THE SAVAGE STING

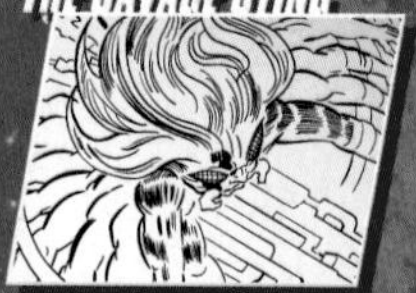

THE TRIAD

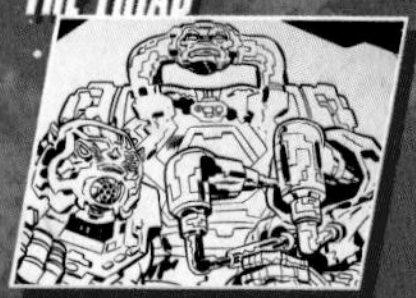

THE STORY SO FAR

Commander ADAM ARCHER is a former NASA astronaut who possesses incredible cosmic powers -- the unexpected result of a failed mission to Mars. He lives in Manhattan with his sisters, NEELA, STELLA and ANGIE, in a hi-tech facility built by the U.S. government known as the INFINITY TOWER.

While investigating a mysterious meteor crash at the Great Wall of China, Commander Archer is the first to encounter a visiting alien lifeform that he soon suspects has come in peace. That peace is shattered when the super-villain junkie, BASIL CRONUS, arrives on the scene to confiscate the alien for his own hallucinogenic experiments. Adam soon launches an all-out assault on Basil's deep sea sub lab, freeing the captive alien, appropriately named MAXIM, in the process. Although he loses his head in the melee, Basil escapes Adam's retribution via blind teleportation. Unfortunately, Basil -- head and body still separated -- falls into the possession of rival super-villain, FRIEDRICH NICKELHEAD.

Meanwhile, Adam discovers that sister NEELA -- also a former NASA astronaut experiencing rising resentment toward her brother -- has embarked on a solo rescue mission to free America's most cherished hero (and Adam's rival for the general public's respect and affection), CRASHMAN, who was kidnapped by the self-styled "Queen of Pain", DISCORDIA. Before Adam can get to her, Neela soon joins Crashman in captivity. Thankfully, Adam rescues them both Discordia is placed into custody. However, after being found guilty by a jury of her peers (yeah, right!) in a Federal court, Discordia shocks the world when her head inexplicably explodes on live television, killing her instantly. Simultaneously, Neela has willfully allied herself with an independent, privately owned space flight program.

As a giant "Eff you" to his former employer, THE TORMENTOR, Nickelhead performs unholy "jar head replacement surgery"... resulting in Basil's head residing on Discordia's body (Discordia being the Tormentor's daughter)! Upon FedEx delivery to the Tormentor's European retreat, both the Tormentor and Basil vow revenge for this twisted affront.

Meanwhile, a group of galactic axe murderers travel to Earth with the explicit intent to destroy it before its cosmic emissary can fully "mature". Fusing their energy patterns with three human hosts, thus is born ED, SUPRA and EEG-OH... collectively known as THE TRIAD. Soon enough, they lay waste to -- and then occupy -- a secret military installation located in the Nevada desert.

To cover up Neela's rocket launch, the scientists behind the program trigger a continent-wide EMP. Unfortunately, this temporarily shuts down Adam Archer's cosmic abilities and he soon finds himself in Friedrich Nickelhead's clutches. Trapped in the basement of Nickelhead's Funhouse, Adam is bombarded by psychotropic imagery from his past, designed to break him down into a quivering puddle of flop sweat and tears. He escapes just in time to save New York City from KING JANUS, a seemingly immortal religious fanatic hell-bent on blowing both himself and his followers to hell in the name of a twisted god-being, using an enormous Pyramid Ship (equipped with a nasty detonation core).

Adam Archer succeeds in removing the detonation core and flying it out over the open sea. But, upon its detonation, Adam -- having been caught in the blast -- mysteriously disappears, along with King Janus' high-powered muscle, THE NEVER. After a surreal prison break from another dimension, Adam returns to Earth but is less than welcomed by the U.S. Army. The corridors of power now view Adam much more as a potential threat than a hero...

Meanwhile, the Triad is slowly moving toward their ultimate plan of planetary annihilation: a DOOMSDAY MISSILE that will burrow to the center of the Earth and trigger a chain reaction that will destroy everything. Simultaneously, NEELA ARCHER is herself transformed into a cosmic being and, using her newly acquired powers, begins to make brief visits to her home planet.

Finally, the government assesses their fractured relationship with Adam Archer and swiftly implements a plan to "contain" his cosmic power. Thus, the true nature of the Infinity Tower is revealed -- as it transforms into a secure prison that traps Adam, Maxim and Stella inside. Not even their combined cosmic abilities are able to spring them. At this point, the government plays their trump card, sending CRASHMAN in to, once and for all, deal with Commander Archer in an all-out grudge match.

Coincidentally, this clash of the titans is unfortunately interrupted by the Tormentor's plan for revenge on Adam -- he has "thawed out" one of Nicklehead's secret science experiments, a deadly beast named THE SAVAGE STING. She's hungry, guys...

(Of course, all this and more can be found in the first three collections in this series, GØDLAND VOL. 1: HELLO, COSMIC!, GØDLAND VOL. 2: ANOTHER SUNNY DELIGHT and GØDLAND VOL. 3: PROTO-PLASTIC PARTY. Available where all graphic novels are sold. Go out and buy it and enjoy the cosmic goodness!)

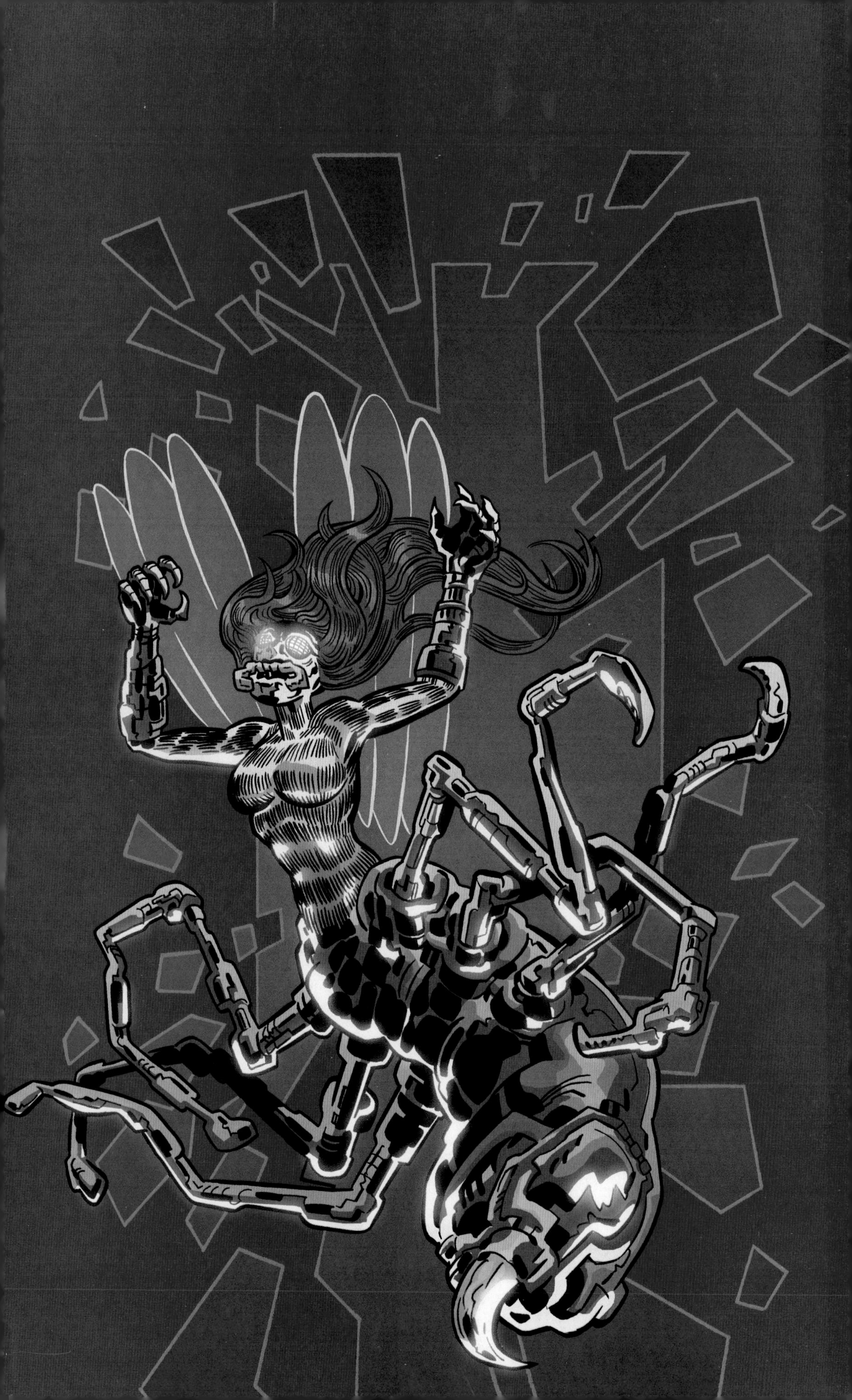

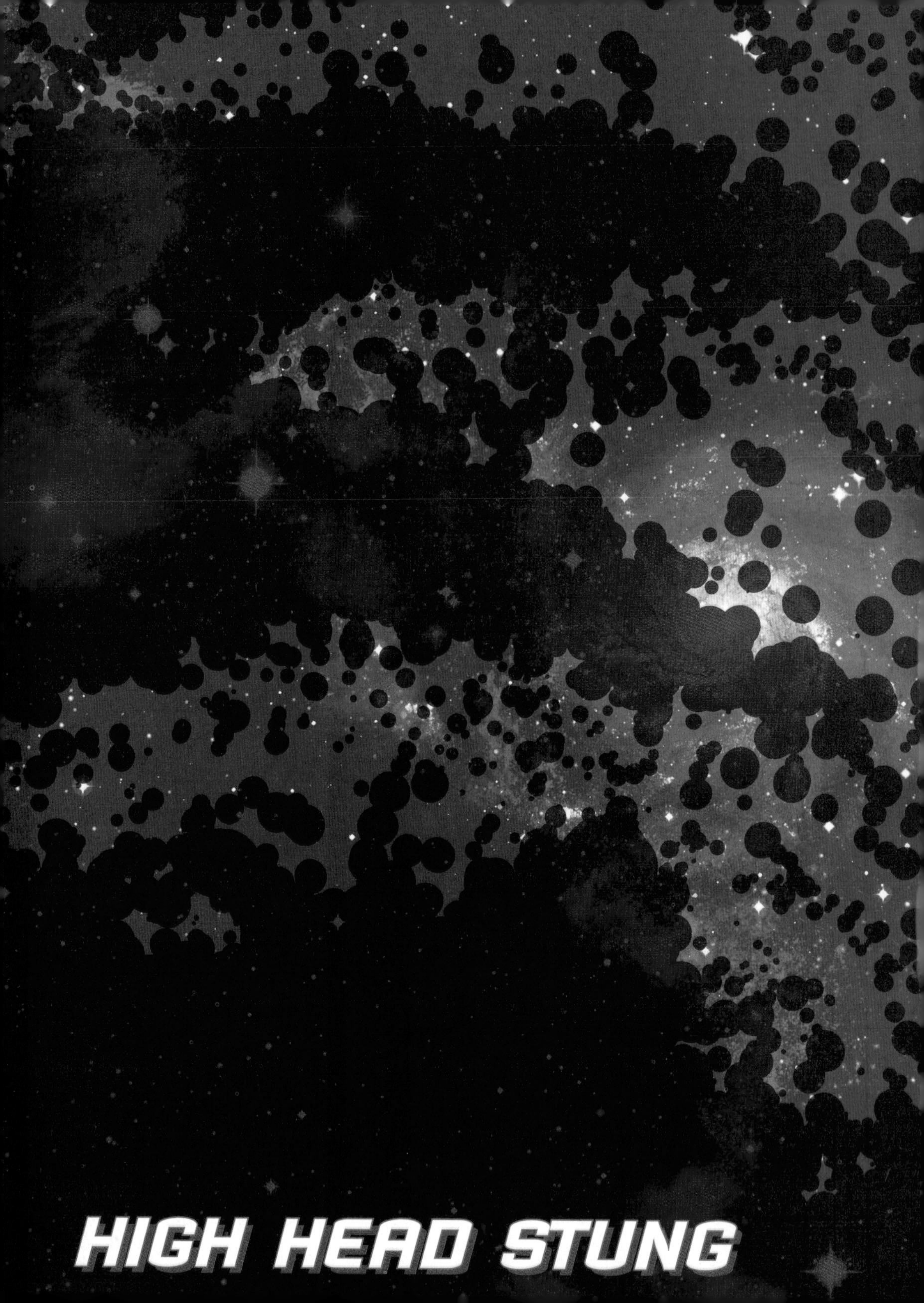

HIGH HEAD STUNG

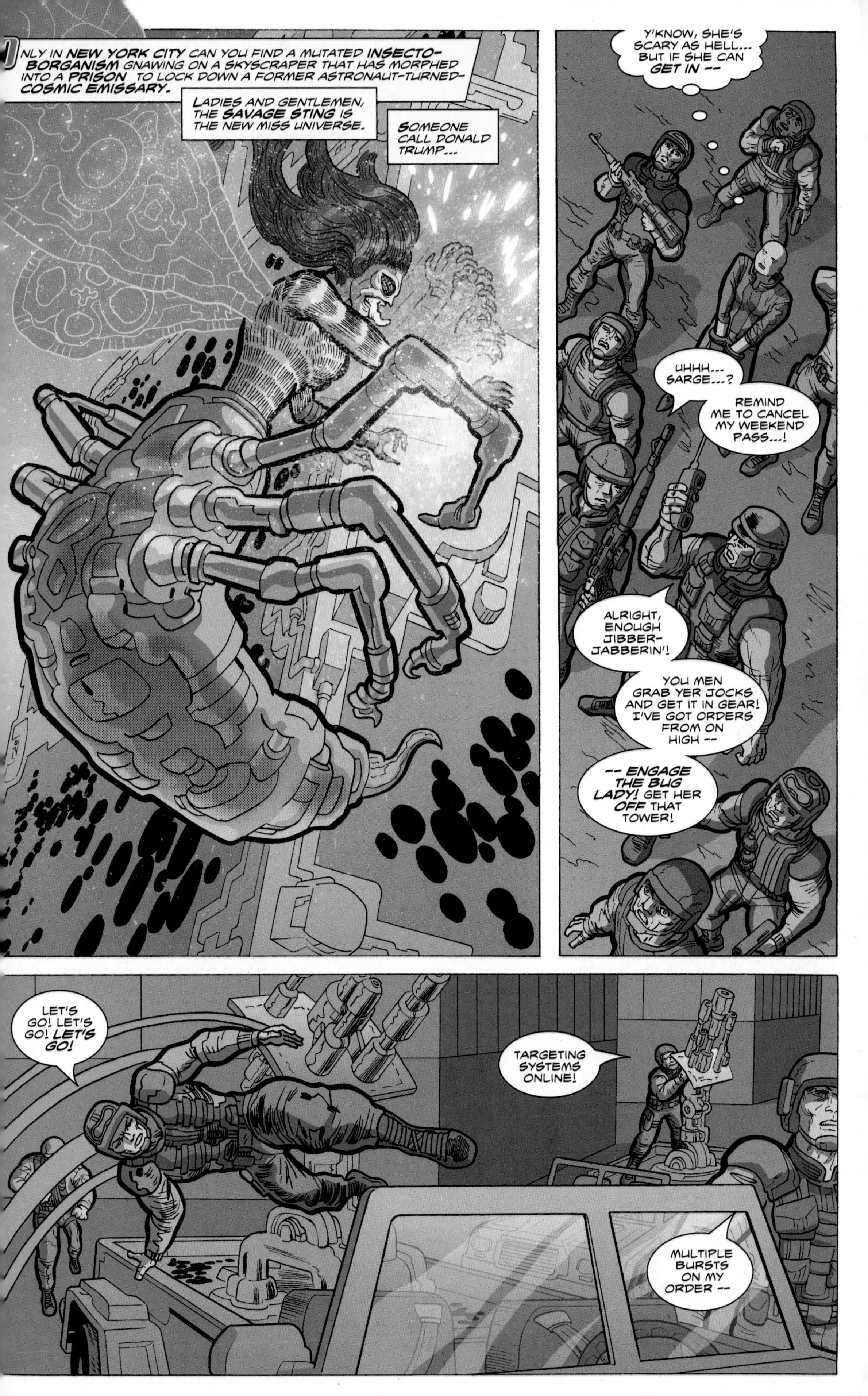
ONLY IN NEW YORK CITY CAN YOU FIND A MUTATED INSECTO-BORGANISM GNAWING ON A SKYSCRAPER THAT HAS MORPHED INTO A PRISON TO LOCK DOWN A FORMER ASTRONAUT-TURNED-COSMIC EMISSARY.
LADIES AND GENTLEMEN, THE SAVAGE STING IS THE NEW MISS UNIVERSE.
SOMEONE CALL DONALD TRUMP...
Y'KNOW, SHE'S SCARY AS HELL... BUT IF SHE CAN GET IN --
UHHH... SARGE...?
REMIND ME TO CANCEL MY WEEKEND PASS...!
ALRIGHT, ENOUGH JIBBER-JABBERIN'!
YOU MEN GRAB YER JOCKS AND GET IT IN GEAR! I'VE GOT ORDERS FROM ON HIGH --
-- ENGAGE THE BUG LADY! GET HER OFF THAT TOWER!
LET'S GO! LET'S GO! LET'S GO!
TARGETING SYSTEMS ONLINE!
MULTIPLE BURSTS ON MY ORDER --

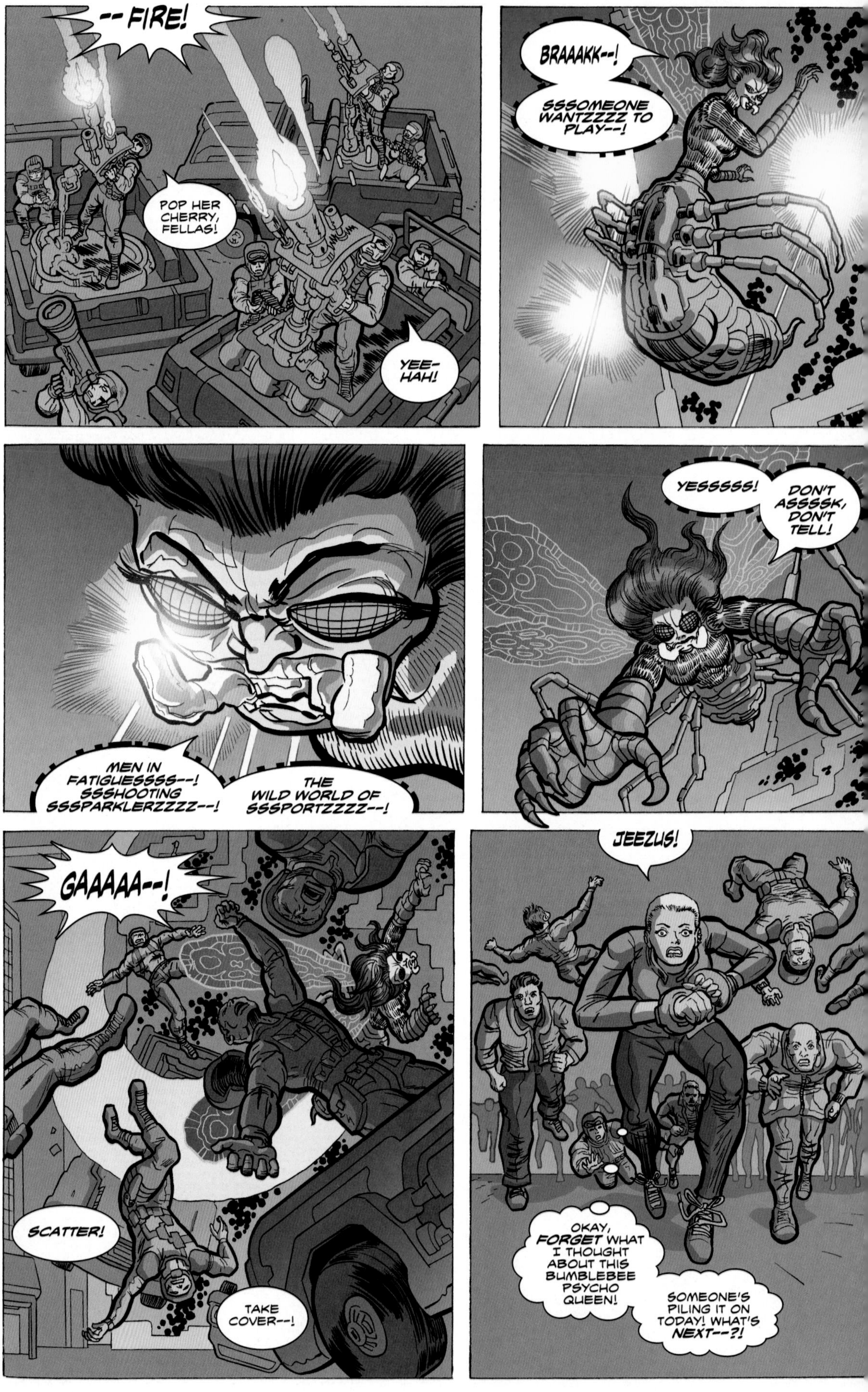
--FIRE!
POP HER CHERRY, FELLAS!
YEE-HAH!
BRAAAKK--!
SSSOMEONE WANTZZZZ TO PLAY--!
MEN IN FATIGUESSSS--! SSSHOOTING SSSPARKLERZZZZ--!
THE WILD WORLD OF SSSPORTZZZZ--!
YESSSSS!
DON'T ASSSSK, DON'T TELL!
GAAAAA--!
SCATTER!
TAKE COVER--!
JEEZUS!
OKAY, FORGET WHAT I THOUGHT ABOUT THIS BUMBLEBEE PSYCHO QUEEN!
SOMEONE'S PILING IT ON TODAY! WHAT'S NEXT--?!

NEVADA'S NOT A BAD PLACE TO VISIT, EITHER...

...ESPECIALLY IF YOU'RE IN THE MOOD TO SEE A GIGANTIC, ALIEN-DESIGNED *DOOMSDAY MISSILE* AIMED TOWARD THE CENTER OF THE EARTH.

NOT TO MENTION, THE THREE GALACTIC WORLD-KILLERS THAT *BUILT* IT...

THE TRIAD ABIDES...

....MOST OF THE TIME.

-ξSOB!ξ- -ξSOB!ξ-

AAHUUU--!

SUPRA! THIS UGLY DISPLAY OF EMOTION... THIS IS NOT THE TIME--!

AND YET... I AM SO *MOVED*...

YOU TWO ARE *PATHETIC!* REMEMBER WHAT YOU *ARE!* REMEMBER WHY WE ARE *HERE!*

OBSERVE AND REVEL IN THE GLORY AS I THROW THE *IGNITION SWITCH!*

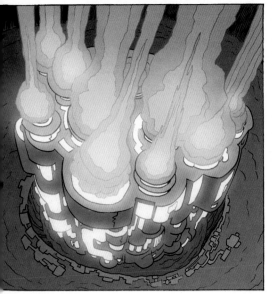

IT'S... BEAUTIFUL....

PIPE DOWN! THIS IS MERELY *STAGE ONE*--

-- IN WHICH THE MECHANISM TECHNOFORMS ITS OWN LAUNCH PLATFORM!

WITNESS, YOU BLUBBERING BABOONS! THE *DIRECTIONAL EXHAUST JETS* HAVE ACTIVATED -- INITIATING THE CLOCKWISE SPIN THAT WILL FACILITATE TERRESTRIAL PENETRATION!

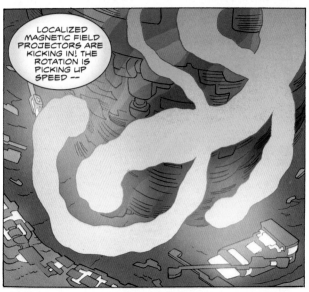

LOCALIZED MAGNETIC FIELD PROJECTORS ARE KICKING IN! THE ROTATION IS PICKING UP SPEED --

-- *SUCCESS!* THIS WEAKENED ROCK HAS OPENED ITSELF UP... THE MISSILE HAS BEGUN ITS DOOMSDAY DESCENT!

BOUNCE LOCATOR TECHNOLOGY ALLOWS US TO TRACK ITS *TRAJECTORY...* SEE HOW IT EASILY PASSES THROUGH THE OUTER LAYERS OF THIS PLANET'S CRUST --

-- SOON IT WILL ENGAGE THE *LITHOSPHERE* WITH SUPERIOR CONFIDENCE!

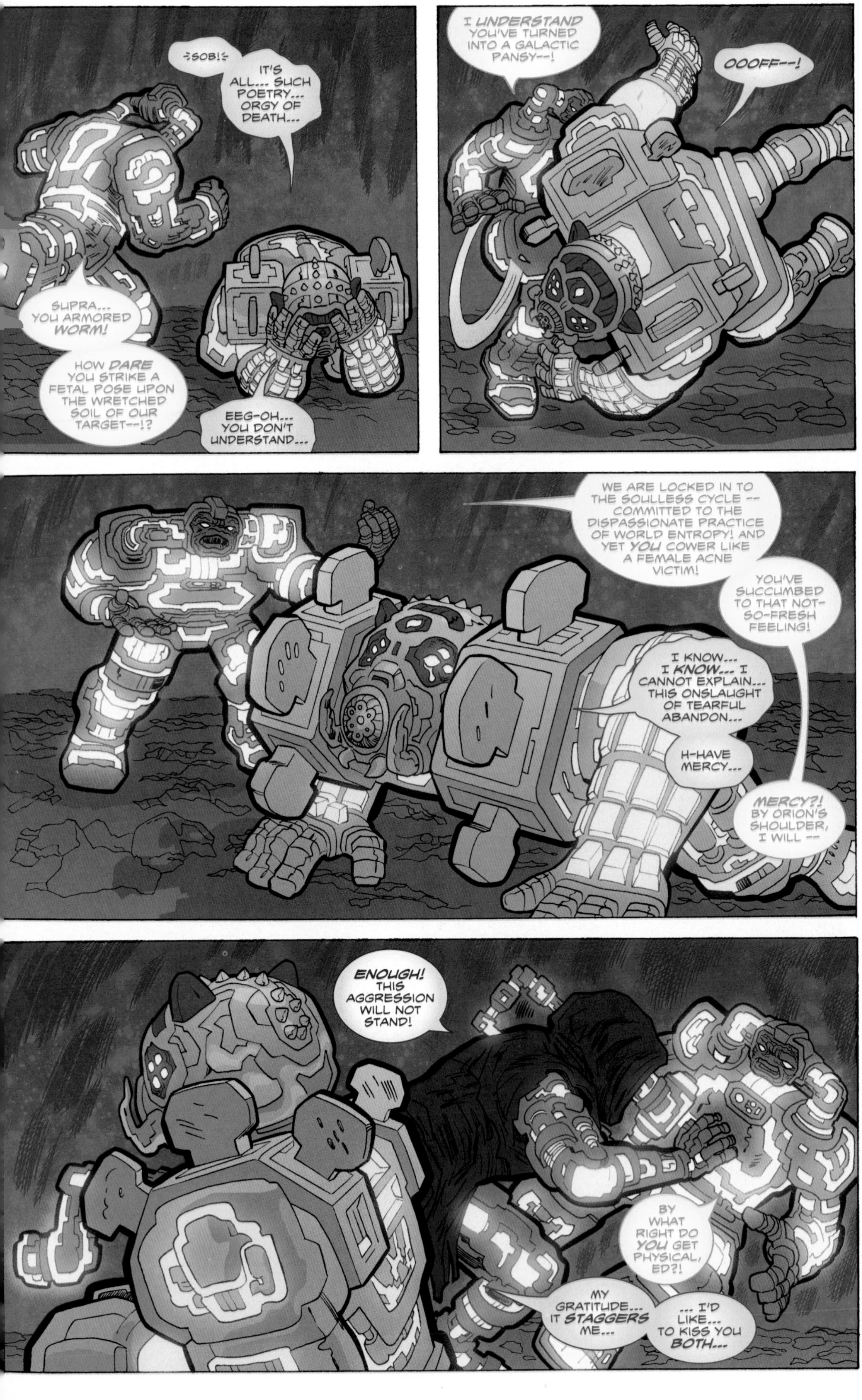

-SOB!-
IT'S ALL... SUCH POETRY... ORGY OF DEATH...
SUPRA... YOU ARMORED WORM!
HOW DARE YOU STRIKE A FETAL POSE UPON THE WRETCHED SOIL OF OUR TARGET--!?
EEG-OH... YOU DON'T UNDERSTAND...
I UNDERSTAND YOU'VE TURNED INTO A GALACTIC PANSY--!
OOOFF--!
WE ARE LOCKED IN TO THE SOULLESS CYCLE -- COMMITTED TO THE DISPASSIONATE PRACTICE OF WORLD ENTROPY! AND YET YOU COWER LIKE A FEMALE ACNE VICTIM!
YOU'VE SUCCUMBED TO THAT NOT-SO-FRESH FEELING!
I KNOW... I KNOW... I CANNOT EXPLAIN... THIS ONSLAUGHT OF TEARFUL ABANDON...
H-HAVE MERCY...
MERCY?! BY ORION'S SHOULDER, I WILL --
ENOUGH! THIS AGGRESSION WILL NOT STAND!
BY WHAT RIGHT DO YOU GET PHYSICAL, ED?!
MY GRATITUDE... IT STAGGERS ME...
... I'D LIKE... TO KISS YOU BOTH...

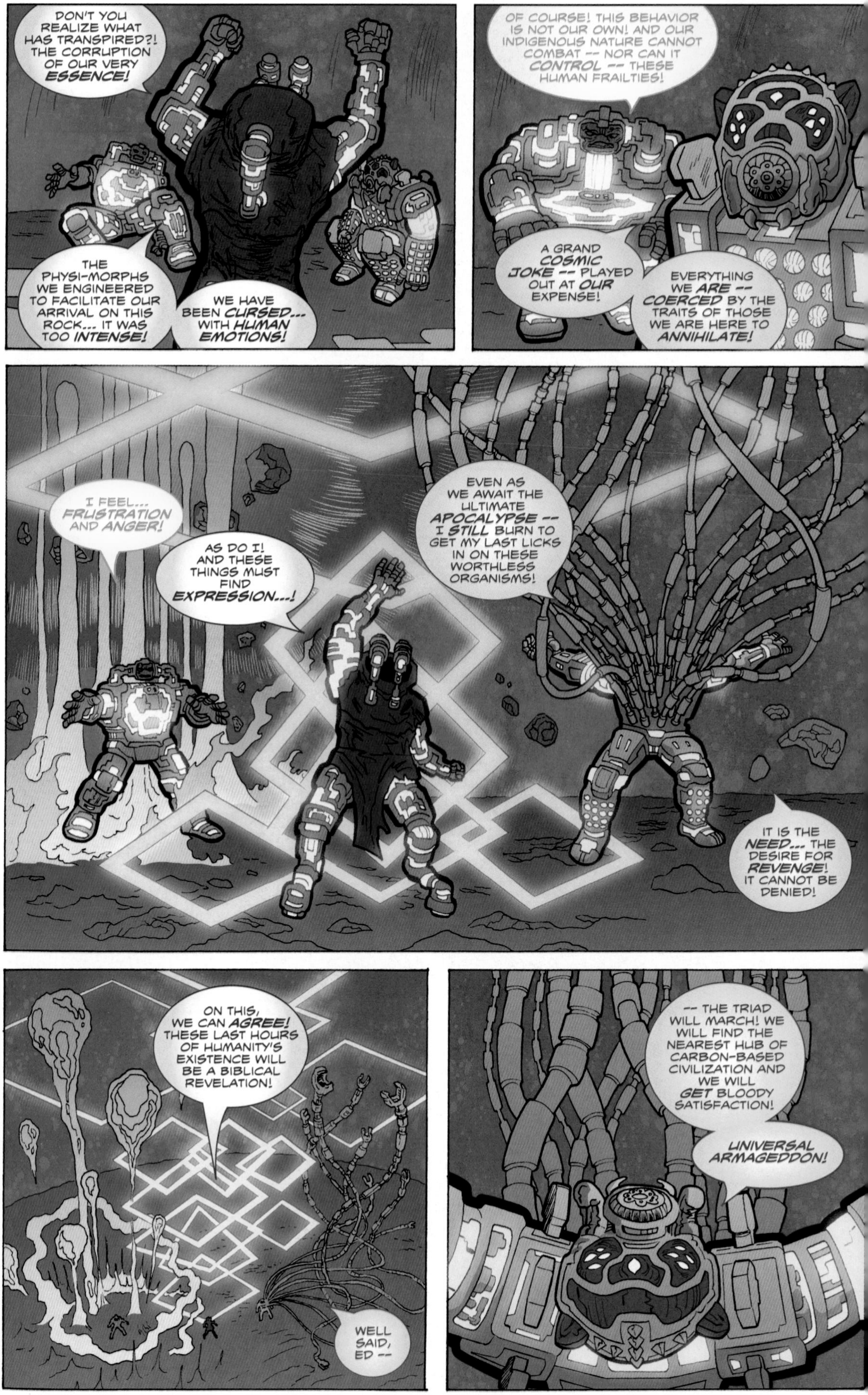
DON'T YOU REALIZE WHAT HAS TRANSPIRED?! THE CORRUPTION OF OUR VERY ESSENCE!
THE PHYSI-MORPHS WE ENGINEERED TO FACILITATE OUR ARRIVAL ON THIS ROCK... IT WAS TOO INTENSE!
WE HAVE BEEN CURSED... WITH HUMAN EMOTIONS!
OF COURSE! THIS BEHAVIOR IS NOT OUR OWN! AND OUR INDIGENOUS NATURE CANNOT COMBAT -- NOR CAN IT CONTROL -- THESE HUMAN FRAILTIES!
A GRAND COSMIC JOKE -- PLAYED OUT AT OUR EXPENSE!
EVERYTHING WE ARE -- COERCED BY THE TRAITS OF THOSE WE ARE HERE TO ANNIHILATE!
I FEEL... FRUSTRATION AND ANGER!
AS DO I! AND THESE THINGS MUST FIND EXPRESSION...!
EVEN AS WE AWAIT THE ULTIMATE APOCALYPSE -- I STILL BURN TO GET MY LAST LICKS IN ON THESE WORTHLESS ORGANISMS!
IT IS THE NEED... THE DESIRE FOR REVENGE! IT CANNOT BE DENIED!
ON THIS, WE CAN AGREE! THESE LAST HOURS OF HUMANITY'S EXISTENCE WILL BE A BIBLICAL REVELATION!
WELL SAID, ED --
-- THE TRIAD WILL MARCH! WE WILL FIND THE NEAREST HUB OF CARBON-BASED CIVILIZATION AND WE WILL GET BLOODY SATISFACTION!
UNIVERSAL ARMAGEDDON!

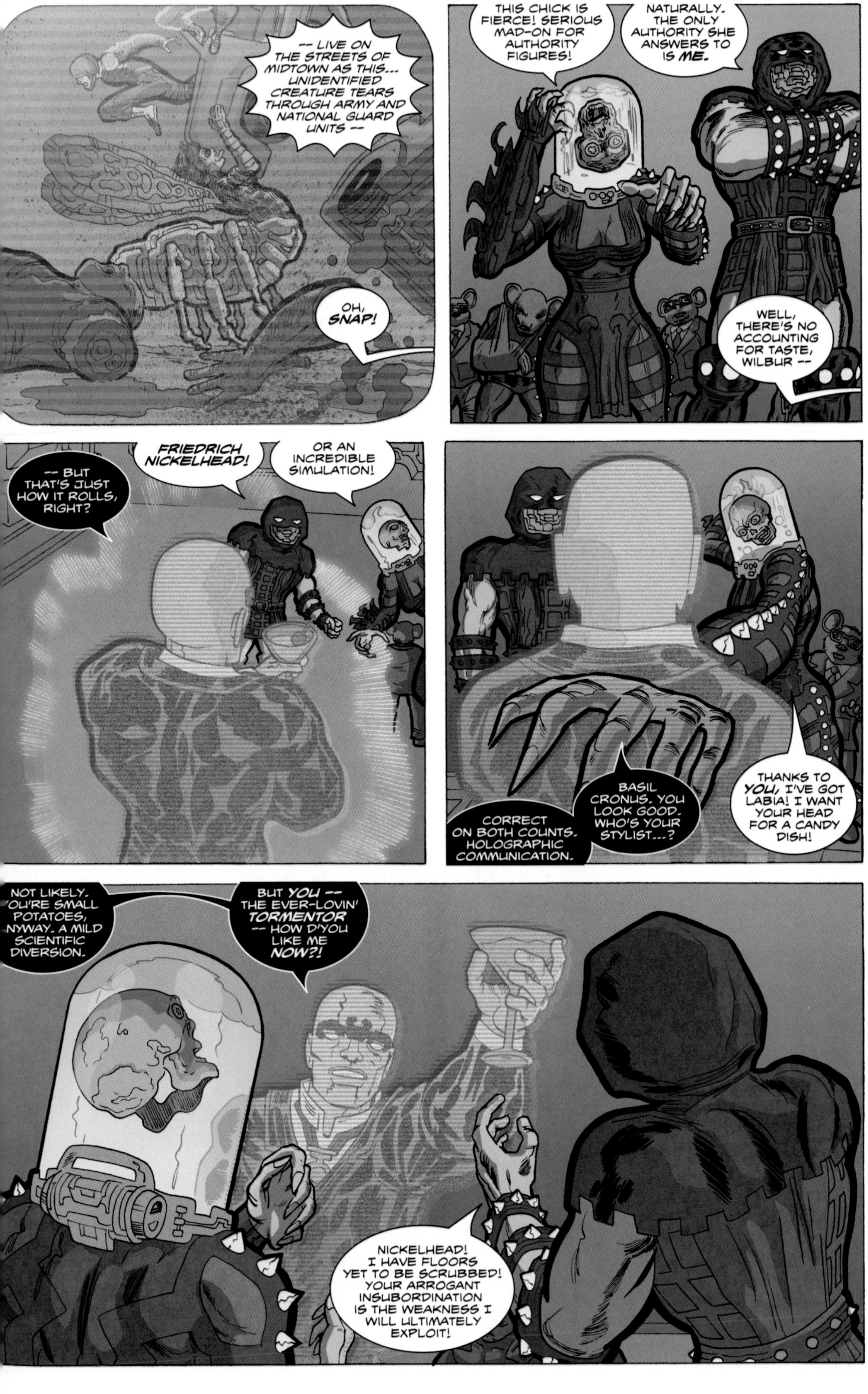
-- LIVE ON THE STREETS OF MIDTOWN AS THIS... UNIDENTIFIED CREATURE TEARS THROUGH ARMY AND NATIONAL GUARD UNITS --
OH, SNAP!
THIS CHICK IS FIERCE! SERIOUS MAD-ON FOR AUTHORITY FIGURES!
NATURALLY. THE ONLY AUTHORITY SHE ANSWERS TO IS ME.
WELL, THERE'S NO ACCOUNTING FOR TASTE, WILBUR --
-- BUT THAT'S JUST HOW IT ROLLS, RIGHT?
FRIEDRICH NICKELHEAD!
OR AN INCREDIBLE SIMULATION!
CORRECT ON BOTH COUNTS. HOLOGRAPHIC COMMUNICATION.
BASIL CRONUS. YOU LOOK GOOD. WHO'S YOUR STYLIST...?
THANKS TO YOU, I'VE GOT LABIA! I WANT YOUR HEAD FOR A CANDY DISH!
BUT YOU -- THE EVER-LOVIN' TORMENTOR -- HOW D'YOU LIKE ME NOW?!
NOT LIKELY. 'OU'RE SMALL POTATOES, NYWAY. A MILD SCIENTIFIC DIVERSION.
NICKELHEAD! I HAVE FLOORS YET TO BE SCRUBBED! YOUR ARROGANT INSUBORDINATION IS THE WEAKNESS I WILL ULTIMATELY EXPLOIT!

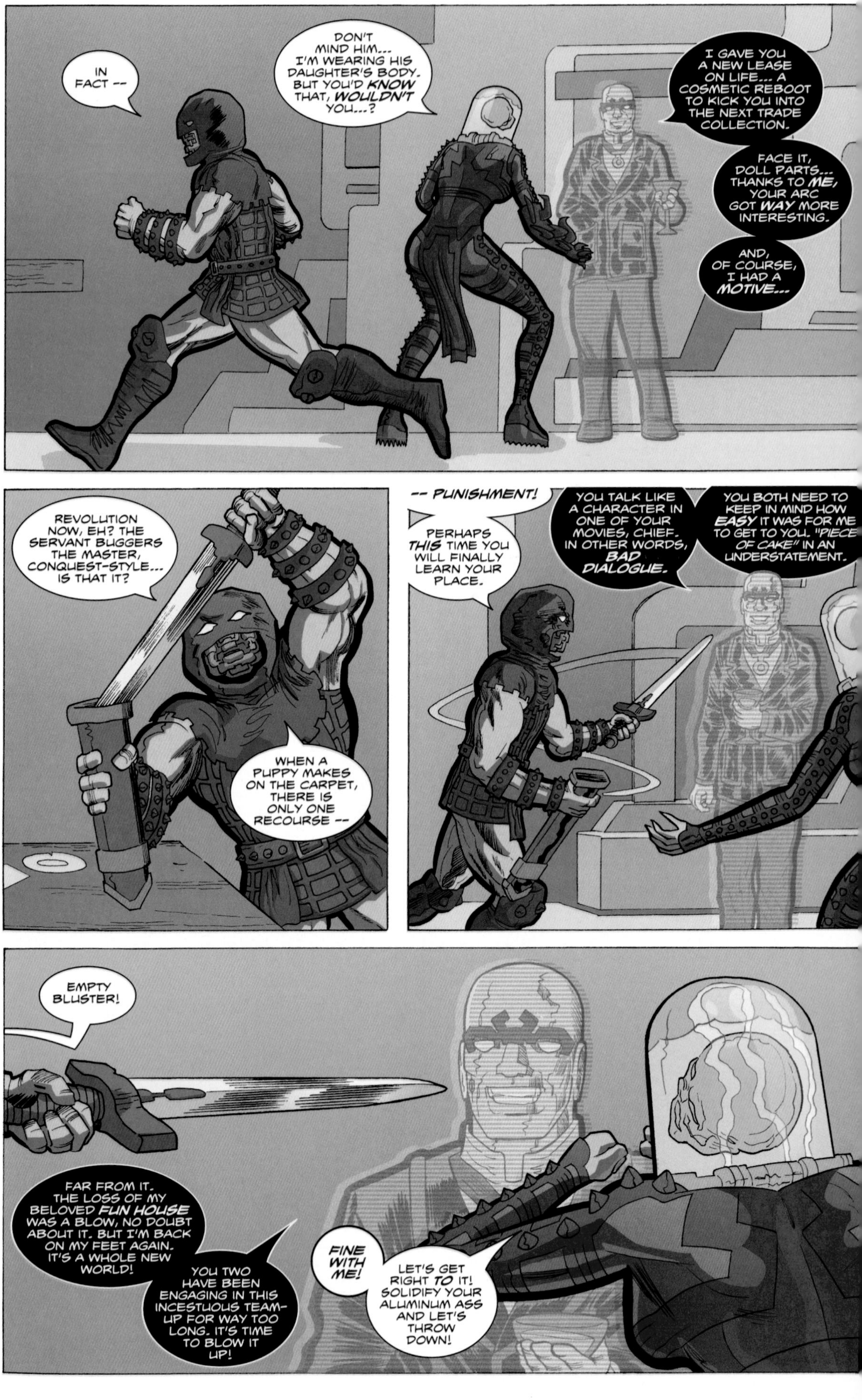

IN FACT --
DON'T MIND HIM... I'M WEARING HIS DAUGHTER'S BODY. BUT YOU'D KNOW THAT, WOULDN'T YOU...?
I GAVE YOU A NEW LEASE ON LIFE... A COSMETIC REBOOT TO KICK YOU INTO THE NEXT TRADE COLLECTION.
FACE IT, DOLL PARTS... THANKS TO ME, YOUR ARC GOT WAY MORE INTERESTING.
AND, OF COURSE, I HAD A MOTIVE...
REVOLUTION NOW, EH? THE SERVANT BUGGERS THE MASTER, CONQUEST-STYLE... IS THAT IT?
WHEN A PUPPY MAKES ON THE CARPET, THERE IS ONLY ONE RECOURSE --
-- PUNISHMENT!
PERHAPS THIS TIME YOU WILL FINALLY LEARN YOUR PLACE.
YOU TALK LIKE A CHARACTER IN ONE OF YOUR MOVIES, CHIEF. IN OTHER WORDS, BAD DIALOGUE.
YOU BOTH NEED TO KEEP IN MIND HOW EASY IT WAS FOR ME TO GET TO YOU. "PIECE OF CAKE" IN AN UNDERSTATEMENT.
EMPTY BLUSTER!
FAR FROM IT. THE LOSS OF MY BELOVED FUN HOUSE WAS A BLOW, NO DOUBT ABOUT IT. BUT I'M BACK ON MY FEET AGAIN. IT'S A WHOLE NEW WORLD!
YOU TWO HAVE BEEN ENGAGING IN THIS INCESTUOUS TEAM-UP FOR WAY TOO LONG. IT'S TIME TO BLOW IT UP!
FINE WITH ME!
LET'S GET RIGHT TO IT! SOLIDIFY YOUR ALUMINUM ASS AND LET'S THROW DOWN!

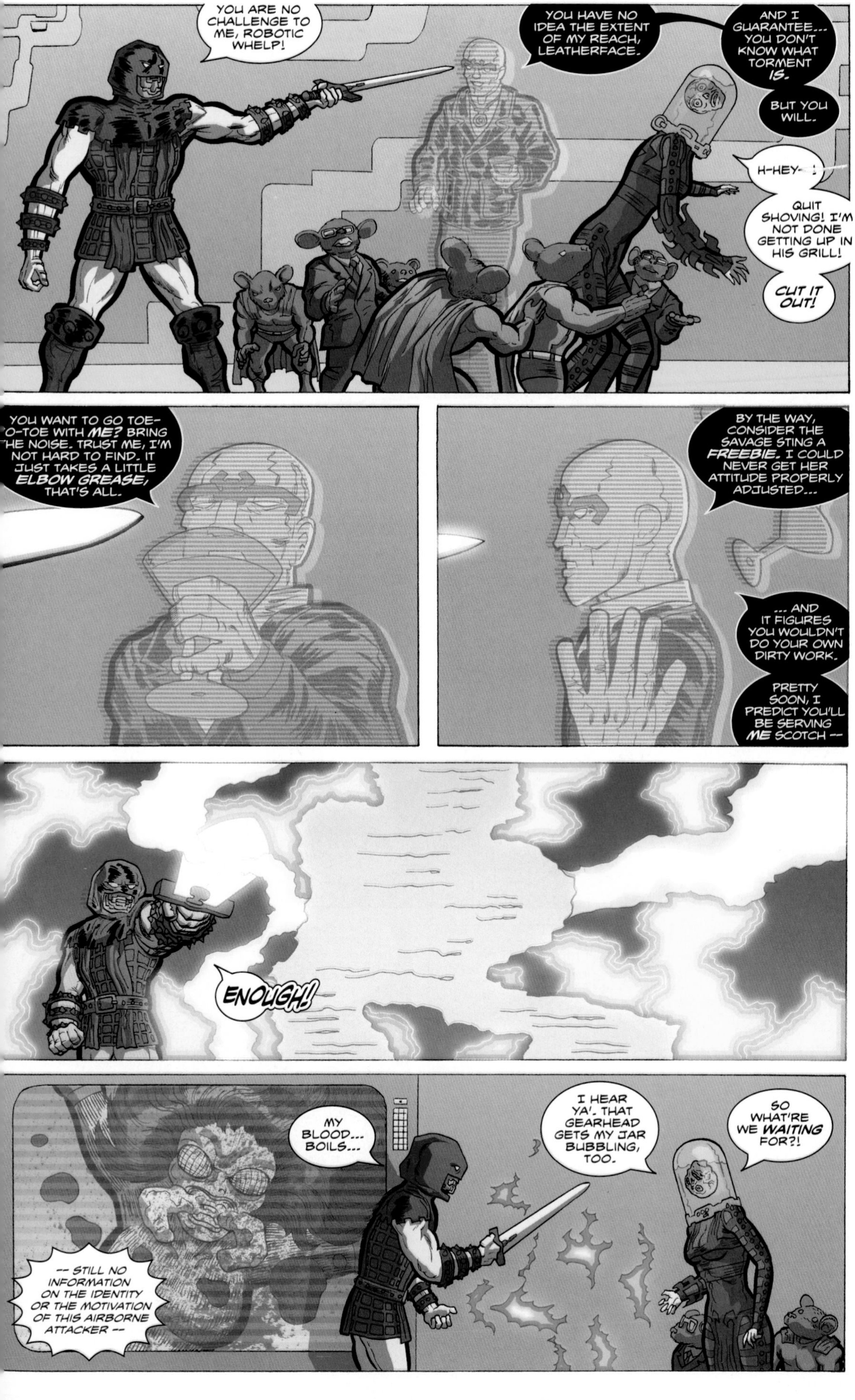
YOU ARE NO CHALLENGE TO ME, ROBOTIC WHELP!
YOU HAVE NO IDEA THE EXTENT OF MY REACH, LEATHERFACE.
AND I GUARANTEE... YOU DON'T KNOW WHAT TORMENT IS.
BUT YOU WILL.
H-HEY--!
QUIT SHOVING! I'M NOT DONE GETTING UP IN HIS GRILL!
CUT IT OUT!
YOU WANT TO GO TOE-O-TOE WITH ME? BRING THE NOISE. TRUST ME, I'M NOT HARD TO FIND. IT JUST TAKES A LITTLE ELBOW GREASE, THAT'S ALL.
BY THE WAY, CONSIDER THE SAVAGE STING A FREEBIE. I COULD NEVER GET HER ATTITUDE PROPERLY ADJUSTED...
... AND IT FIGURES YOU WOULDN'T DO YOUR OWN DIRTY WORK.
PRETTY SOON, I PREDICT YOU'LL BE SERVING ME SCOTCH --
ENOUGH!
-- STILL NO INFORMATION ON THE IDENTITY OR THE MOTIVATION OF THIS AIRBORNE ATTACKER --
MY BLOOD... BOILS...
I HEAR YA'. THAT GEARHEAD GETS MY JAR BUBBLING, TOO.
SO WHAT'RE WE WAITING FOR?!

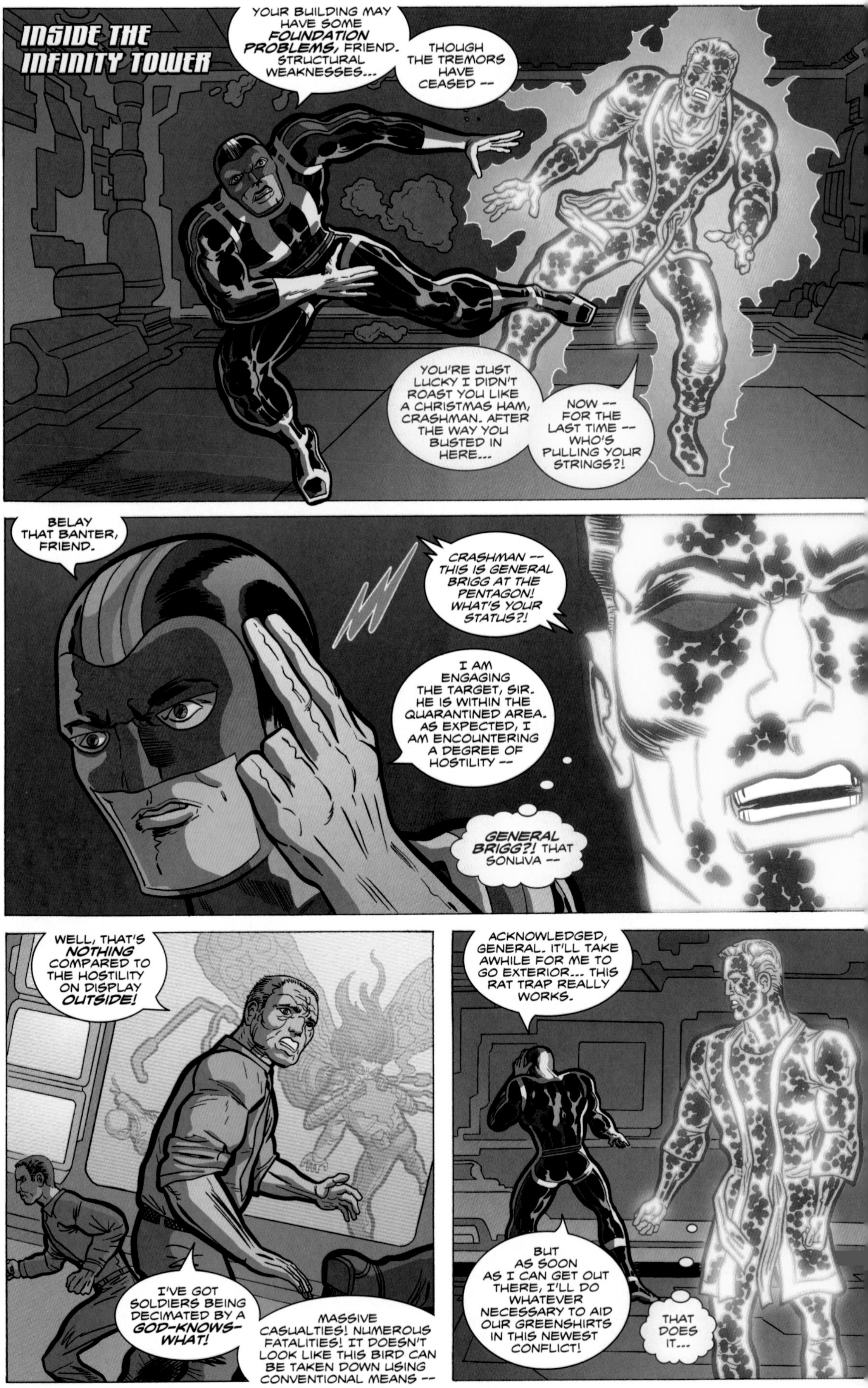
INSIDE THE INFINITY TOWER
YOUR BUILDING MAY HAVE SOME FOUNDATION PROBLEMS, FRIEND. STRUCTURAL WEAKNESSES...
THOUGH THE TREMORS HAVE CEASED --
YOU'RE JUST LUCKY I DIDN'T ROAST YOU LIKE A CHRISTMAS HAM, CRASHMAN. AFTER THE WAY YOU BUSTED IN HERE...
NOW -- FOR THE LAST TIME -- WHO'S PULLING YOUR STRINGS?!
BELAY THAT BANTER, FRIEND.
CRASHMAN -- THIS IS GENERAL BRIGG AT THE PENTAGON! WHAT'S YOUR STATUS?!
I AM ENGAGING THE TARGET, SIR. HE IS WITHIN THE QUARANTINED AREA. AS EXPECTED, I AM ENCOUNTERING A DEGREE OF HOSTILITY --
GENERAL BRIGG?! THAT SONUVA --
WELL, THAT'S NOTHING COMPARED TO THE HOSTILITY ON DISPLAY OUTSIDE!
I'VE GOT SOLDIERS BEING DECIMATED BY A GOD-KNOWS-WHAT!
MASSIVE CASUALTIES! NUMEROUS FATALITIES! IT DOESN'T LOOK LIKE THIS BIRD CAN BE TAKEN DOWN USING CONVENTIONAL MEANS --
ACKNOWLEDGED, GENERAL. IT'LL TAKE AWHILE FOR ME TO GO EXTERIOR... THIS RAT TRAP REALLY WORKS.
BUT AS SOON AS I CAN GET OUT THERE, I'LL DO WHATEVER NECESSARY TO AID OUR GREENSHIRTS IN THIS NEWEST CONFLICT!
THAT DOES IT...

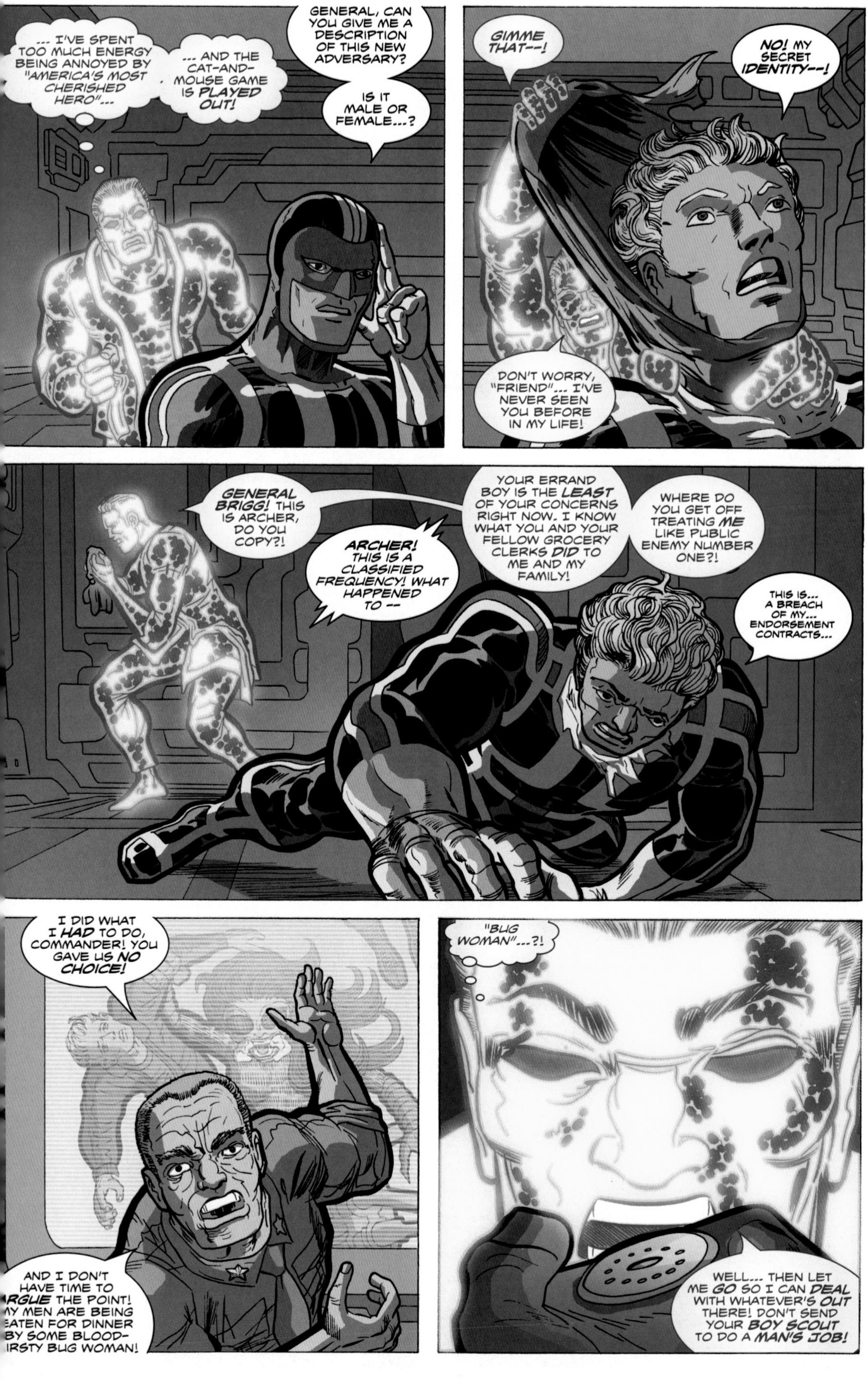
... I'VE SPENT TOO MUCH ENERGY BEING ANNOYED BY "AMERICA'S MOST CHERISHED HERO"...
... AND THE CAT-AND-MOUSE GAME IS PLAYED OUT!
GENERAL, CAN YOU GIVE ME A DESCRIPTION OF THIS NEW ADVERSARY?
IS IT MALE OR FEMALE...?
GIMME THAT--!
NO! MY SECRET IDENTITY--!
DON'T WORRY, "FRIEND"... I'VE NEVER SEEN YOU BEFORE IN MY LIFE!
GENERAL BRIGG! THIS IS ARCHER, DO YOU COPY?!
ARCHER! THIS IS A CLASSIFIED FREQUENCY! WHAT HAPPENED TO --
YOUR ERRAND BOY IS THE LEAST OF YOUR CONCERNS RIGHT NOW. I KNOW WHAT YOU AND YOUR FELLOW GROCERY CLERKS DID TO ME AND MY FAMILY!
WHERE DO YOU GET OFF TREATING ME LIKE PUBLIC ENEMY NUMBER ONE?!
THIS IS... A BREACH OF MY... ENDORSEMENT CONTRACTS...
I DID WHAT I HAD TO DO, COMMANDER! YOU GAVE US NO CHOICE!
AND I DON'T HAVE TIME TO ARGUE THE POINT! MY MEN ARE BEING EATEN FOR DINNER BY SOME BLOOD-THIRSTY BUG WOMAN!
"BUG WOMAN"...?!
WELL... THEN LET ME GO SO I CAN DEAL WITH WHATEVER'S OUT THERE! DON'T SEND YOUR BOY SCOUT TO DO A MAN'S JOB!

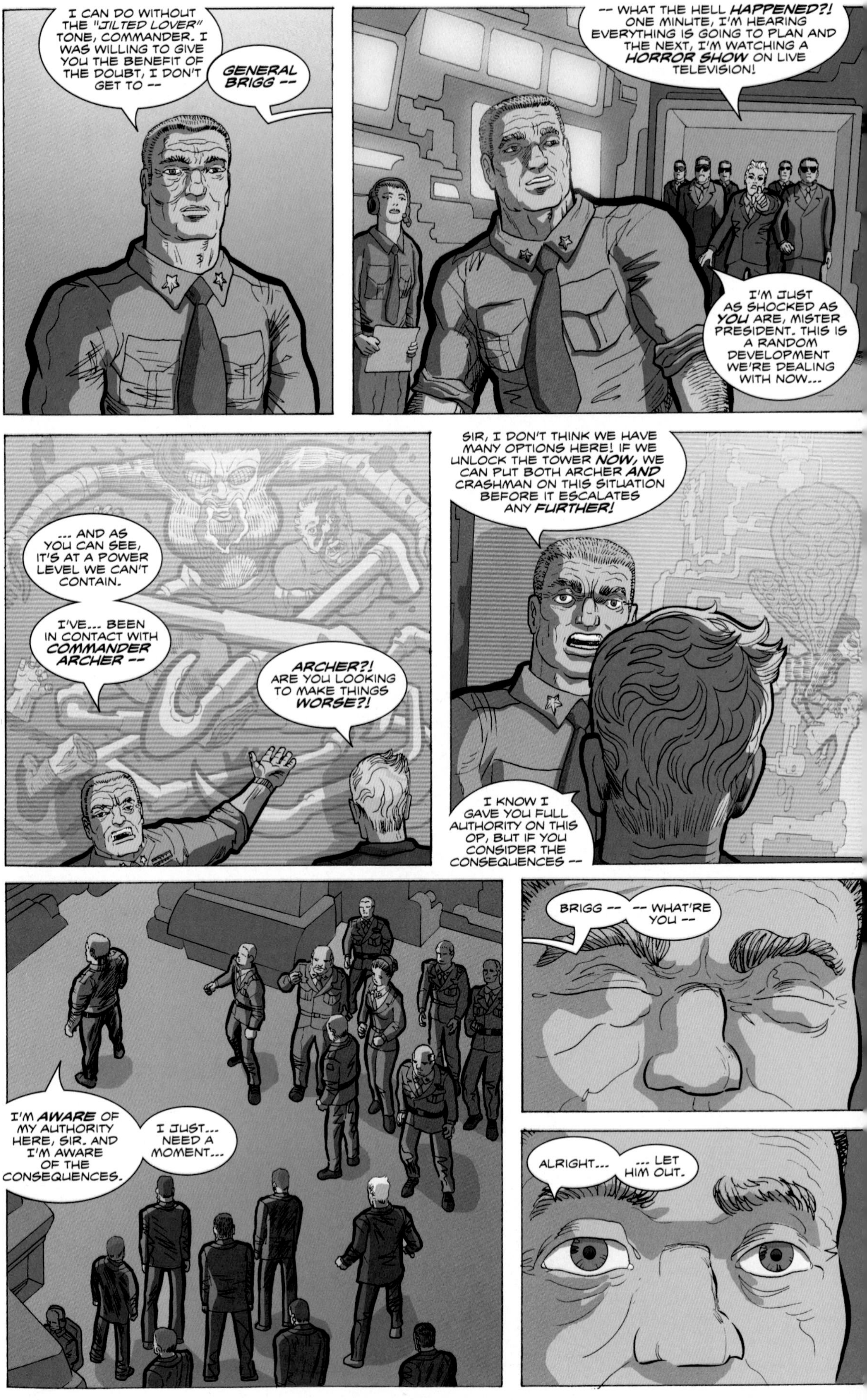
I CAN DO WITHOUT THE "JILTED LOVER" TONE, COMMANDER. I WAS WILLING TO GIVE YOU THE BENEFIT OF THE DOUBT, I DON'T GET TO --
GENERAL BRIGG --
-- WHAT THE HELL HAPPENED?! ONE MINUTE, I'M HEARING EVERYTHING IS GOING TO PLAN AND THE NEXT, I'M WATCHING A HORROR SHOW ON LIVE TELEVISION!
I'M JUST AS SHOCKED AS YOU ARE, MISTER PRESIDENT. THIS IS A RANDOM DEVELOPMENT WE'RE DEALING WITH NOW...
... AND AS YOU CAN SEE, IT'S AT A POWER LEVEL WE CAN'T CONTAIN.
I'VE... BEEN IN CONTACT WITH COMMANDER ARCHER --
ARCHER?! ARE YOU LOOKING TO MAKE THINGS WORSE?!
SIR, I DON'T THINK WE HAVE MANY OPTIONS HERE! IF WE UNLOCK THE TOWER NOW, WE CAN PUT BOTH ARCHER AND CRASHMAN ON THIS SITUATION BEFORE IT ESCALATES ANY FURTHER!
I KNOW I GAVE YOU FULL AUTHORITY ON THIS OP, BUT IF YOU CONSIDER THE CONSEQUENCES --
I'M AWARE OF MY AUTHORITY HERE, SIR. AND I'M AWARE OF THE CONSEQUENCES.
I JUST... NEED A MOMENT...
BRIGG --
-- WHAT'RE YOU --
ALRIGHT...
... LET HIM OUT.

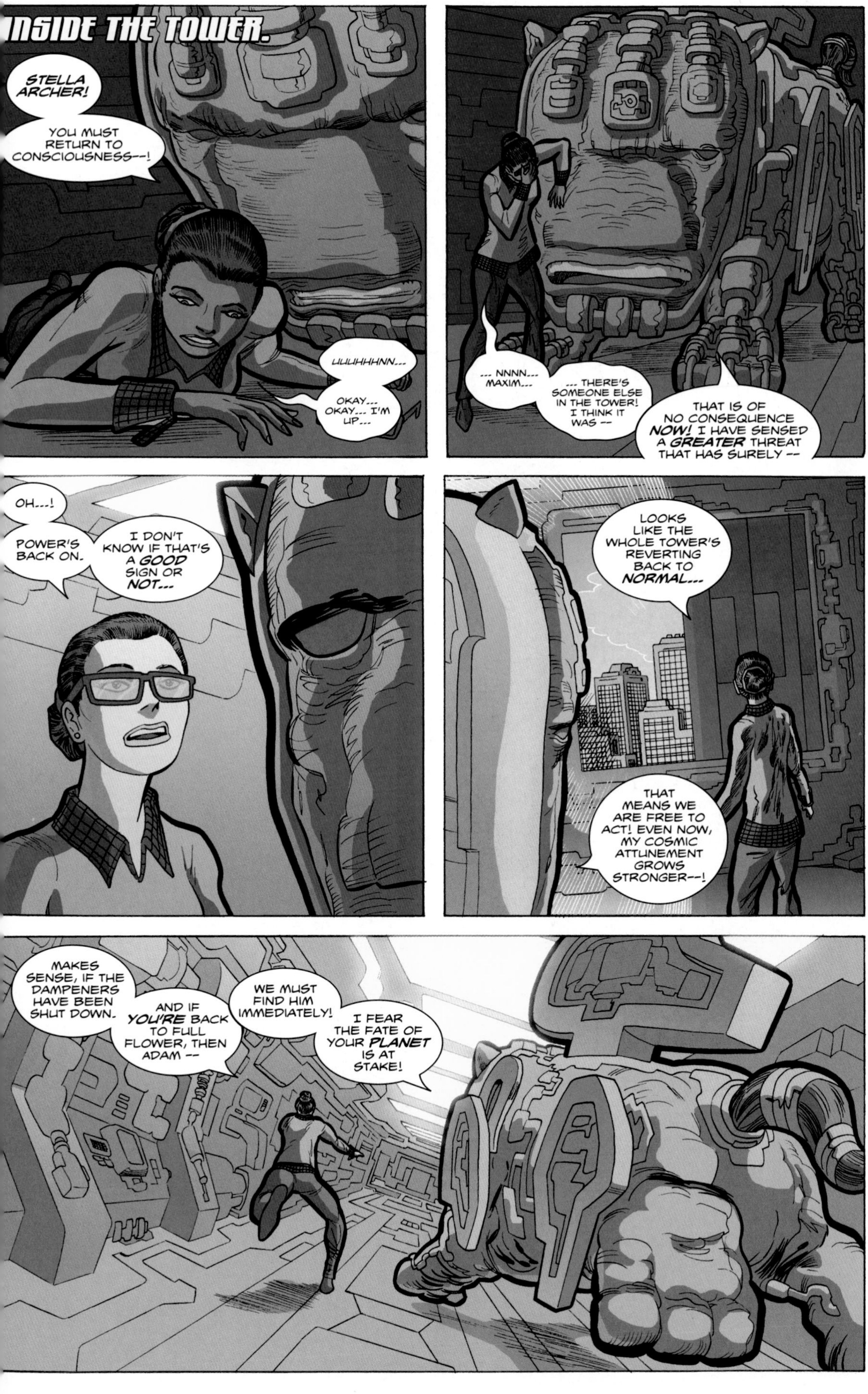
INSIDE THE TOWER.
STELLA ARCHER!
YOU MUST RETURN TO CONSCIOUSNESS--!
UUUHHHNN...
OKAY... OKAY... I'M UP...
... NNNN... MAXIM...
... THERE'S SOMEONE ELSE IN THE TOWER! I THINK IT WAS --
THAT IS OF NO CONSEQUENCE NOW! I HAVE SENSED A GREATER THREAT THAT HAS SURELY --
OH...!
POWER'S BACK ON.
I DON'T KNOW IF THAT'S A GOOD SIGN OR NOT...
LOOKS LIKE THE WHOLE TOWER'S REVERTING BACK TO NORMAL...
THAT MEANS WE ARE FREE TO ACT! EVEN NOW, MY COSMIC ATTUNEMENT GROWS STRONGER--!
MAKES SENSE, IF THE DAMPENERS HAVE BEEN SHUT DOWN.
AND IF YOU'RE BACK TO FULL FLOWER, THEN ADAM --
WE MUST FIND HIM IMMEDIATELY!
I FEAR THE FATE OF YOUR PLANET IS AT STAKE!

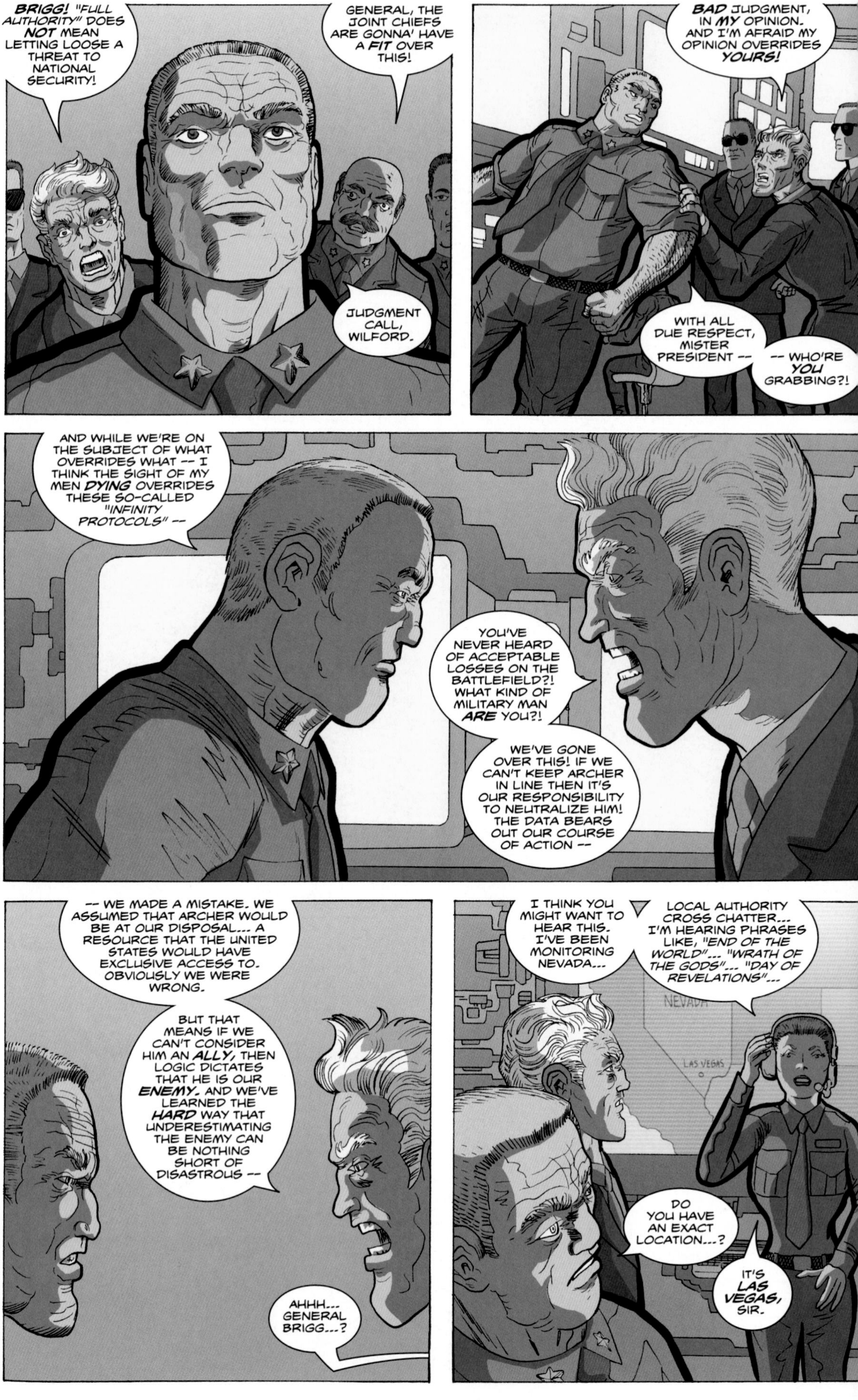

BRIGG! "FULL AUTHORITY" DOES NOT MEAN LETTING LOOSE A THREAT TO NATIONAL SECURITY!
GENERAL, THE JOINT CHIEFS ARE GONNA' HAVE A FIT OVER THIS!
JUDGMENT CALL, WILFORD.
BAD JUDGMENT, IN MY OPINION. AND I'M AFRAID MY OPINION OVERRIDES YOURS!
WITH ALL DUE RESPECT, MISTER PRESIDENT --
-- WHO'RE YOU GRABBING?!
AND WHILE WE'RE ON THE SUBJECT OF WHAT OVERRIDES WHAT -- I THINK THE SIGHT OF MY MEN DYING OVERRIDES THESE SO-CALLED "INFINITY PROTOCOLS" --
YOU'VE NEVER HEARD OF ACCEPTABLE LOSSES ON THE BATTLEFIELD?! WHAT KIND OF MILITARY MAN ARE YOU?!
WE'VE GONE OVER THIS! IF WE CAN'T KEEP ARCHER IN LINE THEN IT'S OUR RESPONSIBILITY TO NEUTRALIZE HIM! THE DATA BEARS OUT OUR COURSE OF ACTION --
-- WE MADE A MISTAKE. WE ASSUMED THAT ARCHER WOULD BE AT OUR DISPOSAL... A RESOURCE THAT THE UNITED STATES WOULD HAVE EXCLUSIVE ACCESS TO. OBVIOUSLY WE WERE WRONG.
BUT THAT MEANS IF WE CAN'T CONSIDER HIM AN ALLY, THEN LOGIC DICTATES THAT HE IS OUR ENEMY. AND WE'VE LEARNED THE HARD WAY THAT UNDERESTIMATING THE ENEMY CAN BE NOTHING SHORT OF DISASTROUS --
AHHH... GENERAL BRIGG...?
I THINK YOU MIGHT WANT TO HEAR THIS. I'VE BEEN MONITORING NEVADA...
LOCAL AUTHORITY CROSS CHATTER... I'M HEARING PHRASES LIKE, "END OF THE WORLD"... "WRATH OF THE GODS"... "DAY OF REVELATIONS"...
NEVADA
LAS VEGAS
DO YOU HAVE AN EXACT LOCATION...?
IT'S LAS VEGAS, SIR.

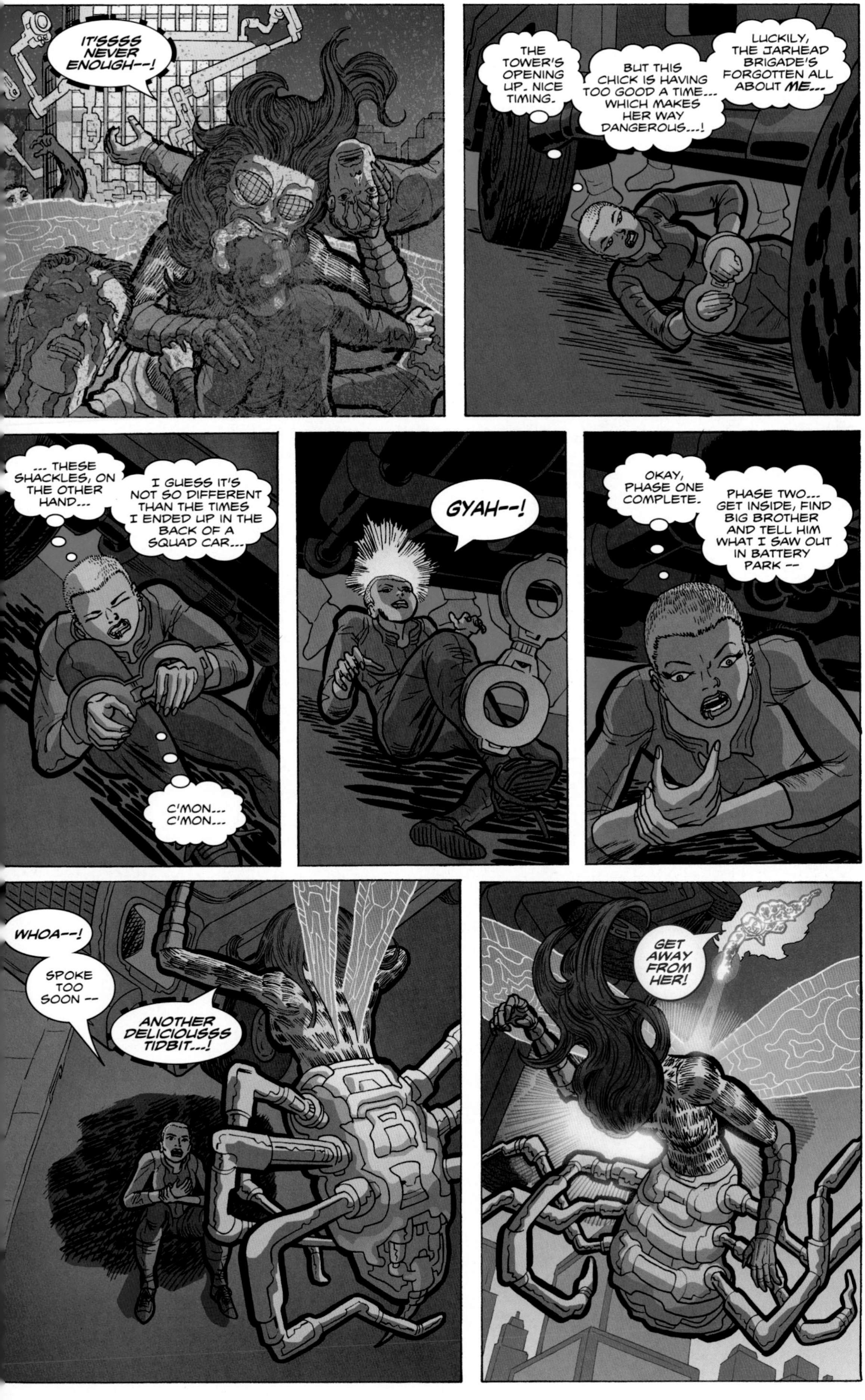
IT'SSSS NEVER ENOUGH--!
THE TOWER'S OPENING UP. NICE TIMING.
BUT THIS CHICK IS HAVING TOO GOOD A TIME... WHICH MAKES HER WAY DANGEROUS...!
LUCKILY, THE JARHEAD BRIGADE'S FORGOTTEN ALL ABOUT ME...
... THESE SHACKLES, ON THE OTHER HAND...
I GUESS IT'S NOT SO DIFFERENT THAN THE TIMES I ENDED UP IN THE BACK OF A SQUAD CAR...
C'MON... C'MON...
GYAH--!
OKAY, PHASE ONE COMPLETE.
PHASE TWO... GET INSIDE, FIND BIG BROTHER AND TELL HIM WHAT I SAW OUT IN BATTERY PARK --
WHOA--!
SPOKE TOO SOON --
ANOTHER DELICIOUSSS TIDBIT...!
GET AWAY FROM HER!

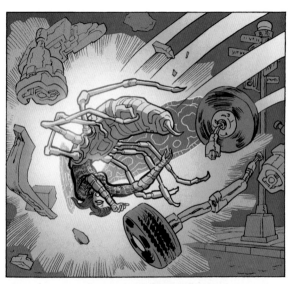

THAT... WAZZZZ FUN!

AN OUTLET FOR MY SSSEXUAL TENSION--!

LANGUAGE, YOUNG LADY...!

THERE ARE IMPRESSIONABLE AMERICAN CHILDREN WATCHING LIVE ON T.V...!

I WOULD BE REMISS IF I DIDN'T GIVE YOU A CHANCE TO SURRENDER.

YOU SEEM LIKE YOU MIGHT BE A NICE GIRL... UNDERNEATH ALL THAT SLIME. BUT I MAKE NO JUDGMENTS...

I SSSEE LUSSST IN YOUR EYESSSS. HOW VERY SSSAD...

--- LET'SSSS SSSEE IF YOU CAN GET OFF ON THISSS --

CAN YOU FEEL MY FRUSSSTRATION...?!

I... CAN FEEL...

... SOMETHING --

SSSSSSS

HURRUUUH --

≥URK≤

I GOT BLOOD ON YOUR PRETTY COSSSTUME...

SSSSSUCH A SSSHAME...

OMIGOD--!

CRASHMAN!

IS HE--?!

DID YOU GET THAT?!

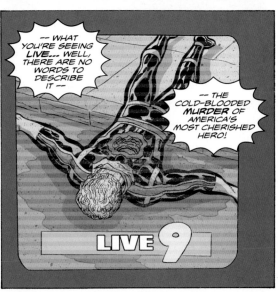

-- WHAT YOU'RE SEEING LIVE... WELL, THERE ARE NO WORDS TO DESCRIBE IT --

-- THE COLD-BLOODED MURDER OF AMERICA'S MOST CHERISHED HERO!

LIVE 9

SSSSOMEONE ELSSSE WANTZZZ TO PLAY--!

YOU COULD SAY THAT --

OOOOO... SSSO SSSHINY...!

THAT'S RIGHT--!

DAMN! HER JAW'S LIKE SOLID GRANITE!

I CAN'T IMAGINE WHAT THIS'LL LOOK LIKE ON TELEVISION -- LIKE I'M AVENGING MY "GOOD BUDDY", CRASHMAN'S DEATH.

JUST GOES TO SHOW YOU... YOU CAN'T BELIEVE THE MEDIA ANYMORE.

MAYBE THEY'VE ALREADY BRANDED ME THE ENEMY... COMPLETE WITH A LOGO AND MUSICAL STING --

GAAAAA--!

FEELSSSS LIKE CHRISTMASSSS MORNING, EH---?!

CAN'T SEE A THING!

NO IDEA WHICH DIRECTION I'M --

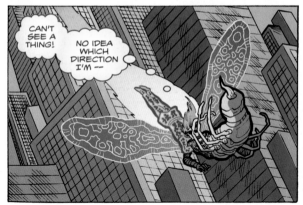

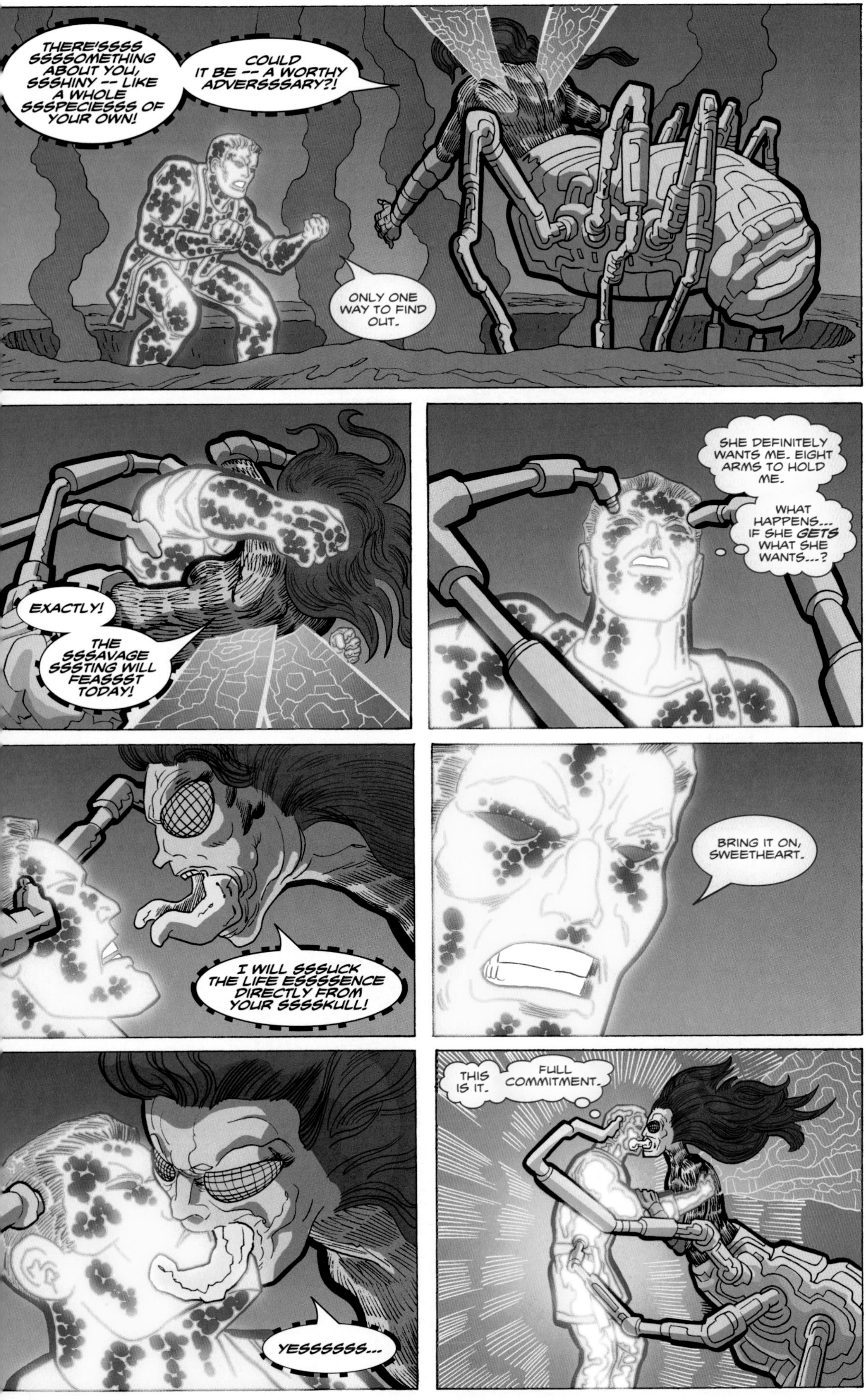
THERE'SSSS SSSSOMETHING ABOUT YOU, SSSHINY -- LIKE A WHOLE SSSPECIESSS OF YOUR OWN!
COULD IT BE -- A WORTHY ADVERSSSARY?!
ONLY ONE WAY TO FIND OUT.
EXACTLY!
THE SSSAVAGE SSSTING WILL FEASSST TODAY!
SHE DEFINITELY WANTS ME. EIGHT ARMS TO HOLD ME.
WHAT HAPPENS... IF SHE GETS WHAT SHE WANTS...?
I WILL SSSUCK THE LIFE ESSSSENCE DIRECTLY FROM YOUR SSSSKULL!
BRING IT ON, SWEETHEART.
YESSSSSS...
THIS IS IT.
FULL COMMITMENT.

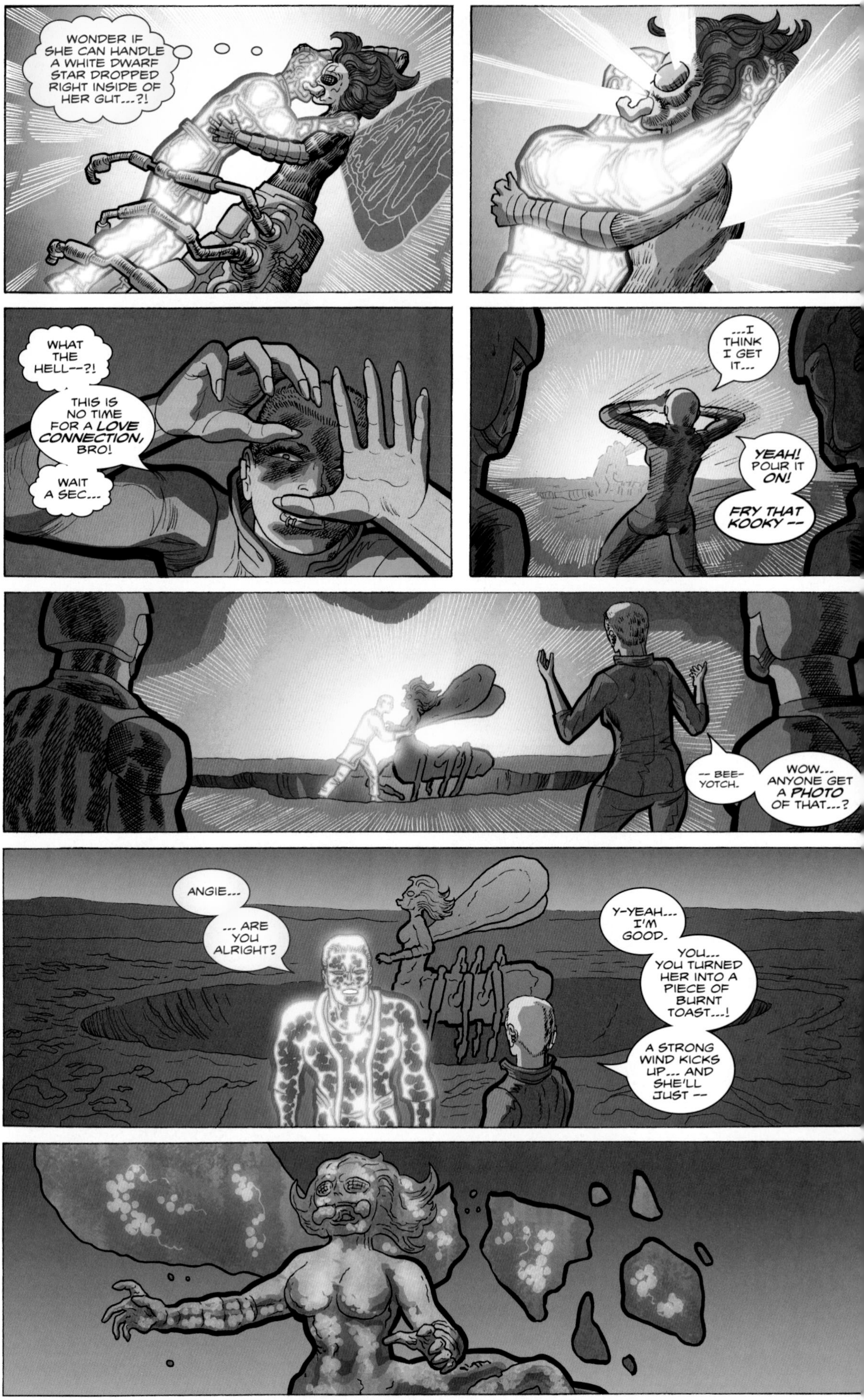
WONDER IF SHE CAN HANDLE A WHITE DWARF STAR DROPPED RIGHT INSIDE OF HER GUT...?!
WHAT THE HELL--?!
THIS IS NO TIME FOR A LOVE CONNECTION, BRO!
WAIT A SEC...
...I THINK I GET IT...
YEAH! POUR IT ON!
FRY THAT KOOKY --
-- BEE-YOTCH.
WOW... ANYONE GET A PHOTO OF THAT...?
ANGIE...
... ARE YOU ALRIGHT?
Y-YEAH... I'M GOOD.
YOU... YOU TURNED HER INTO A PIECE OF BURNT TOAST...!
A STRONG WIND KICKS UP... AND SHE'LL JUST --

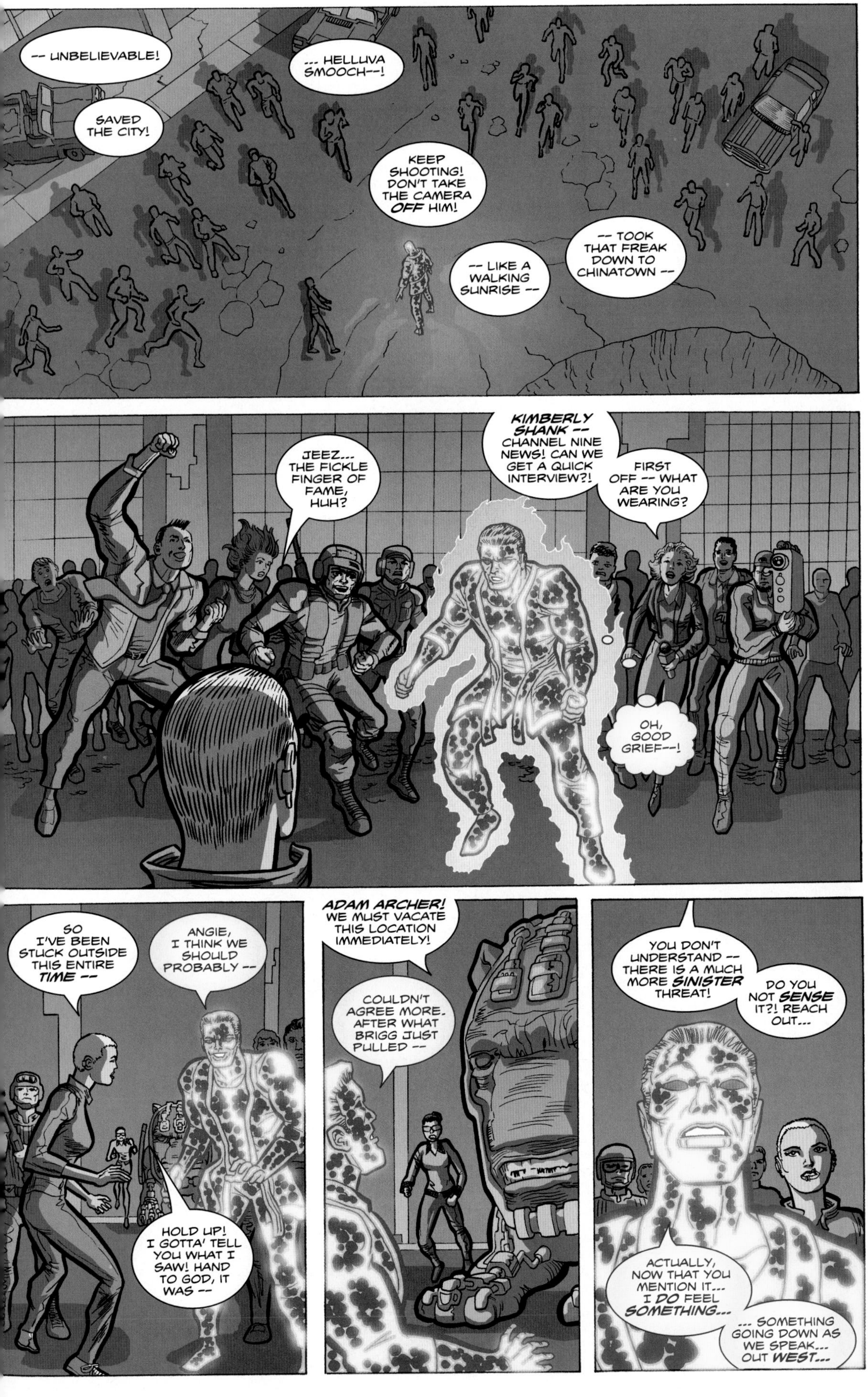
-- UNBELIEVABLE!
SAVED THE CITY!
... HELLUVA SMOOCH--!
KEEP SHOOTING! DON'T TAKE THE CAMERA OFF HIM!
-- LIKE A WALKING SUNRISE --
-- TOOK THAT FREAK DOWN TO CHINATOWN --
JEEZ... THE FICKLE FINGER OF FAME, HUH?
KIMBERLY SHANK -- CHANNEL NINE NEWS! CAN WE GET A QUICK INTERVIEW?!
FIRST OFF -- WHAT ARE YOU WEARING?
OH, GOOD GRIEF--!
SO I'VE BEEN STUCK OUTSIDE THIS ENTIRE TIME --
ANGIE, I THINK WE SHOULD PROBABLY --
HOLD UP! I GOTTA' TELL YOU WHAT I SAW! HAND TO GOD, IT WAS --
ADAM ARCHER! WE MUST VACATE THIS LOCATION IMMEDIATELY!
COULDN'T AGREE MORE. AFTER WHAT BRIGG JUST PULLED --
YOU DON'T UNDERSTAND -- THERE IS A MUCH MORE SINISTER THREAT!
DO YOU NOT SENSE IT?! REACH OUT...
ACTUALLY, NOW THAT YOU MENTION IT... I DO FEEL SOMETHING...
... SOMETHING GOING DOWN AS WE SPEAK... OUT WEST...

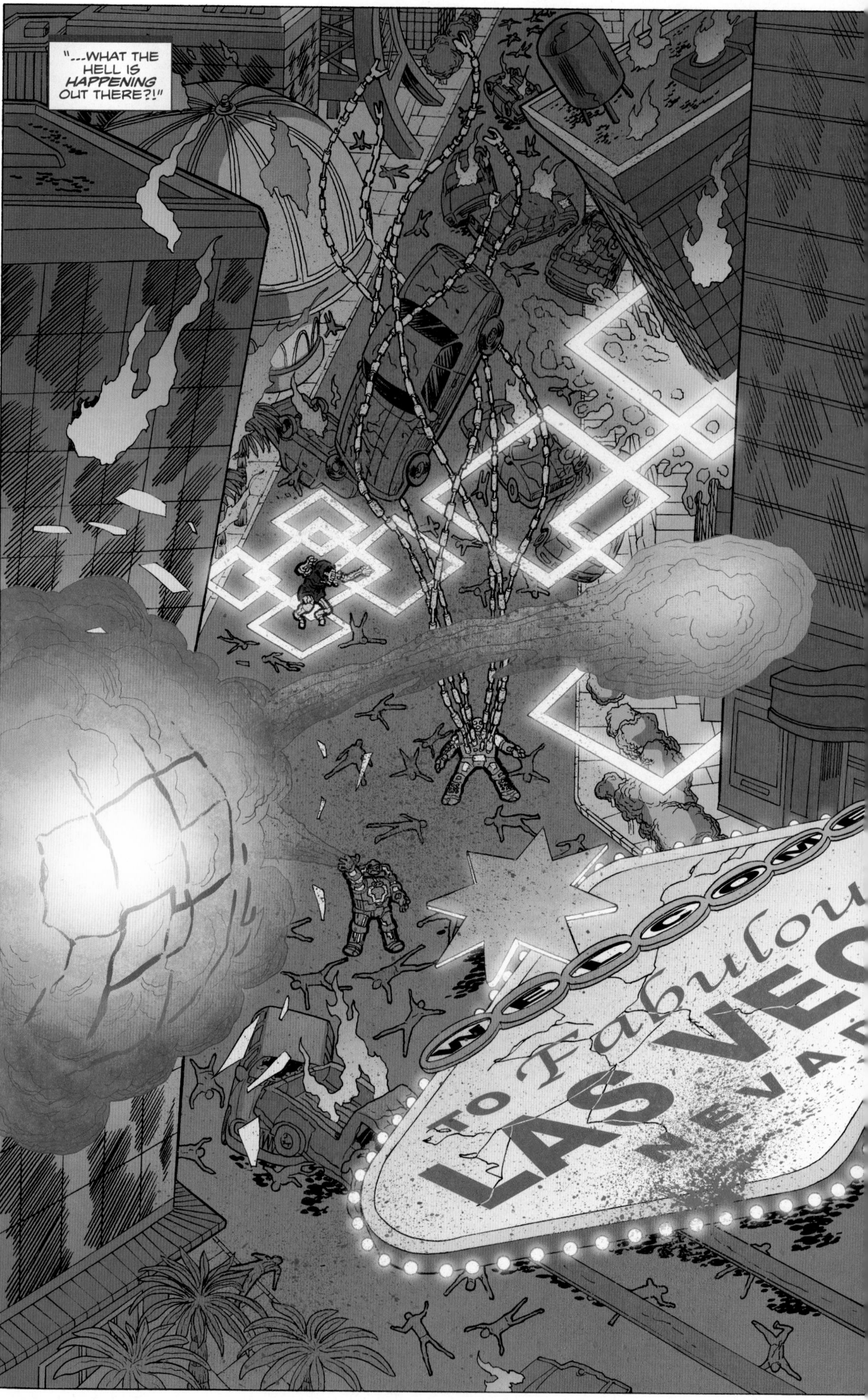
"...WHAT THE HELL IS *HAPPENING* OUT THERE?!"
WELCOME
to Fabulou
LAS VEG
NEVA

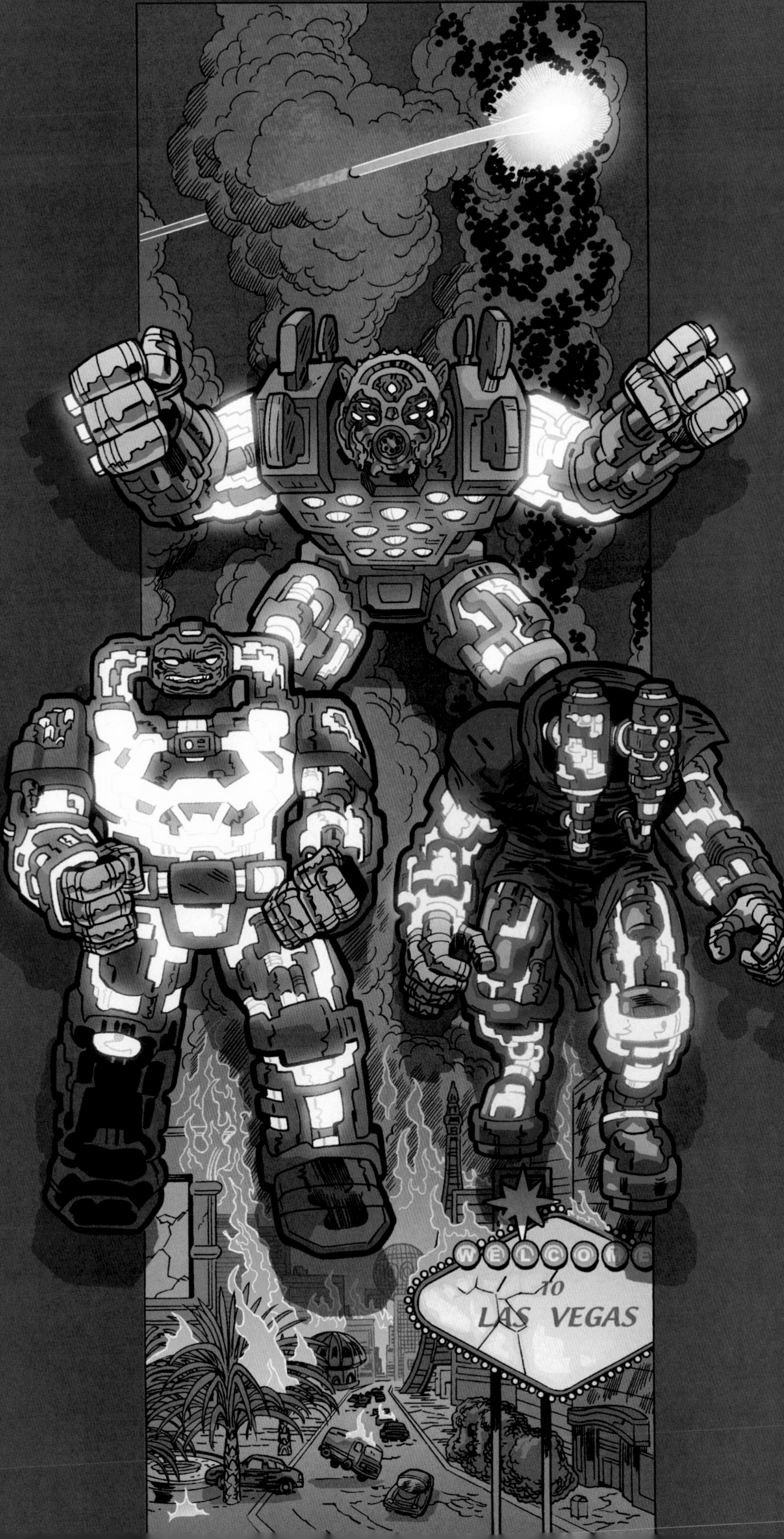
WELCOME
TO
LAS VEGAS

VIVA LAS VULGAR

BOOK TWENTY

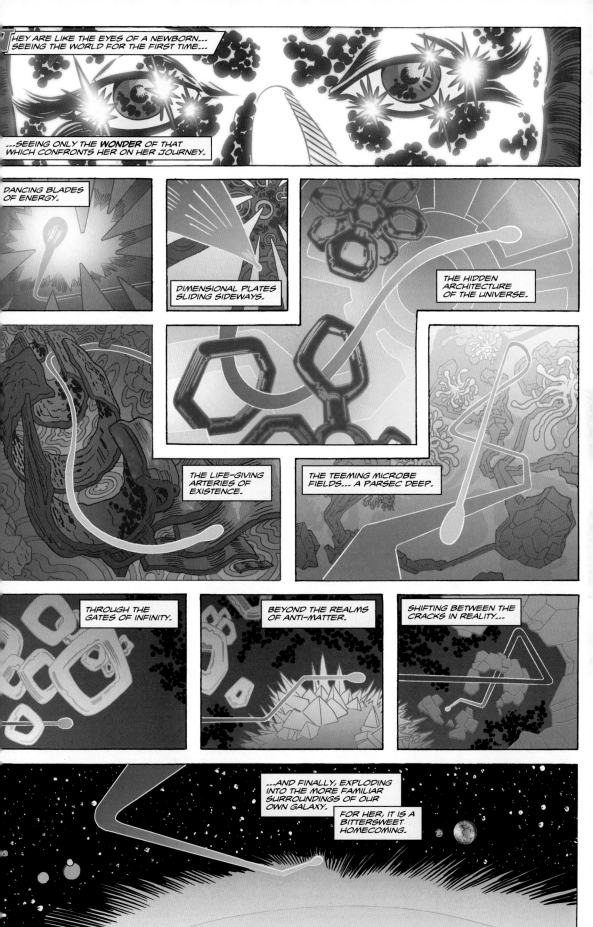

THEY ARE LIKE THE EYES OF A NEWBORN... SEEING THE WORLD FOR THE FIRST TIME...

...SEEING ONLY THE **WONDER** OF THAT WHICH CONFRONTS HER ON HER JOURNEY.

DANCING BLADES OF ENERGY.

DIMENSIONAL PLATES SLIDING SIDEWAYS.

THE HIDDEN ARCHITECTURE OF THE UNIVERSE.

THE LIFE-GIVING ARTERIES OF EXISTENCE.

THE TEEMING MICROBE FIELDS... A PARSEC DEEP.

THROUGH THE GATES OF INFINITY.

BEYOND THE REALMS OF ANTI-MATTER.

SHIFTING BETWEEN THE CRACKS IN REALITY...

...AND FINALLY, EXPLODING INTO THE MORE FAMILIAR SURROUNDINGS OF OUR OWN GALAXY.

FOR HER, IT IS A BITTERSWEET HOMECOMING.

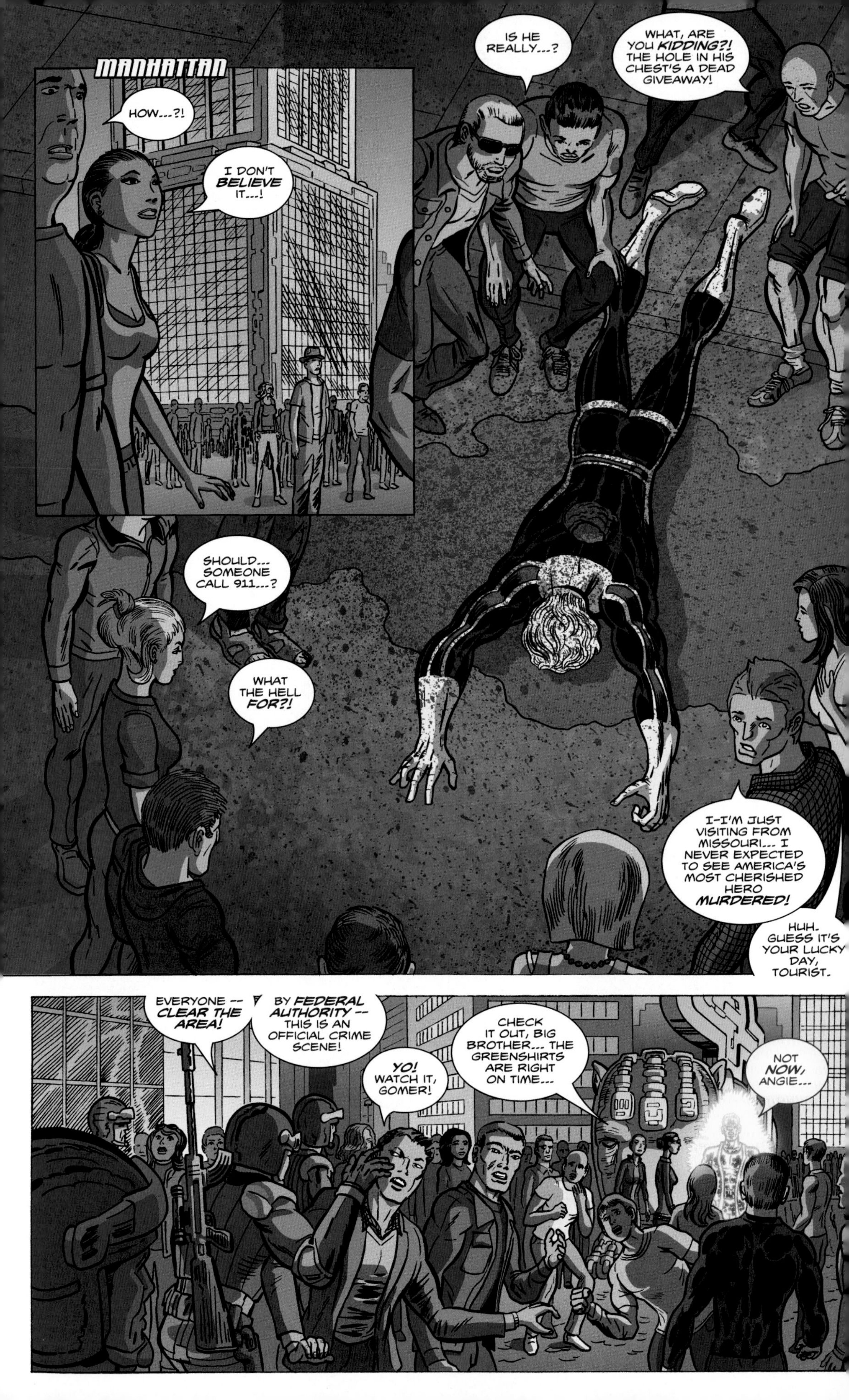
MANHATTAN
HOW...?!
I DON'T BELIEVE IT...!
IS HE REALLY...?
WHAT, ARE YOU KIDDING?! THE HOLE IN HIS CHEST'S A DEAD GIVEAWAY!
SHOULD... SOMEONE CALL 911...?
WHAT THE HELL FOR?!
I-I'M JUST VISITING FROM MISSOURI... I NEVER EXPECTED TO SEE AMERICA'S MOST CHERISHED HERO MURDERED!
HUH. GUESS IT'S YOUR LUCKY DAY, TOURIST.
EVERYONE -- CLEAR THE AREA!
BY FEDERAL AUTHORITY -- THIS IS AN OFFICIAL CRIME SCENE!
YO! WATCH IT, GOMER!
CHECK IT OUT, BIG BROTHER... THE GREENSHIRTS ARE RIGHT ON TIME...
NOT NOW, ANGIE...

COMMANDER ARCHER, YOU'RE GOING TO HAVE TO POWER DOWN AND COME WITH US --

ARE YOU *NUTS*?! HE JUST *SAVED* THIS CITY FROM A KILL-CRAZY *BUG LADY* AND *YOU GUYS* WANNA' --

ADAM ARCHER, CAN YOU NOT SENSE THE GROWING THREAT *ELSEWHERE*?! WE MUST --

I KNOW, MAXIM... BELIEVE ME.

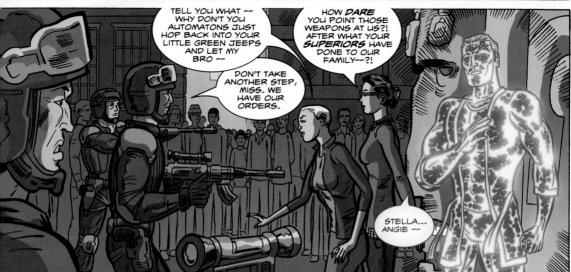

TELL YOU WHAT -- WHY DON'T YOU AUTOMATONS JUST HOP BACK INTO YOUR LITTLE GREEN JEEPS AND LET MY BRO --

DON'T TAKE ANOTHER STEP, MISS. WE HAVE OUR ORDERS.

HOW *DARE* YOU POINT THOSE WEAPONS AT US?! AFTER WHAT YOUR *SUPERIORS* HAVE DONE TO OUR FAMILY--?!

STELLA... ANGIE --

-- LET ME HANDLE THIS.

THERE IS NO TIME FOR SUCH POSTURING!

I AGREE. BUT I WANT TO SAY *ONE THING* TO THESE SOLDIERS...

COMMANDER --

... YOU GO BACK AND YOU TELL *GENERAL BRIGG* THAT I'M GOING TO LIVE UP TO MY END OF THE DEAL... *DESPITE* WHAT HE OR THE PRESIDENT THINKS OF ME!

BUT IF THEY COME AFTER ME *AGAIN* --

ADAM ARCHER!

RIGHT, RIGHT... LET'S DO THIS.

WHAT--?!

DAMMIT!

OKAY, OKAY... YOU KNOW WE'VE GOTTA' SAY IT. LOOK WHERE **ARE**... LOOK AT WHAT'S **GOING ON** HERE... HOW COULD WE **NOT** SAY IT? SO HERE GOES...

WHAT HAPPENS IN VEGAS... STAYS IN VEGAS.

APPARENTLY.... THIS INCLUDES **ARMAGEDDON.**

AMERICA'S PLAYGROUND HAS BECOME HELL ON EARTH.

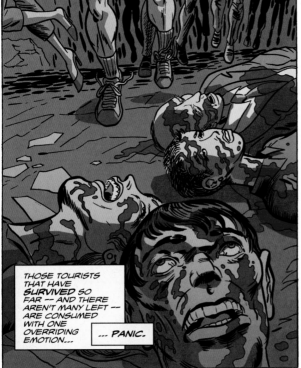

THOSE TOURISTS THAT HAVE **SURVIVED** SO FAR -- AND THERE AREN'T MANY LEFT -- ARE CONSUMED WITH ONE OVERRIDING EMOTION...

... PANIC.

AND WITH GOOD REASON...

... THE **TRIAD** IS ON AN INEXPLICABLE TEAR.

AND EVEN **THEY** DON'T KNOW WHY....

THEY RUN... THEY **SCREAM**... THEY PRAY TO THEIR CHOSEN DEITIES...

I TASTE EACH FIERY DEATH ON MY PHYSIC-MORPHED TONGUE AND YET --

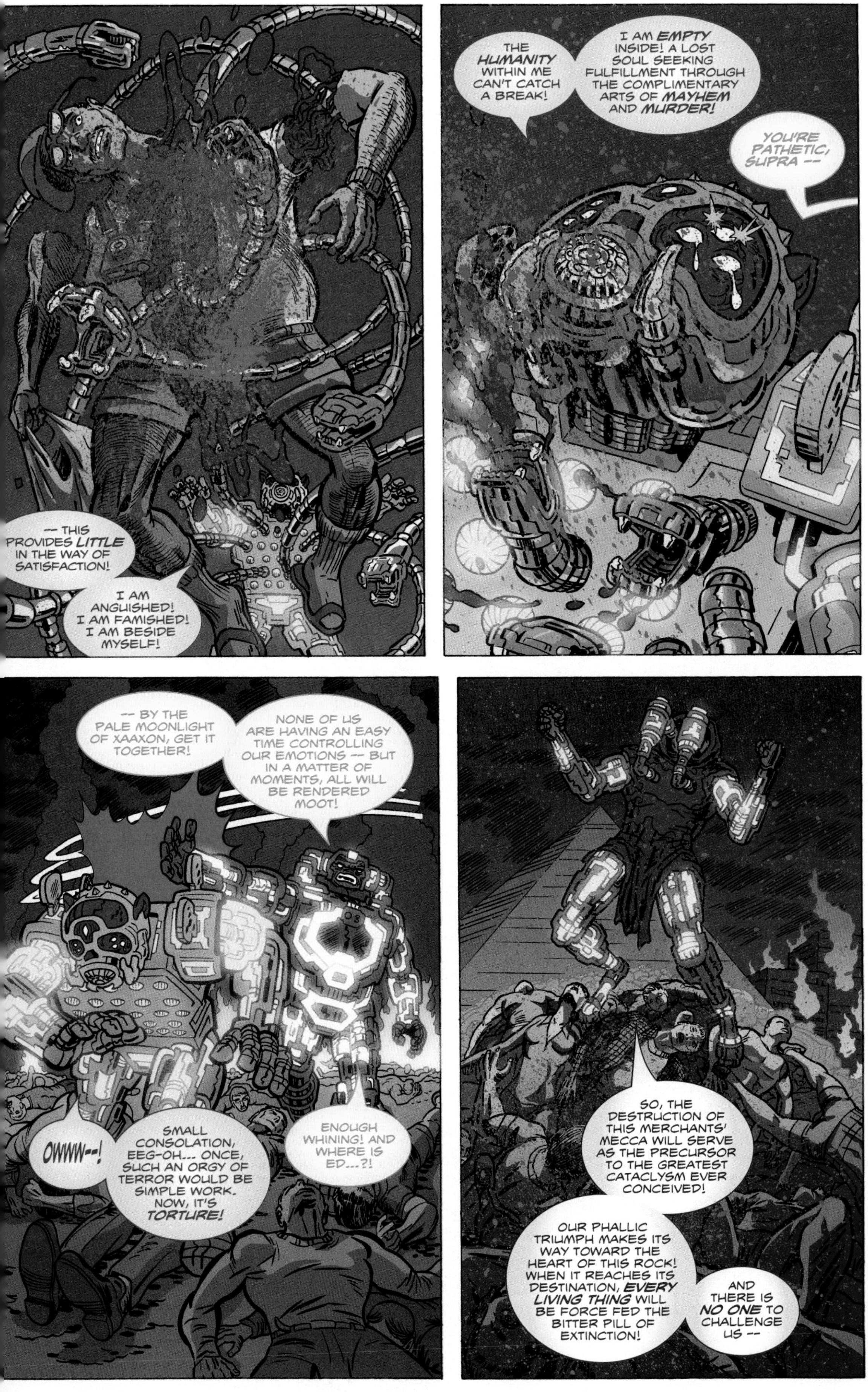
-- THIS PROVIDES LITTLE IN THE WAY OF SATISFACTION!
I AM ANGUISHED! I AM FAMISHED! I AM BESIDE MYSELF!
THE HUMANITY WITHIN ME CAN'T CATCH A BREAK!
I AM EMPTY INSIDE! A LOST SOUL SEEKING FULFILLMENT THROUGH THE COMPLIMENTARY ARTS OF MAYHEM AND MURDER!
YOU'RE PATHETIC, SUPRA --
-- BY THE PALE MOONLIGHT OF XAAXON, GET IT TOGETHER!
NONE OF US ARE HAVING AN EASY TIME CONTROLLING OUR EMOTIONS -- BUT IN A MATTER OF MOMENTS, ALL WILL BE RENDERED MOOT!
OWWW--!
SMALL CONSOLATION, EEG-OH... ONCE, SUCH AN ORGY OF TERROR WOULD BE SIMPLE WORK. NOW, IT'S TORTURE!
ENOUGH WHINING! AND WHERE IS ED...?!
SO, THE DESTRUCTION OF THIS MERCHANTS' MECCA WILL SERVE AS THE PRECURSOR TO THE GREATEST CATACLYSM EVER CONCEIVED!
OUR PHALLIC TRIUMPH MAKES ITS WAY TOWARD THE HEART OF THIS ROCK! WHEN IT REACHES ITS DESTINATION, EVERY LIVING THING WILL BE FORCE FED THE BITTER PILL OF EXTINCTION!
AND THERE IS NO ONE TO CHALLENGE US --

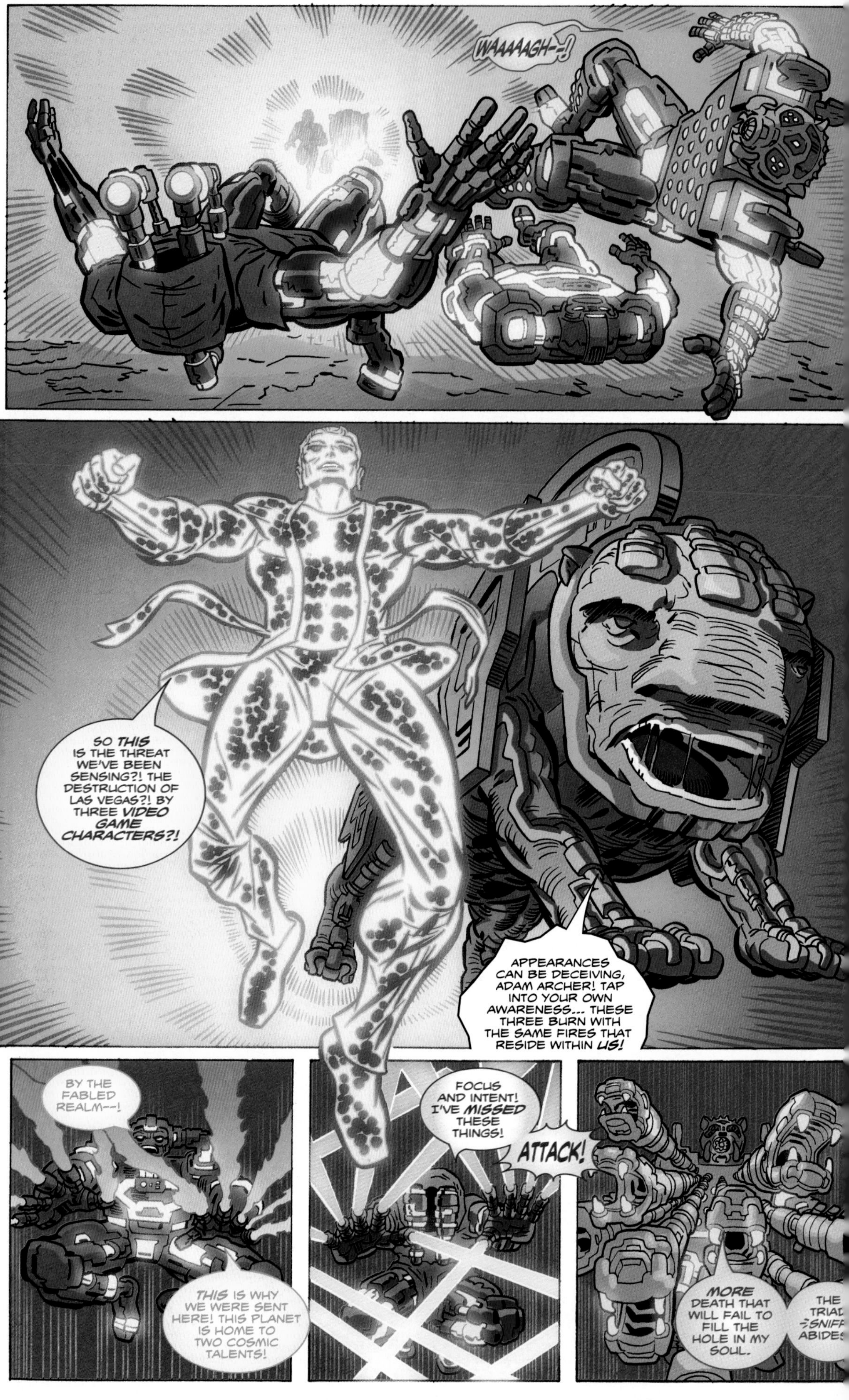
WAAAAAGH--!
SO THIS IS THE THREAT WE'VE BEEN SENSING?! THE DESTRUCTION OF LAS VEGAS?! BY THREE VIDEO GAME CHARACTERS?!
APPEARANCES CAN BE DECEIVING, ADAM ARCHER! TAP INTO YOUR OWN AWARENESS... THESE THREE BURN WITH THE SAME FIRES THAT RESIDE WITHIN US!
BY THE FABLED REALM--!
THIS IS WHY WE WERE SENT HERE! THIS PLANET IS HOME TO TWO COSMIC TALENTS!
FOCUS AND INTENT! I'VE MISSED THESE THINGS!
ATTACK!
MORE DEATH THAT WILL FAIL TO FILL THE HOLE IN MY SOUL.
THE TRIAD =SNIFF= ABIDES

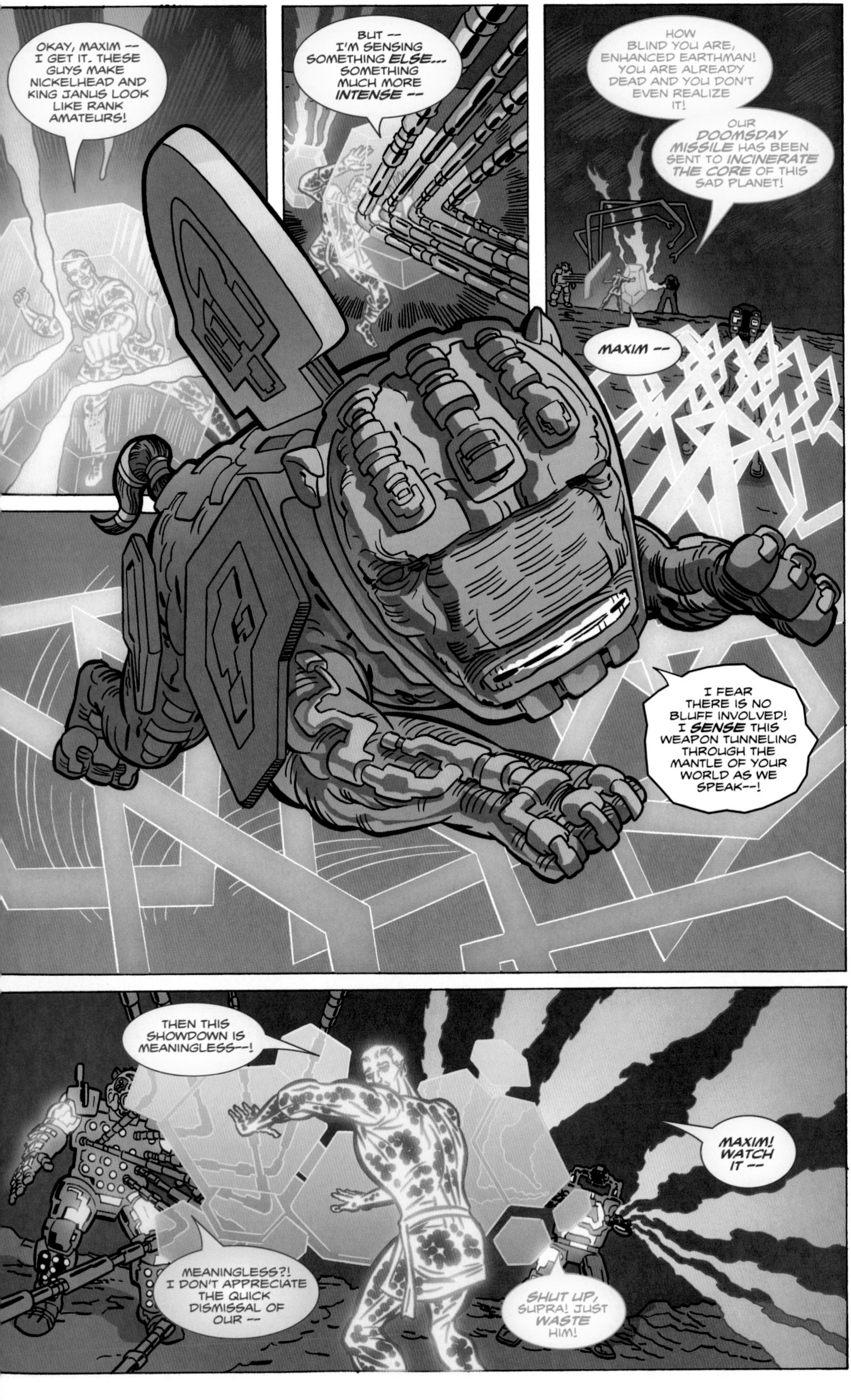

OKAY, MAXIM -- I GET IT. THESE GUYS MAKE NICKELHEAD AND KING JANUS LOOK LIKE RANK AMATEURS!
BUT -- I'M SENSING SOMETHING ELSE... SOMETHING MUCH MORE INTENSE --
HOW BLIND YOU ARE, ENHANCED EARTHMAN! YOU ARE ALREADY DEAD AND YOU DON'T EVEN REALIZE IT!
OUR DOOMSDAY MISSILE HAS BEEN SENT TO INCINERATE THE CORE OF THIS SAD PLANET!
MAXIM --
I FEAR THERE IS NO BLUFF INVOLVED! I SENSE THIS WEAPON TUNNELING THROUGH THE MANTLE OF YOUR WORLD AS WE SPEAK--!
THEN THIS SHOWDOWN IS MEANINGLESS--!
MAXIM! WATCH IT --
MEANINGLESS?! I DON'T APPRECIATE THE QUICK DISMISSAL OF OUR --
SHUT UP, SUPRA! JUST WASTE HIM!

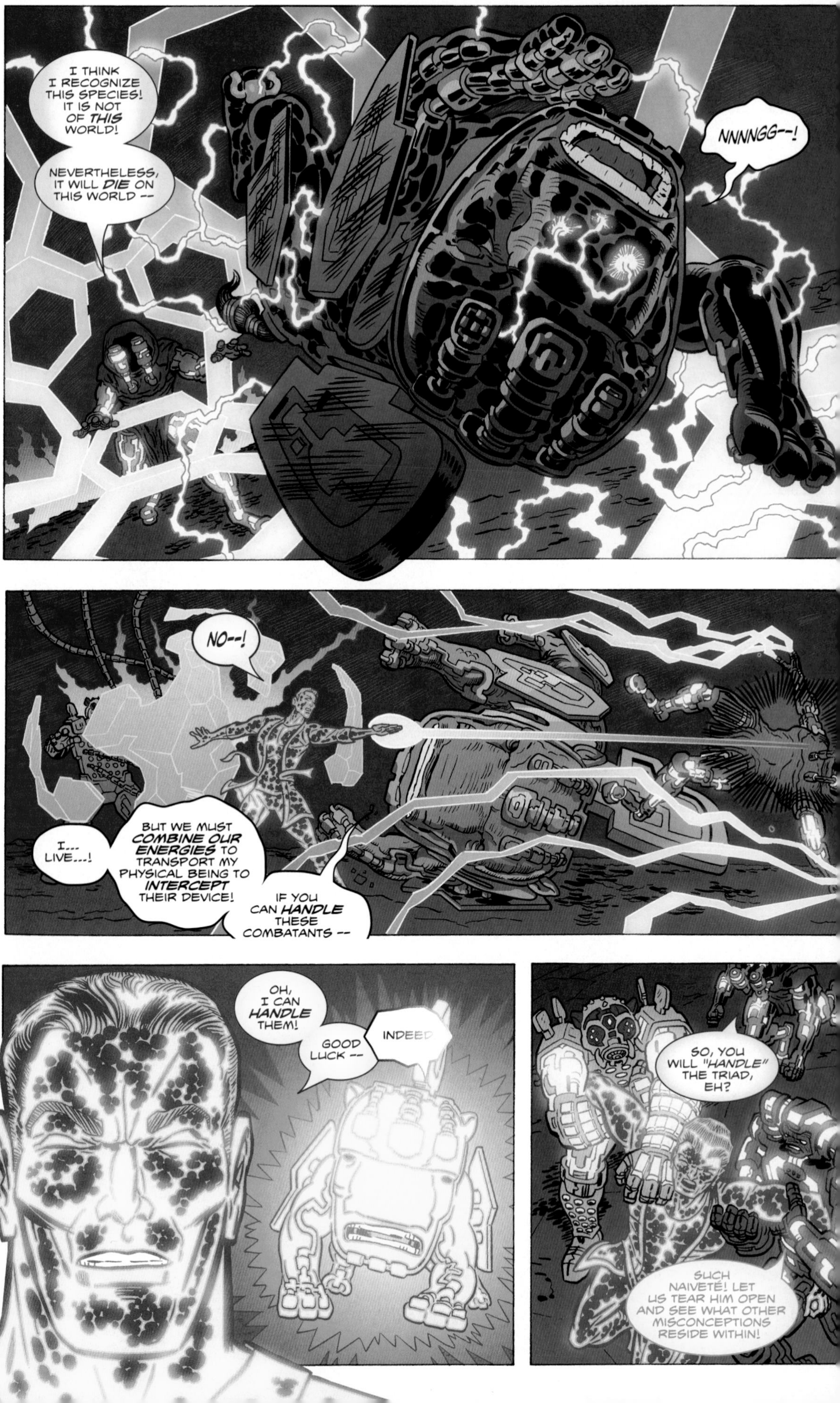

I THINK I RECOGNIZE THIS SPECIES! IT IS NOT OF THIS WORLD!
NEVERTHELESS, IT WILL DIE ON THIS WORLD --
NNNNGG--!
NO--!
I... LIVE...!
BUT WE MUST COMBINE OUR ENERGIES TO TRANSPORT MY PHYSICAL BEING TO INTERCEPT THEIR DEVICE!
IF YOU CAN HANDLE THESE COMBATANTS --
OH, I CAN HANDLE THEM!
GOOD LUCK --
SO, YOU WILL "HANDLE" THE TRIAD, EH?
SUCH NAIVETÉ! LET US TEAR HIM OPEN AND SEE WHAT OTHER MISCONCEPTIONS RESIDE WITHIN!

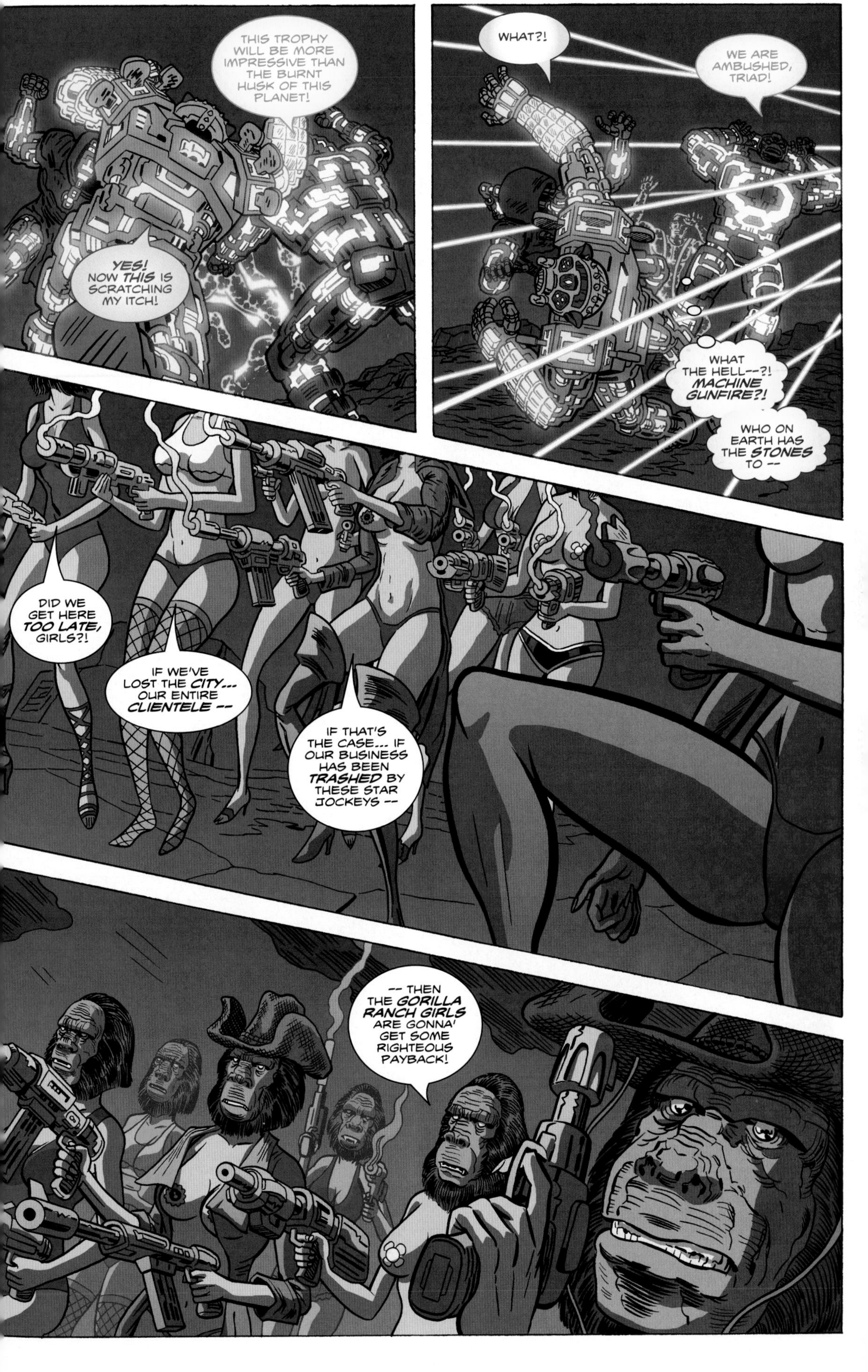
THIS TROPHY WILL BE MORE IMPRESSIVE THAN THE BURNT HUSK OF THIS PLANET!
YES! NOW THIS IS SCRATCHING MY ITCH!
WHAT?!
WE ARE AMBUSHED, TRIAD!
WHAT THE HELL--?! MACHINE GUNFIRE?!
WHO ON EARTH HAS THE STONES TO --
DID WE GET HERE TOO LATE, GIRLS?!
IF WE'VE LOST THE CITY--- OUR ENTIRE CLIENTELE --
IF THAT'S THE CASE--- IF OUR BUSINESS HAS BEEN TRASHED BY THESE STAR JOCKEYS --
-- THEN THE GORILLA RANCH GIRLS ARE GONNA' GET SOME RIGHTEOUS PAYBACK!

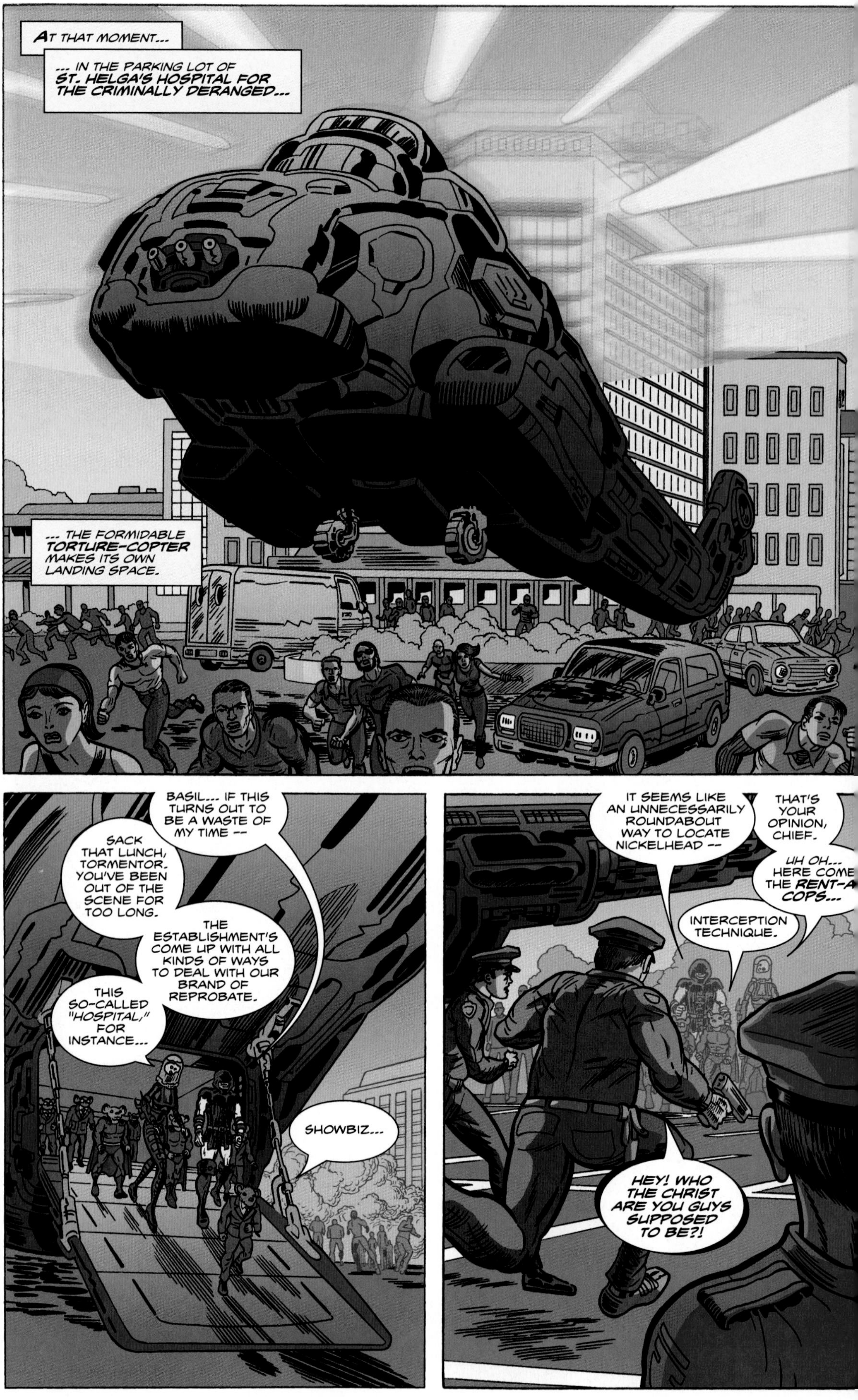
AT THAT MOMENT...
... IN THE PARKING LOT OF ST. HELGA'S HOSPITAL FOR THE CRIMINALLY DERANGED...
... THE FORMIDABLE TORTURE-COPTER MAKES ITS OWN LANDING SPACE.
BASIL... IF THIS TURNS OUT TO BE A WASTE OF MY TIME --
SACK THAT LUNCH, TORMENTOR. YOU'VE BEEN OUT OF THE SCENE FOR TOO LONG.
THE ESTABLISHMENT'S COME UP WITH ALL KINDS OF WAYS TO DEAL WITH OUR BRAND OF REPROBATE.
THIS SO-CALLED "HOSPITAL," FOR INSTANCE...
SHOWBIZ...
IT SEEMS LIKE AN UNNECESSARILY ROUNDABOUT WAY TO LOCATE NICKELHEAD --
THAT'S YOUR OPINION, CHIEF.
INTERCEPTION TECHNIQUE.
UH OH... HERE COME THE RENT-A COPS...
HEY! WHO THE CHRIST ARE YOU GUYS SUPPOSED TO BE?!

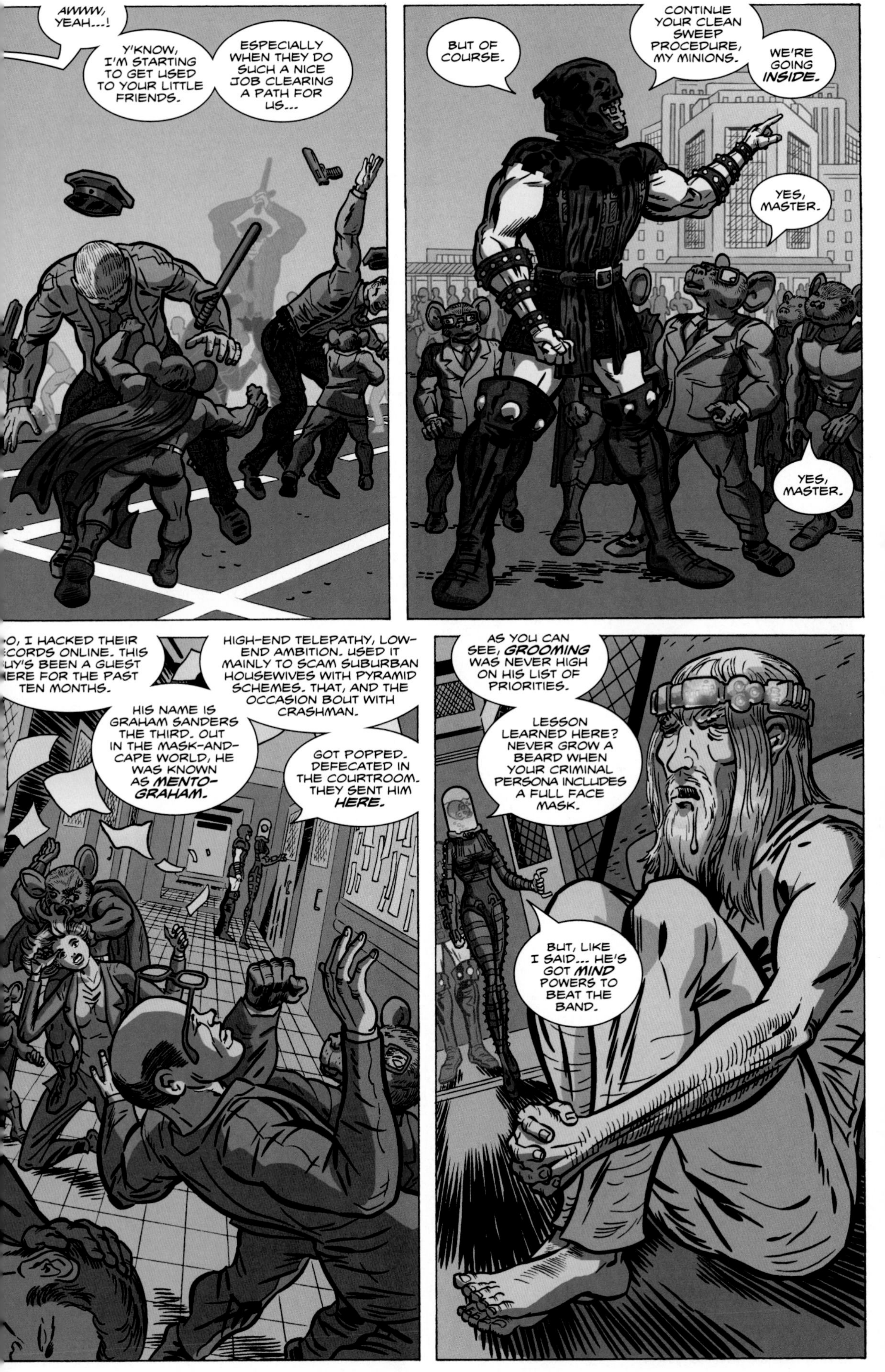
AWWW, YEAH...!
Y'KNOW, I'M STARTING TO GET USED TO YOUR LITTLE FRIENDS.
ESPECIALLY WHEN THEY DO SUCH A NICE JOB CLEARING A PATH FOR US...
BUT OF COURSE.
CONTINUE YOUR CLEAN SWEEP PROCEDURE, MY MINIONS.
WE'RE GOING INSIDE.
YES, MASTER.
YES, MASTER.
O, I HACKED THEIR ECORDS ONLINE. THIS UY'S BEEN A GUEST ERE FOR THE PAST TEN MONTHS.
HIS NAME IS GRAHAM SANDERS THE THIRD. OUT IN THE MASK-AND-CAPE WORLD, HE WAS KNOWN AS MENTO-GRAHAM.
HIGH-END TELEPATHY, LOW-END AMBITION. USED IT MAINLY TO SCAM SUBURBAN HOUSEWIVES WITH PYRAMID SCHEMES. THAT, AND THE OCCASION BOUT WITH CRASHMAN.
GOT POPPED. DEFECATED IN THE COURTROOM. THEY SENT HIM HERE.
AS YOU CAN SEE, GROOMING WAS NEVER HIGH ON HIS LIST OF PRIORITIES.
LESSON LEARNED HERE? NEVER GROW A BEARD WHEN YOUR CRIMINAL PERSONA INCLUDES A FULL FACE MASK.
BUT, LIKE I SAID... HE'S GOT MIND POWERS TO BEAT THE BAND.

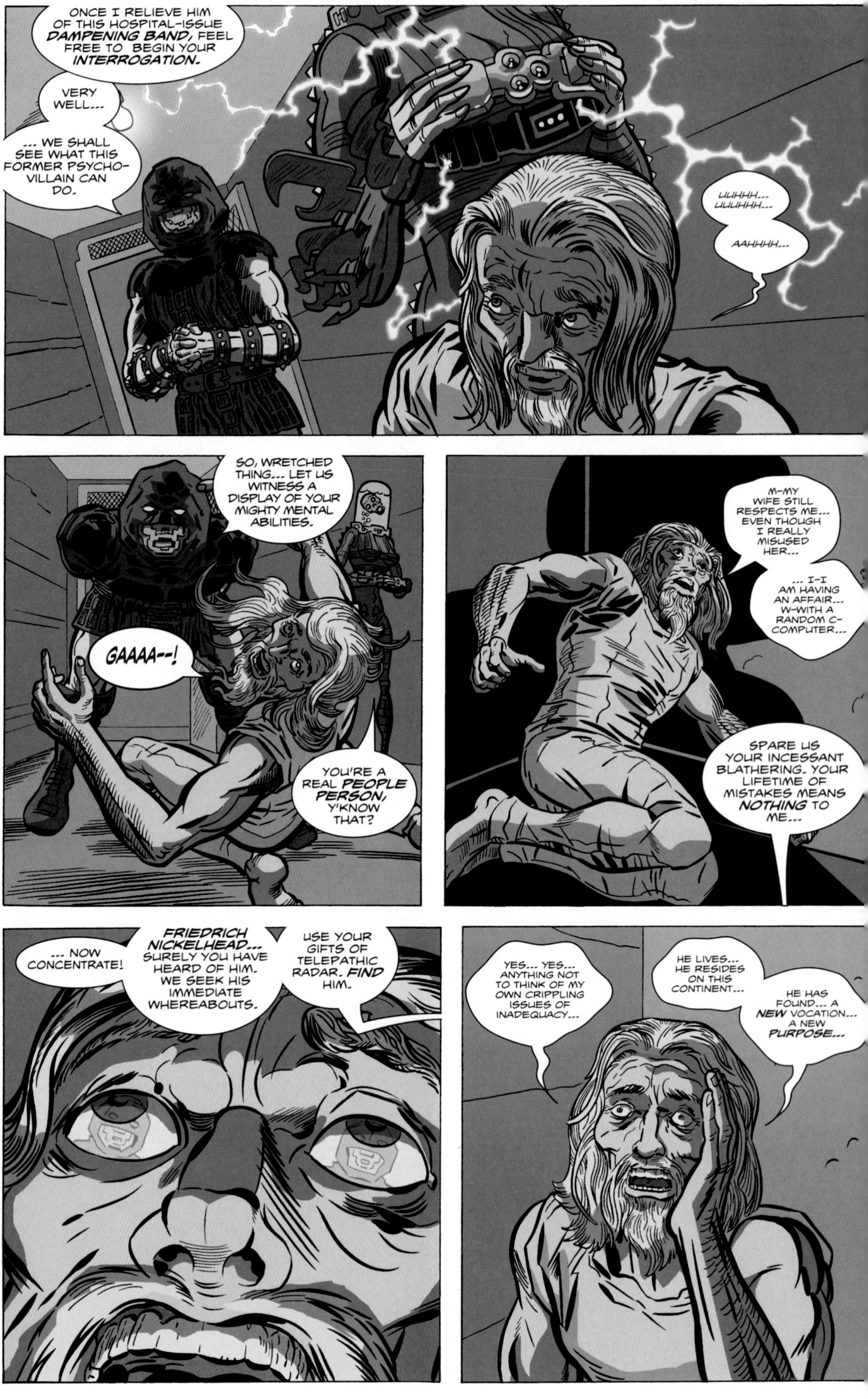
ONCE I RELIEVE HIM OF THIS HOSPITAL-ISSUE DAMPENING BAND, FEEL FREE TO BEGIN YOUR INTERROGATION.
VERY WELL...
... WE SHALL SEE WHAT THIS FORMER PSYCHO-VILLAIN CAN DO.
UUHHH... UUUHHH...
AAHHHH...
SO, WRETCHED THING... LET US WITNESS A DISPLAY OF YOUR MIGHTY MENTAL ABILITIES.
GAAAA--!
YOU'RE A REAL PEOPLE PERSON, Y'KNOW THAT?
M-MY WIFE STILL RESPECTS ME... EVEN THOUGH I REALLY MISUSED HER...
... I-I AM HAVING AN AFFAIR... W-WITH A RANDOM C-COMPUTER...
SPARE US YOUR INCESSANT BLATHERING. YOUR LIFETIME OF MISTAKES MEANS NOTHING TO ME...
... NOW CONCENTRATE!
FRIEDRICH NICKELHEAD... SURELY YOU HAVE HEARD OF HIM. WE SEEK HIS IMMEDIATE WHEREABOUTS.
USE YOUR GIFTS OF TELEPATHIC RADAR. FIND HIM.
YES... YES... ANYTHING NOT TO THINK OF MY OWN CRIPPLING ISSUES OF INADEQUACY...
HE LIVES... HE RESIDES ON THIS CONTINENT...
HE HAS FOUND... A NEW VOCATION... A NEW PURPOSE...

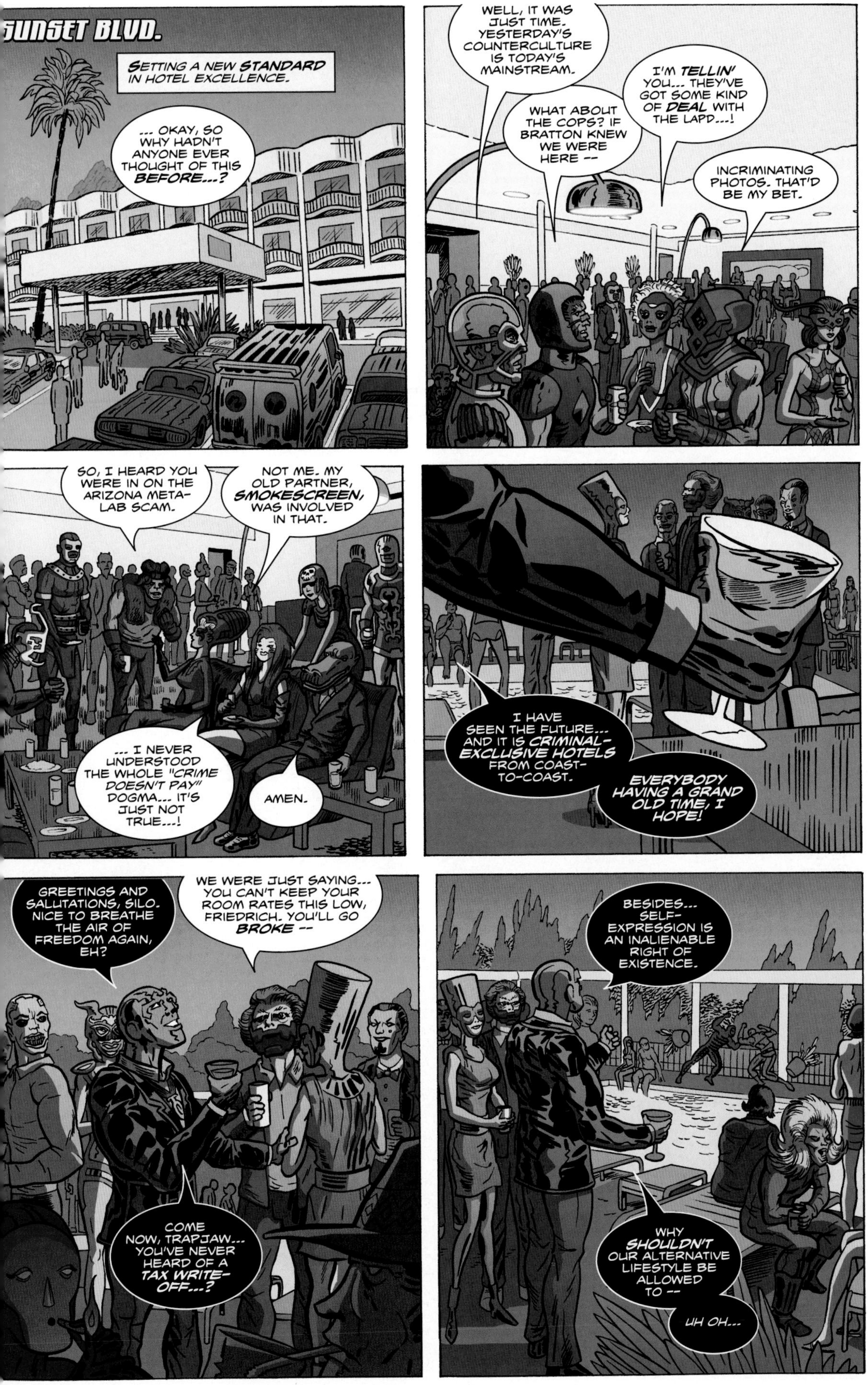
SUNSET BLVD.
SETTING A NEW STANDARD IN HOTEL EXCELLENCE.
... OKAY, SO WHY HADN'T ANYONE EVER THOUGHT OF THIS BEFORE...?
WELL, IT WAS JUST TIME. YESTERDAY'S COUNTERCULTURE IS TODAY'S MAINSTREAM.
WHAT ABOUT THE COPS? IF BRATTON KNEW WE WERE HERE --
I'M TELLIN' YOU... THEY'VE GOT SOME KIND OF DEAL WITH THE LAPD...!
INCRIMINATING PHOTOS. THAT'D BE MY BET.
SO, I HEARD YOU WERE IN ON THE ARIZONA META-LAB SCAM.
NOT ME. MY OLD PARTNER, SMOKESCREEN, WAS INVOLVED IN THAT.
... I NEVER UNDERSTOOD THE WHOLE "CRIME DOESN'T PAY" DOGMA... IT'S JUST NOT TRUE...!
AMEN.
I HAVE SEEN THE FUTURE... AND IT IS CRIMINAL-EXCLUSIVE HOTELS FROM COAST-TO-COAST.
EVERYBODY HAVING A GRAND OLD TIME, I HOPE!
GREETINGS AND SALUTATIONS, SILO. NICE TO BREATHE THE AIR OF FREEDOM AGAIN, EH?
WE WERE JUST SAYING... YOU CAN'T KEEP YOUR ROOM RATES THIS LOW, FRIEDRICH. YOU'LL GO BROKE --
COME NOW, TRAPJAW... YOU'VE NEVER HEARD OF A TAX WRITE-OFF...?
BESIDES... SELF-EXPRESSION IS AN INALIENABLE RIGHT OF EXISTENCE.
WHY SHOULDN'T OUR ALTERNATIVE LIFESTYLE BE ALLOWED TO --
UH OH...

... WELL, AS THEY *SAY*, A LITTLE RAIN MUST FALL.

ADMIT IT, BITCH! YOU SLEPT WITH AQUA VELVET!

HEY -- *SHE* CAME ON TO *ME*! YOU PIECE OF --

NOW, THIS IS NO WAY TO BUILD A BRIDGE.

SECURITY! POOLSIDE MELEE...!

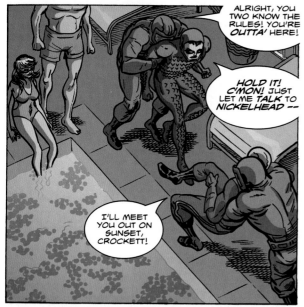

ALRIGHT, YOU TWO KNOW THE RULES! YOU'RE *OUTTA'* HERE!

HOLD IT! C'MON! JUST LET ME *TALK* TO *NICKELHEAD* --

I'LL MEET YOU OUT ON *SUNSET*, CROCKETT!

EXCUSE ME, SIR. BUT THERE'S A *SITUATION* IN ROOM 206 --

AHHH... YOU KNOW THE PROTOCOL, VIVICA. BUSINESS MATTERS ARE TO BE *WHISPERED* AT POOLSIDE...

I SEE. THANK YOU, VIV.

GENTLEMEN... LADIES... IF YOU'LL *EXCUSE* ME, THERE'S A GUEST RELATIONS ISSUE THAT NEEDS MY IMMEDIATE ATTENTION...

IN HERE, SIR...

OH, FOR THE LOVE OF JAGGER'S LIPS...!

THIS IS TRULY EMBARRASSING...

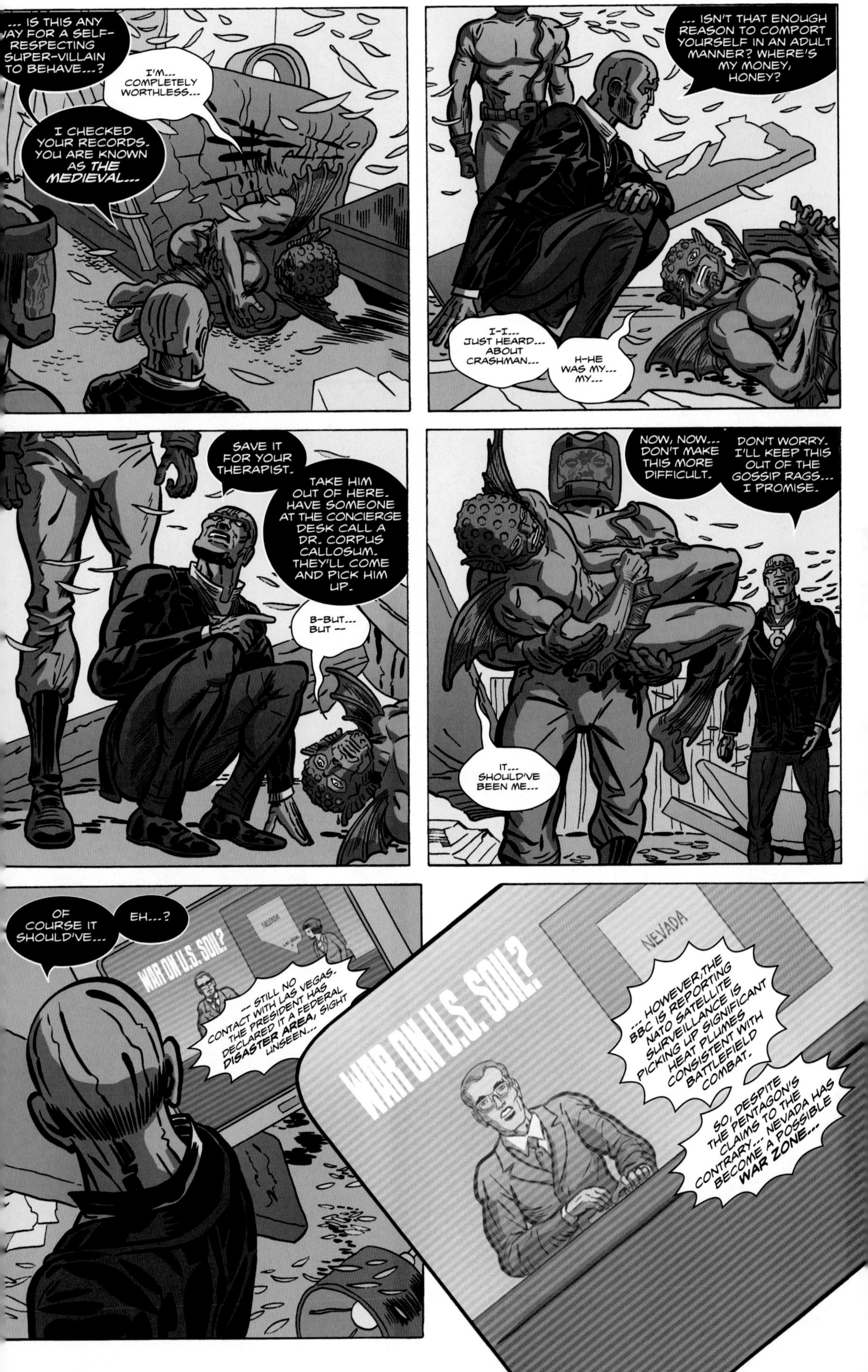
... IS THIS ANY WAY FOR A SELF-RESPECTING SUPER-VILLAIN TO BEHAVE...?
I'M... COMPLETELY WORTHLESS...
I CHECKED YOUR RECORDS. YOU ARE KNOWN AS THE MEDIEVAL...
... ISN'T THAT ENOUGH REASON TO COMPORT YOURSELF IN AN ADULT MANNER? WHERE'S MY MONEY, HONEY?
I-I... JUST HEARD... ABOUT CRASHMAN...
H-HE WAS MY... MY...
SAVE IT FOR YOUR THERAPIST.
TAKE HIM OUT OF HERE. HAVE SOMEONE AT THE CONCIERGE DESK CALL A DR. CORPUS CALLOSUM. THEY'LL COME AND PICK HIM UP.
B-BUT... BUT --
NOW, NOW... DON'T MAKE THIS MORE DIFFICULT.
DON'T WORRY. I'LL KEEP THIS OUT OF THE GOSSIP RAGS... I PROMISE.
IT... SHOULD'VE BEEN ME...
OF COURSE IT SHOULD'VE...
EH...?
WAR ON U.S. SOIL?
-- STILL NO CONTACT WITH LAS VEGAS. THE PRESIDENT HAS DECLARED IT A FEDERAL DISASTER AREA, SIGHT UNSEEN...
NEVADA
WAR ON U.S. SOIL?
... HOWEVER, THE BBC IS REPORTING NATO SATELLITE SURVEILLANCE IS PICKING UP SIGNIFICANT HEAT PLUMES CONSISTENT WITH BATTLEFIELD COMBAT.
SO, DESPITE THE PENTAGON'S CLAIMS TO THE CONTRARY... NEVADA HAS BECOME A POSSIBLE WAR ZONE...

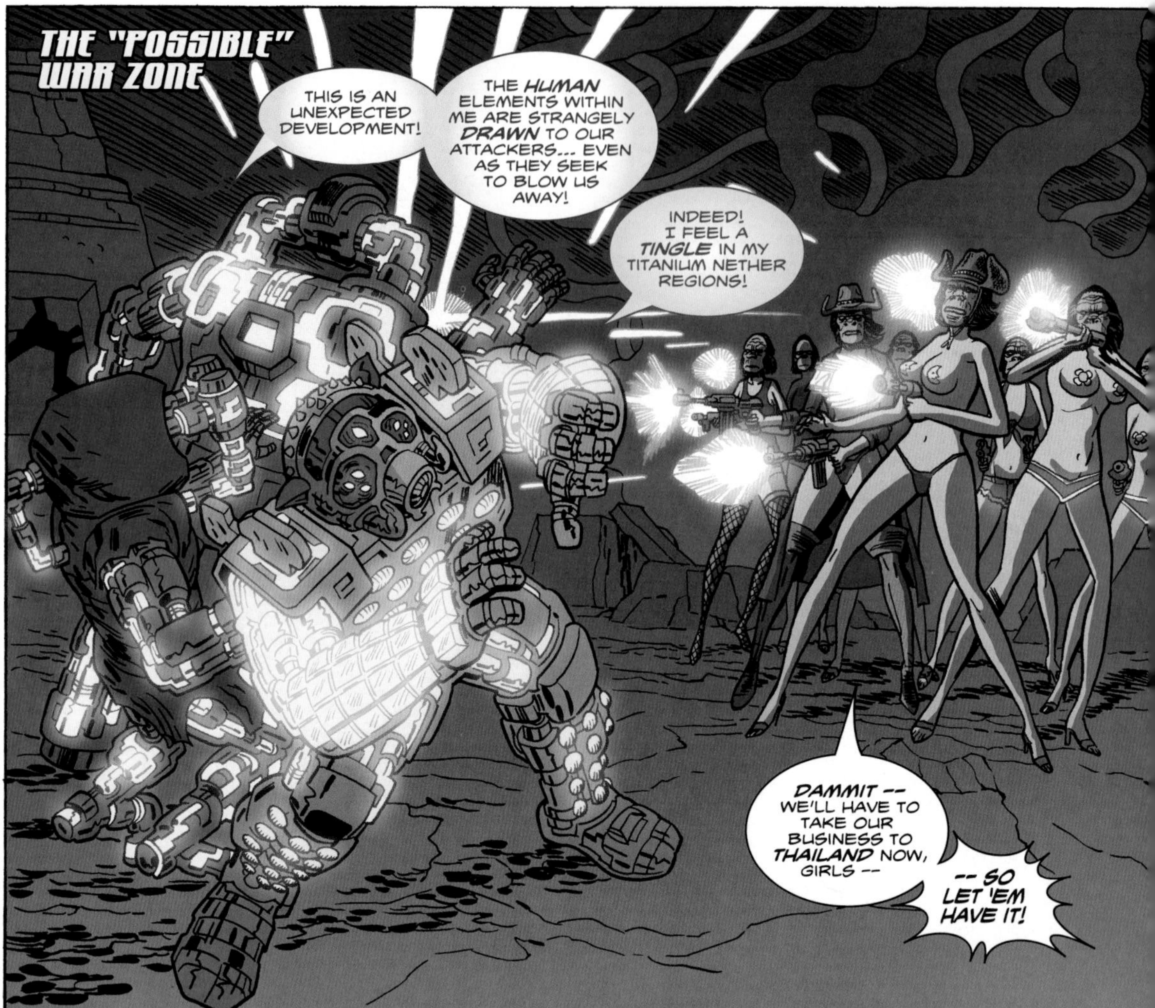
THE "POSSIBLE" WAR ZONE
THIS IS AN UNEXPECTED DEVELOPMENT!
THE HUMAN ELEMENTS WITHIN ME ARE STRANGELY DRAWN TO OUR ATTACKERS... EVEN AS THEY SEEK TO BLOW US AWAY!
INDEED! I FEEL A TINGLE IN MY TITANIUM NETHER REGIONS!
DAMMIT -- WE'LL HAVE TO TAKE OUR BUSINESS TO THAILAND NOW, GIRLS --
-- SO LET 'EM HAVE IT!

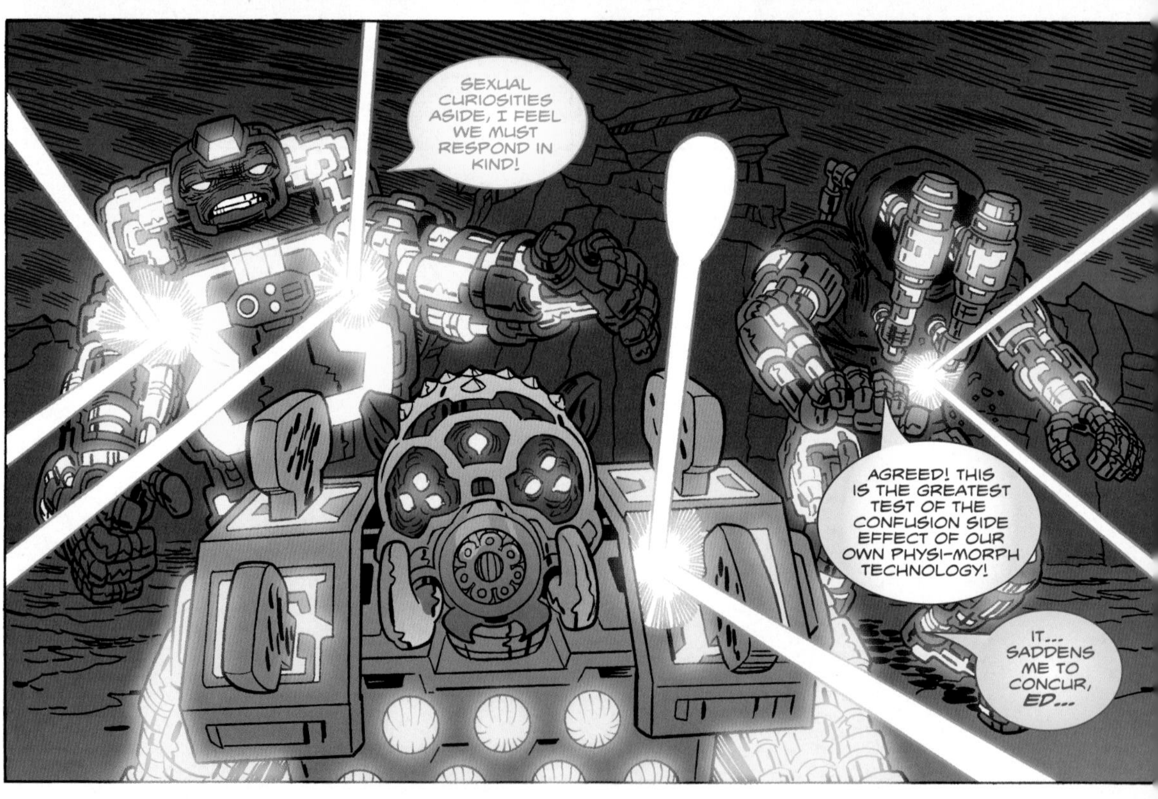
SEXUAL CURIOSITIES ASIDE, I FEEL WE MUST RESPOND IN KIND!
AGREED! THIS IS THE GREATEST TEST OF THE CONFUSION SIDE EFFECT OF OUR OWN PHYSI-MORPH TECHNOLOGY!
IT... SADDENS ME TO CONCUR, ED...

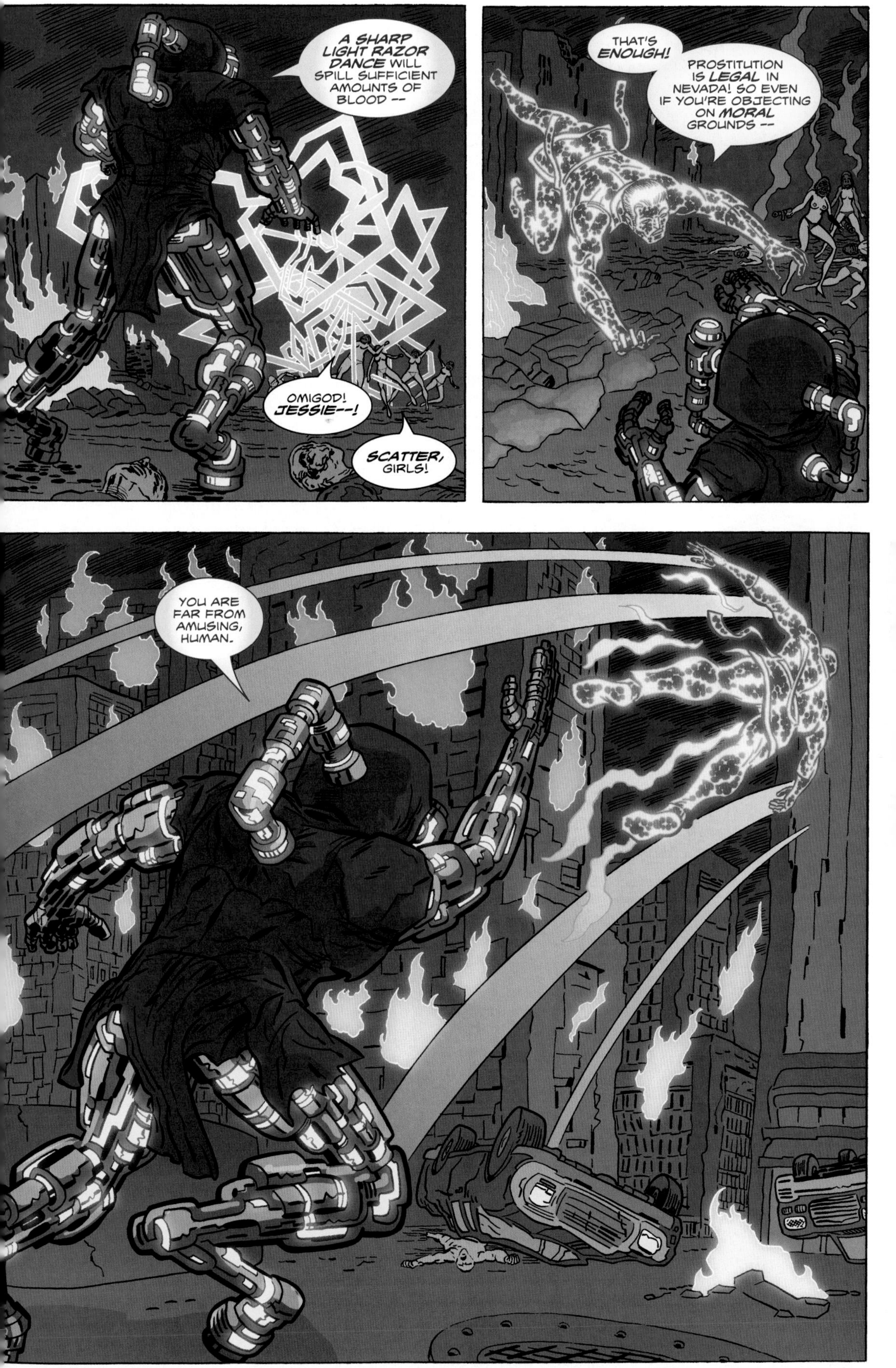
A SHARP LIGHT RAZOR DANCE WILL SPILL SUFFICIENT AMOUNTS OF BLOOD --
OMIGOD! JESSIE--!
SCATTER, GIRLS!
THAT'S ENOUGH!
PROSTITUTION IS LEGAL IN NEVADA! SO EVEN IF YOU'RE OBJECTING ON MORAL GROUNDS --
YOU ARE FAR FROM AMUSING, HUMAN.

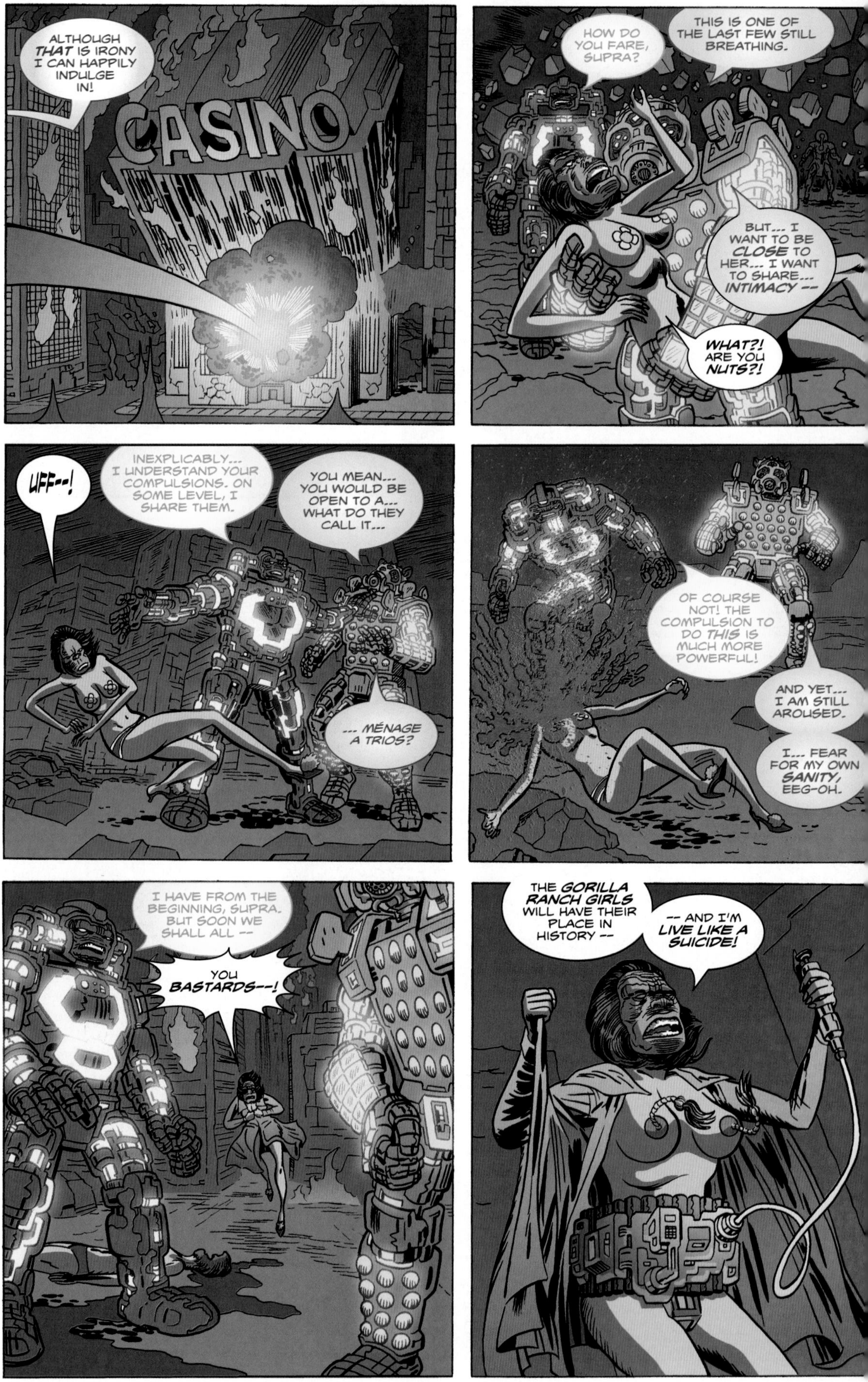
ALTHOUGH THAT IS IRONY I CAN HAPPILY INDULGE IN!
CASINO
HOW DO YOU FARE, SUPRA?
THIS IS ONE OF THE LAST FEW STILL BREATHING.
BUT... I WANT TO BE CLOSE TO HER... I WANT TO SHARE... INTIMACY --
WHAT?! ARE YOU NUTS?!
UFF--!
INEXPLICABLY... I UNDERSTAND YOUR COMPULSIONS. ON SOME LEVEL, I SHARE THEM.
YOU MEAN... YOU WOULD BE OPEN TO A... WHAT DO THEY CALL IT...
... MÉNAGE A TRIOS?
OF COURSE NOT! THE COMPULSION TO DO THIS IS MUCH MORE POWERFUL!
AND YET... I AM STILL AROUSED.
I... FEAR FOR MY OWN SANITY, EEG-OH.
I HAVE FROM THE BEGINNING, SUPRA. BUT SOON WE SHALL ALL --
YOU BASTARDS--!
THE GORILLA RANCH GIRLS WILL HAVE THEIR PLACE IN HISTORY --
-- AND I'M LIVE LIKE A SUICIDE!

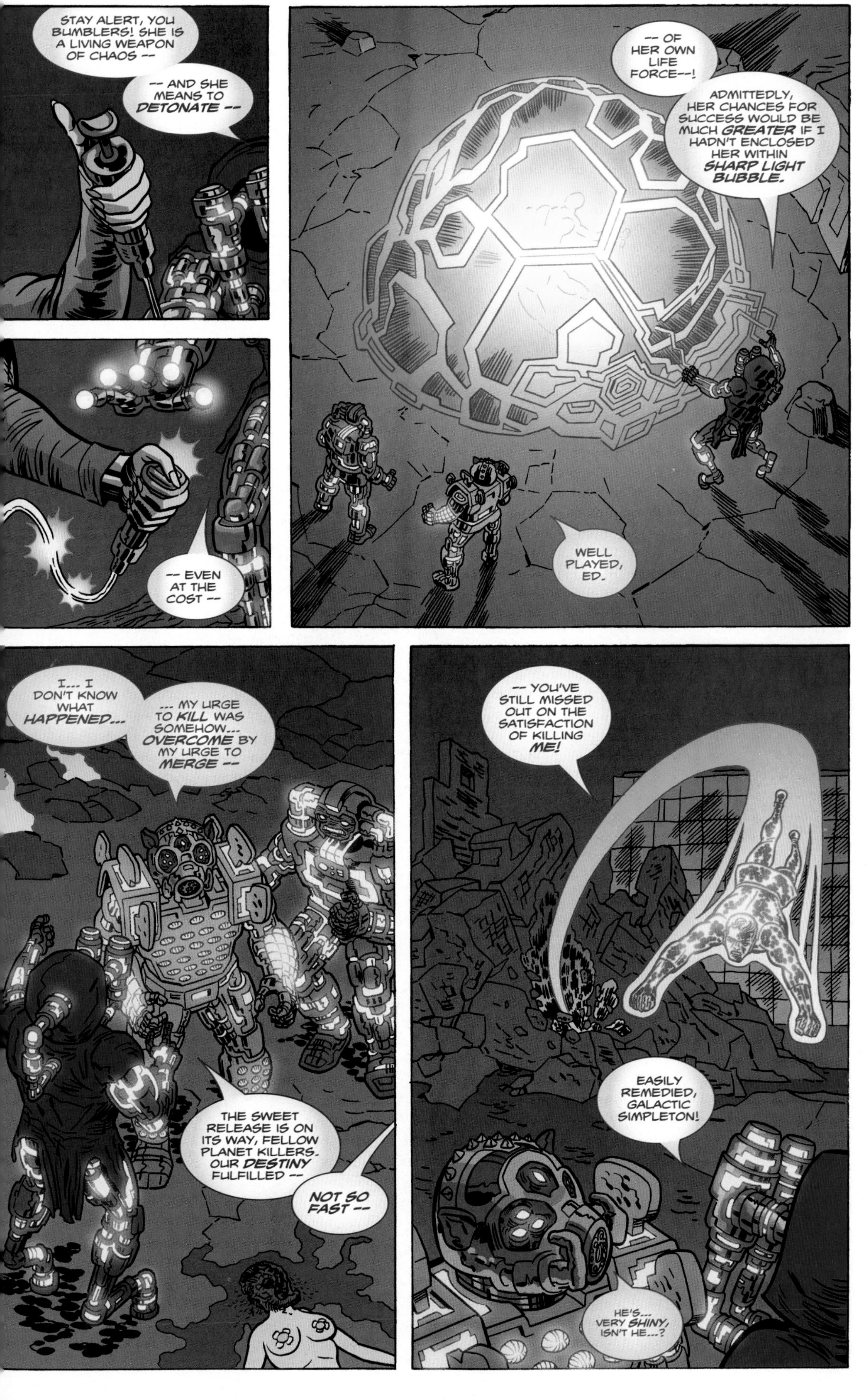
STAY ALERT, YOU BUMBLERS! SHE IS A LIVING WEAPON OF CHAOS --
-- AND SHE MEANS TO DETONATE --
-- EVEN AT THE COST --
-- OF HER OWN LIFE FORCE--!
ADMITTEDLY, HER CHANCES FOR SUCCESS WOULD BE MUCH GREATER IF I HADN'T ENCLOSED HER WITHIN SHARP LIGHT BUBBLE.
WELL PLAYED, ED.
I... I DON'T KNOW WHAT HAPPENED...
... MY URGE TO KILL WAS SOMEHOW... OVERCOME BY MY URGE TO MERGE --
THE SWEET RELEASE IS ON ITS WAY, FELLOW PLANET KILLERS. OUR DESTINY FULFILLED --
NOT SO FAST --
-- YOU'VE STILL MISSED OUT ON THE SATISFACTION OF KILLING ME!
EASILY REMEDIED, GALACTIC SIMPLETON!
HE'S... VERY SHINY, ISN'T HE...?

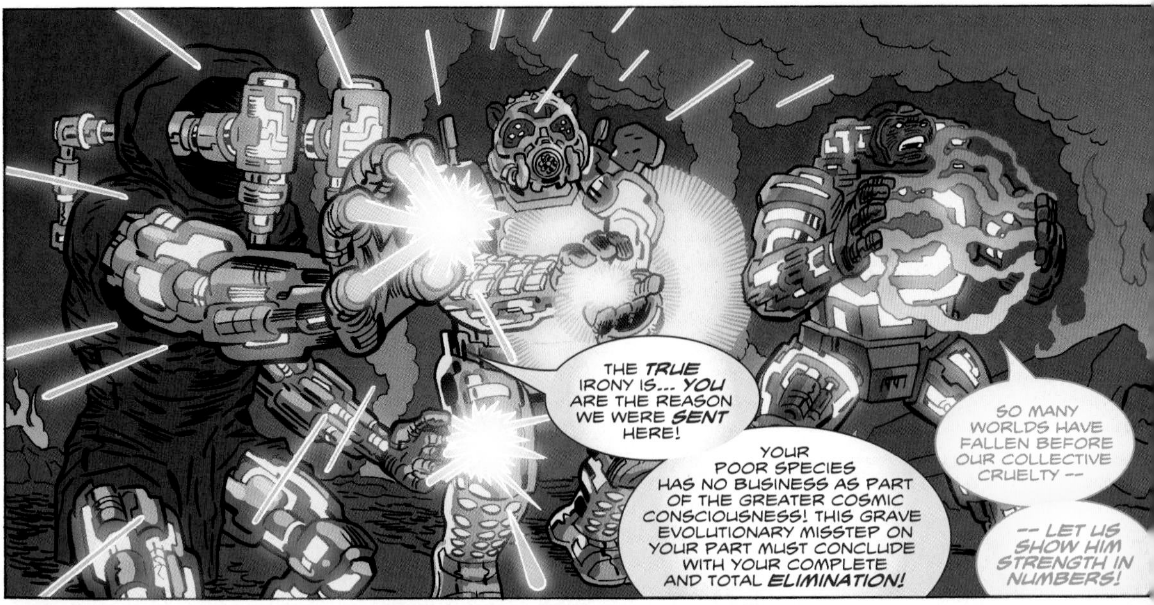
THE TRUE IRONY IS... YOU ARE THE REASON WE WERE SENT HERE!
YOUR POOR SPECIES HAS NO BUSINESS AS PART OF THE GREATER COSMIC CONSCIOUSNESS! THIS GRAVE EVOLUTIONARY MISSTEP ON YOUR PART MUST CONCLUDE WITH YOUR COMPLETE AND TOTAL ELIMINATION!
SO MANY WORLDS HAVE FALLEN BEFORE OUR COLLECTIVE CRUELTY --
-- LET US SHOW HIM STRENGTH IN NUMBERS!

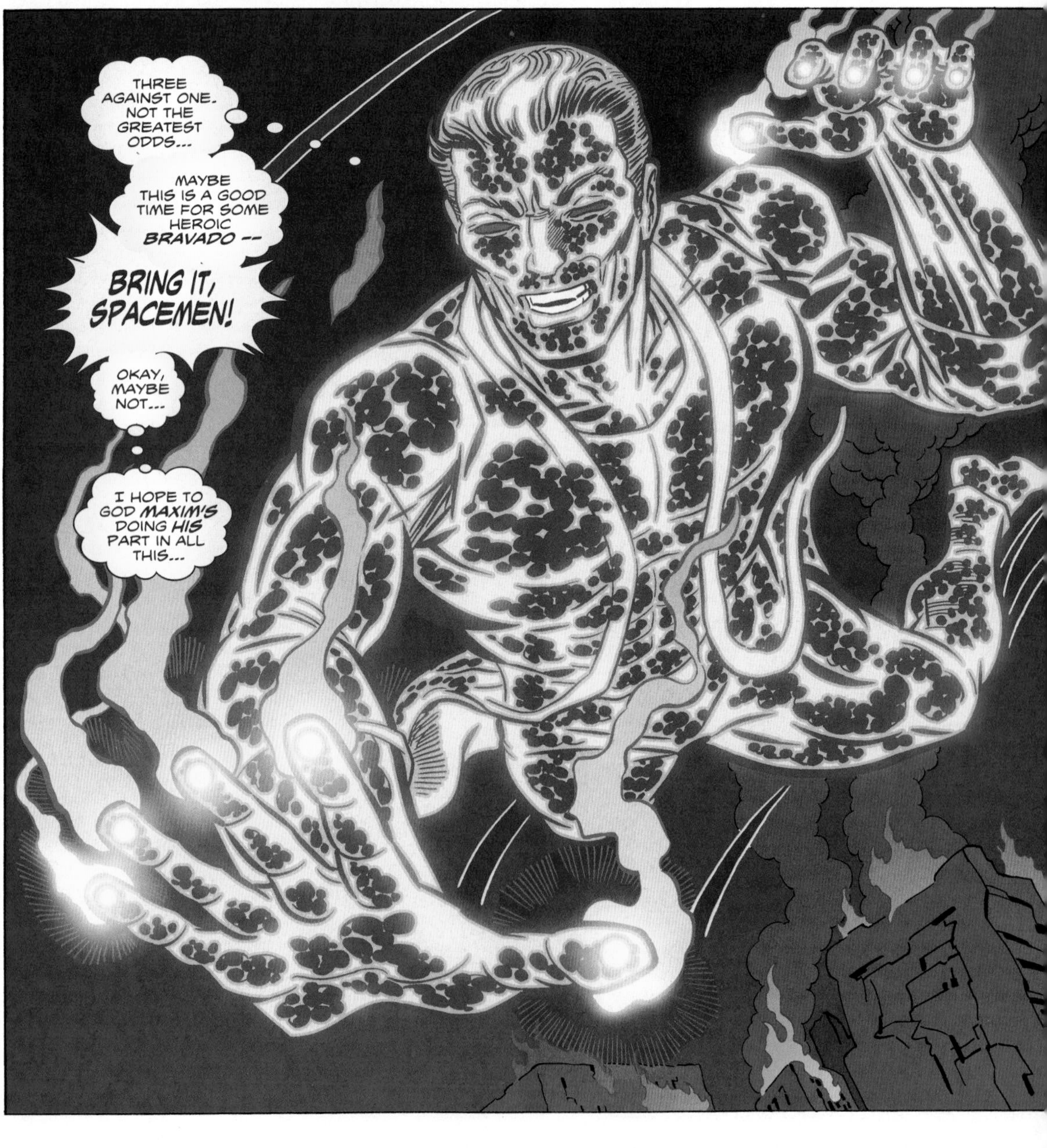
THREE AGAINST ONE. NOT THE GREATEST ODDS...
MAYBE THIS IS A GOOD TIME FOR SOME HEROIC BRAVADO --
BRING IT, SPACEMEN!
OKAY, MAYBE NOT...
I HOPE TO GOD MAXIM'S DOING HIS PART IN ALL THIS...

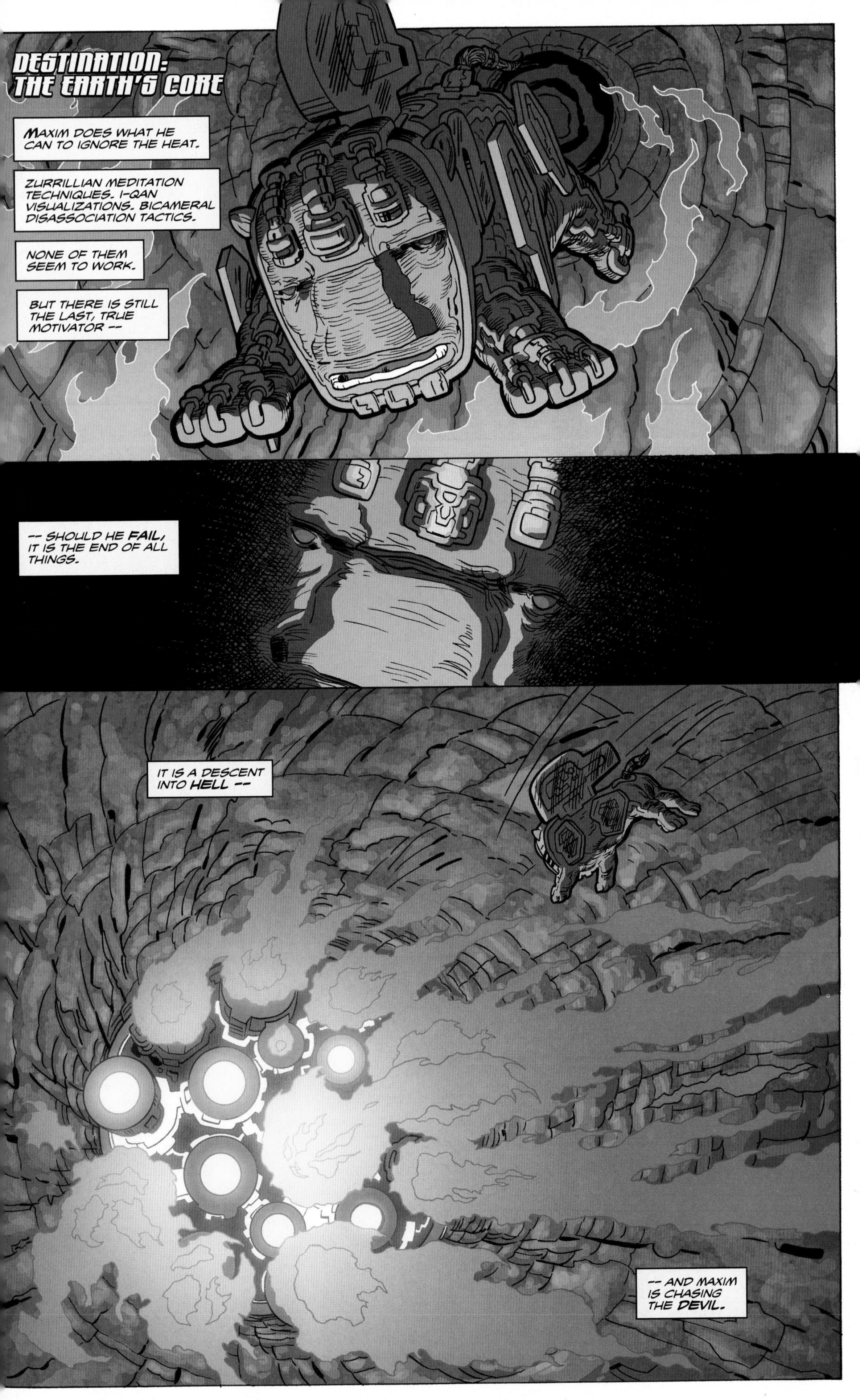
DESTINATION: THE EARTH'S CORE
MAXIM DOES WHAT HE CAN TO IGNORE THE HEAT.
ZURRILLIAN MEDITATION TECHNIQUES. I-QAN VISUALIZATIONS. BICAMERAL DISASSOCIATION TACTICS.
NONE OF THEM SEEM TO WORK.
BUT THERE IS STILL THE LAST, TRUE MOTIVATOR --
-- SHOULD HE FAIL, IT IS THE END OF ALL THINGS.
IT IS A DESCENT INTO HELL --
-- AND MAXIM IS CHASING THE DEVIL.

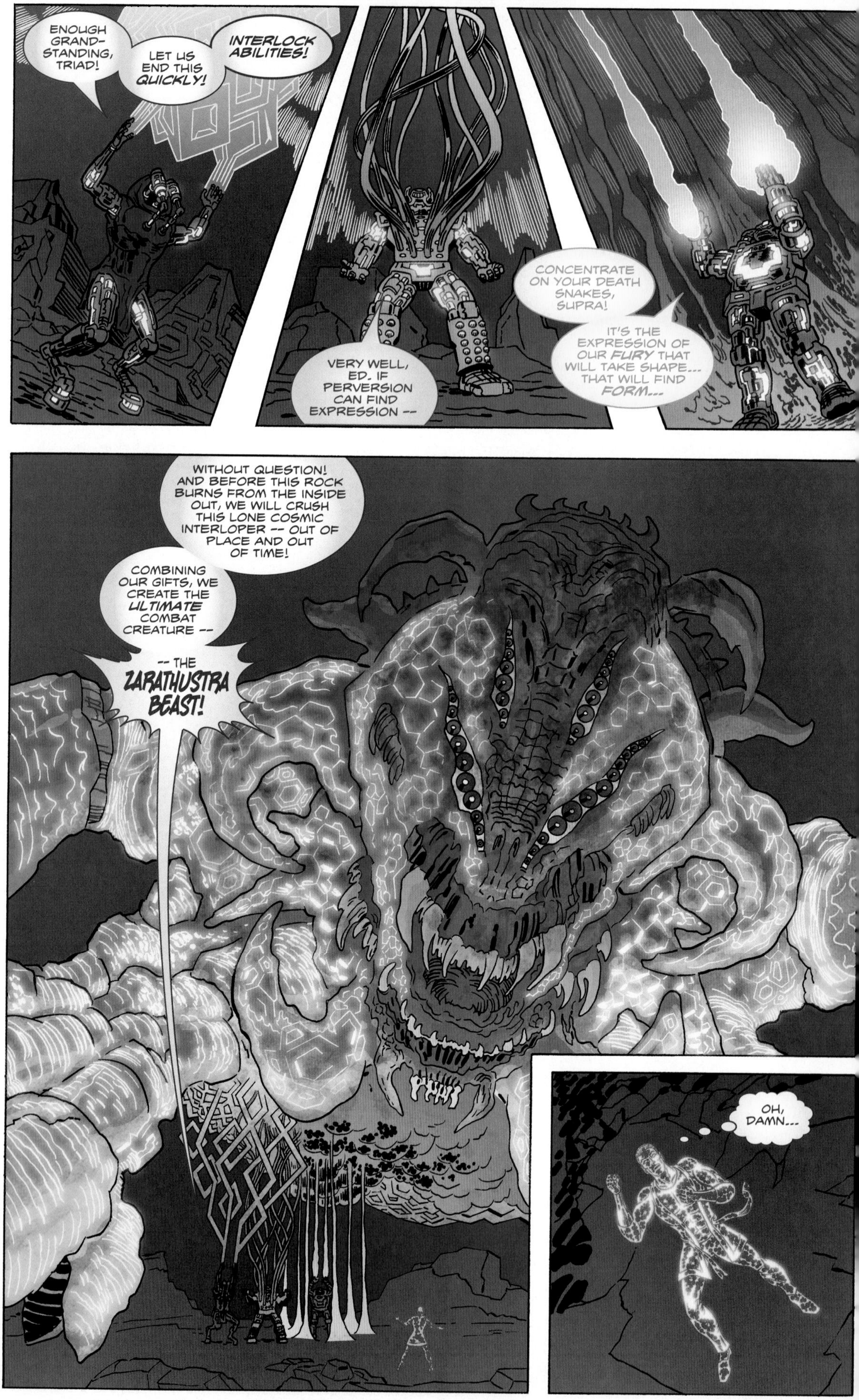
ENOUGH GRAND-STANDING, TRIAD!
LET US END THIS QUICKLY!
INTERLOCK ABILITIES!
VERY WELL, ED. IF PERVERSION CAN FIND EXPRESSION --
CONCENTRATE ON YOUR DEATH SNAKES, SUPRA!
IT'S THE EXPRESSION OF OUR FURY THAT WILL TAKE SHAPE... THAT WILL FIND FORM...
WITHOUT QUESTION! AND BEFORE THIS ROCK BURNS FROM THE INSIDE OUT, WE WILL CRUSH THIS LONE COSMIC INTERLOPER -- OUT OF PLACE AND OUT OF TIME!
COMBINING OUR GIFTS, WE CREATE THE ULTIMATE COMBAT CREATURE --
-- THE ZARATHUSTRA BEAST!
OH, DAMN...

UNSPEAKABLE

BOOK TWENTY-ONE

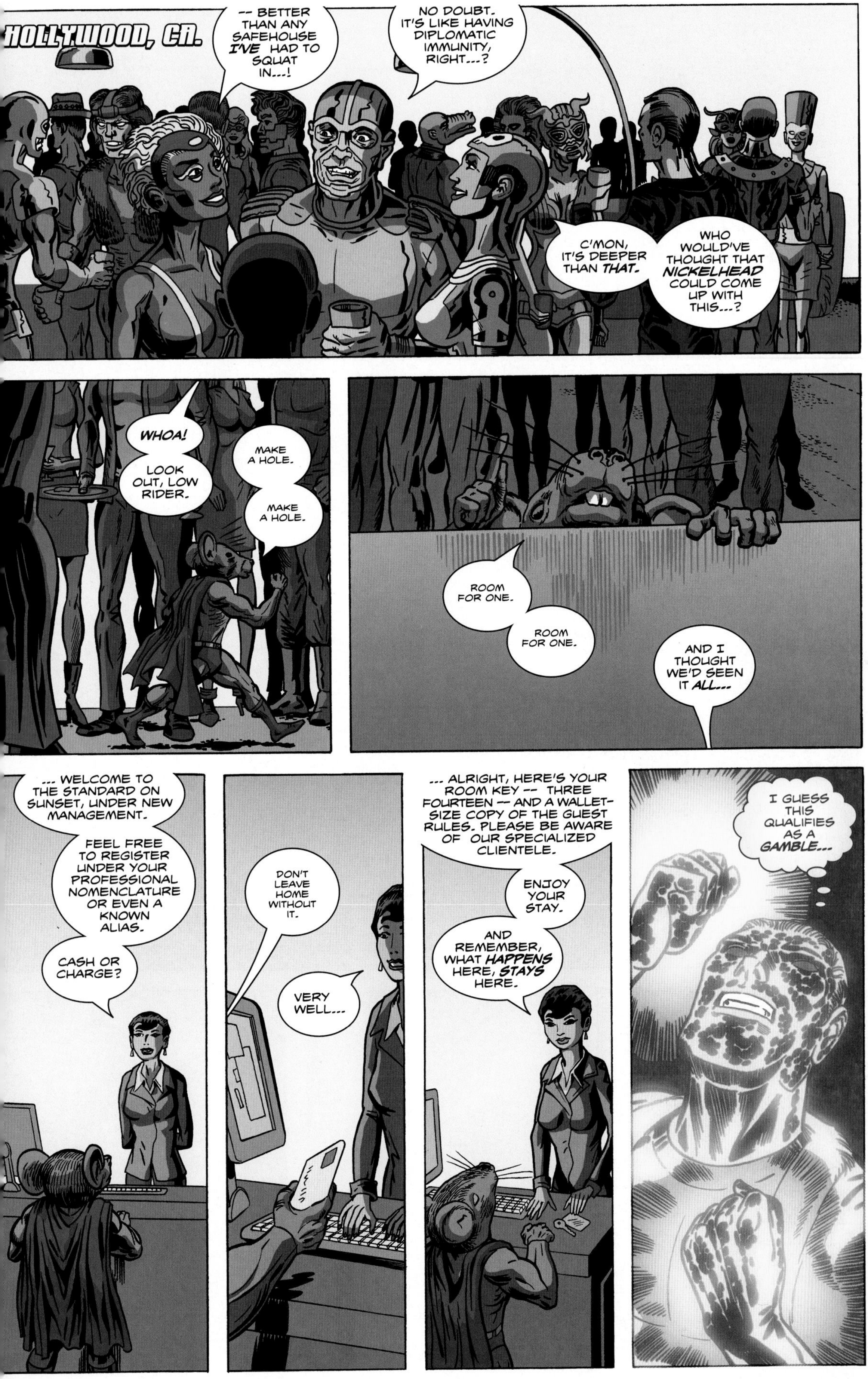
HOLLYWOOD, CA.
-- BETTER THAN ANY SAFEHOUSE I'VE HAD TO SQUAT IN...!
NO DOUBT. IT'S LIKE HAVING DIPLOMATIC IMMUNITY, RIGHT...?
C'MON, IT'S DEEPER THAN THAT.
WHO WOULD'VE THOUGHT THAT NICKELHEAD COULD COME UP WITH THIS...?
WHOA!
LOOK OUT, LOW RIDER.
MAKE A HOLE.
MAKE A HOLE.
ROOM FOR ONE.
ROOM FOR ONE.
AND I THOUGHT WE'D SEEN IT ALL...
... WELCOME TO THE STANDARD ON SUNSET, UNDER NEW MANAGEMENT.
FEEL FREE TO REGISTER UNDER YOUR PROFESSIONAL NOMENCLATURE OR EVEN A KNOWN ALIAS.
CASH OR CHARGE?
DON'T LEAVE HOME WITHOUT IT.
VERY WELL...
... ALRIGHT, HERE'S YOUR ROOM KEY -- THREE FOURTEEN -- AND A WALLET-SIZE COPY OF THE GUEST RULES. PLEASE BE AWARE OF OUR SPECIALIZED CLIENTELE.
ENJOY YOUR STAY.
AND REMEMBER, WHAT HAPPENS HERE, STAYS HERE.
I GUESS THIS QUALIFIES AS A GAMBLE...

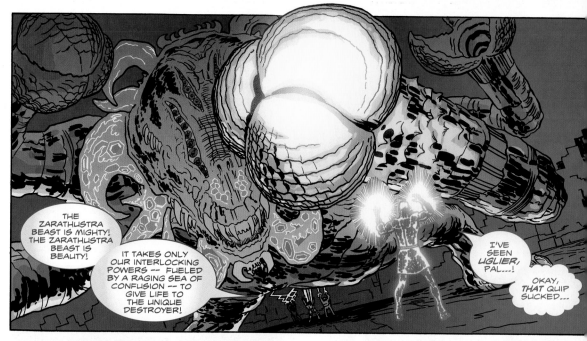

THE ZARATHUSTRA BEAST IS MIGHTY! THE ZARATHUSTRA BEAST IS BEAUTY!

IT TAKES ONLY OUR INTERLOCKING POWERS -- FUELED BY A RAGING SEA OF CONFUSION -- TO GIVE LIFE TO THE UNIQUE DESTROYER!

I'VE SEEN *UGLIER*, PAL....!

OKAY, *THAT* QUIP SUCKED...

THE *TRIAD* POSSESSES PRIDE OF OWNERSHIP!

FEEL THE FEROCITY!

GGGNNN--!

THIS... ISN'T GOING TO BE A CAKE WALK...

SEE HOW HE RESISTS --

-- MY PHYSI-MORPHED HEART IS BURSTING WITH FULFILLMENT!

OH, THIS IS PERFECT --

-- INSANELY POWERFUL *AND* POWERFULLY INSANE! NOT A PROMISING COMBO....!

CAN'T... KEEP UP... MY DEFENSES...

I CAN'T --

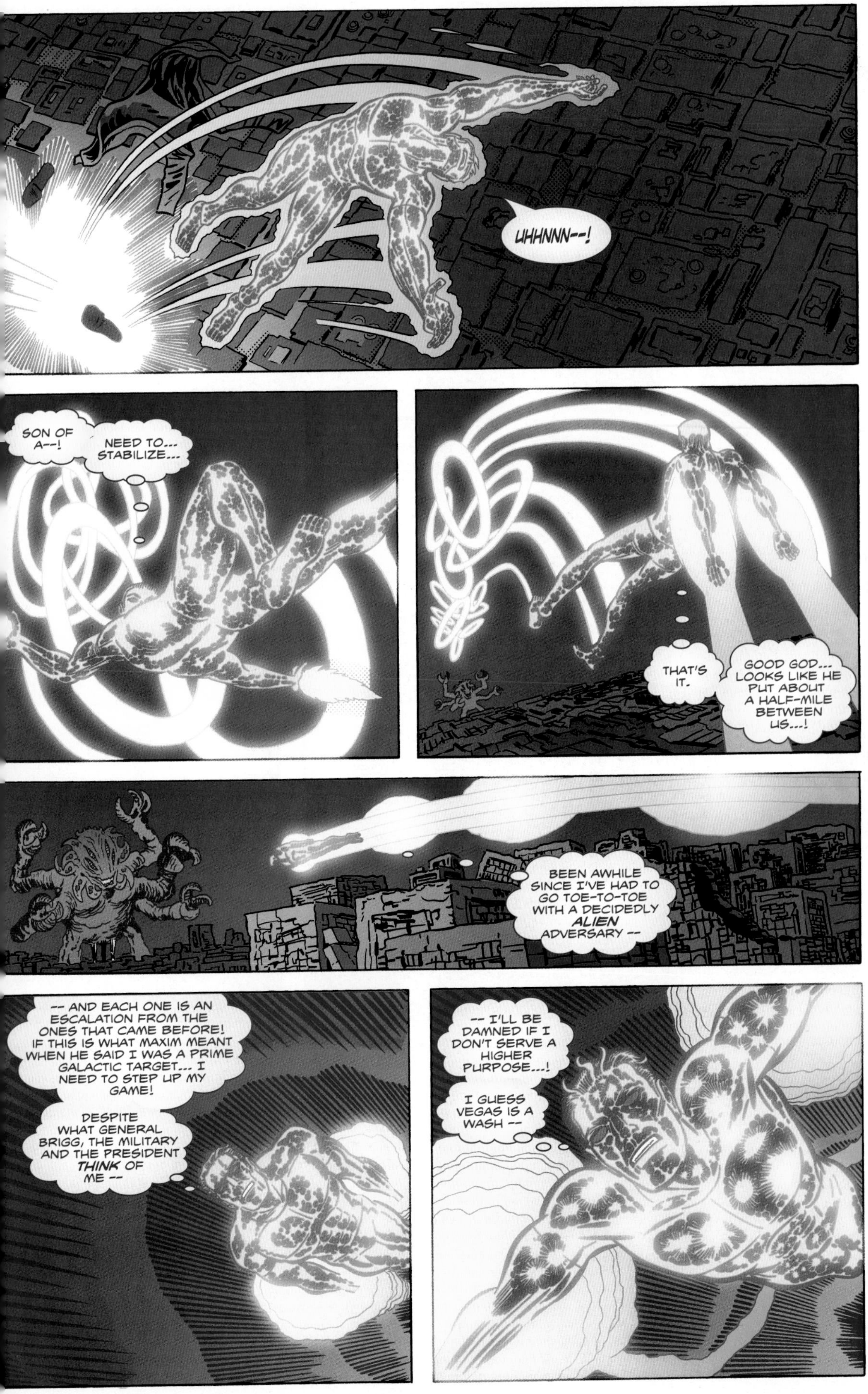
UHHNNN--!
SON OF A--!
NEED TO... STABILIZE...
THAT'S IT.
GOOD GOD... LOOKS LIKE HE PUT ABOUT A HALF-MILE BETWEEN US...!
BEEN AWHILE SINCE I'VE HAD TO GO TOE-TO-TOE WITH A DECIDEDLY ALIEN ADVERSARY --
-- AND EACH ONE IS AN ESCALATION FROM THE ONES THAT CAME BEFORE! IF THIS IS WHAT MAXIM MEANT WHEN HE SAID I WAS A PRIME GALACTIC TARGET... I NEED TO STEP UP MY GAME!
DESPITE WHAT GENERAL BRIGG, THE MILITARY AND THE PRESIDENT THINK OF ME --
-- I'LL BE DAMNED IF I DON'T SERVE A HIGHER PURPOSE...!
I GUESS VEGAS IS A WASH --

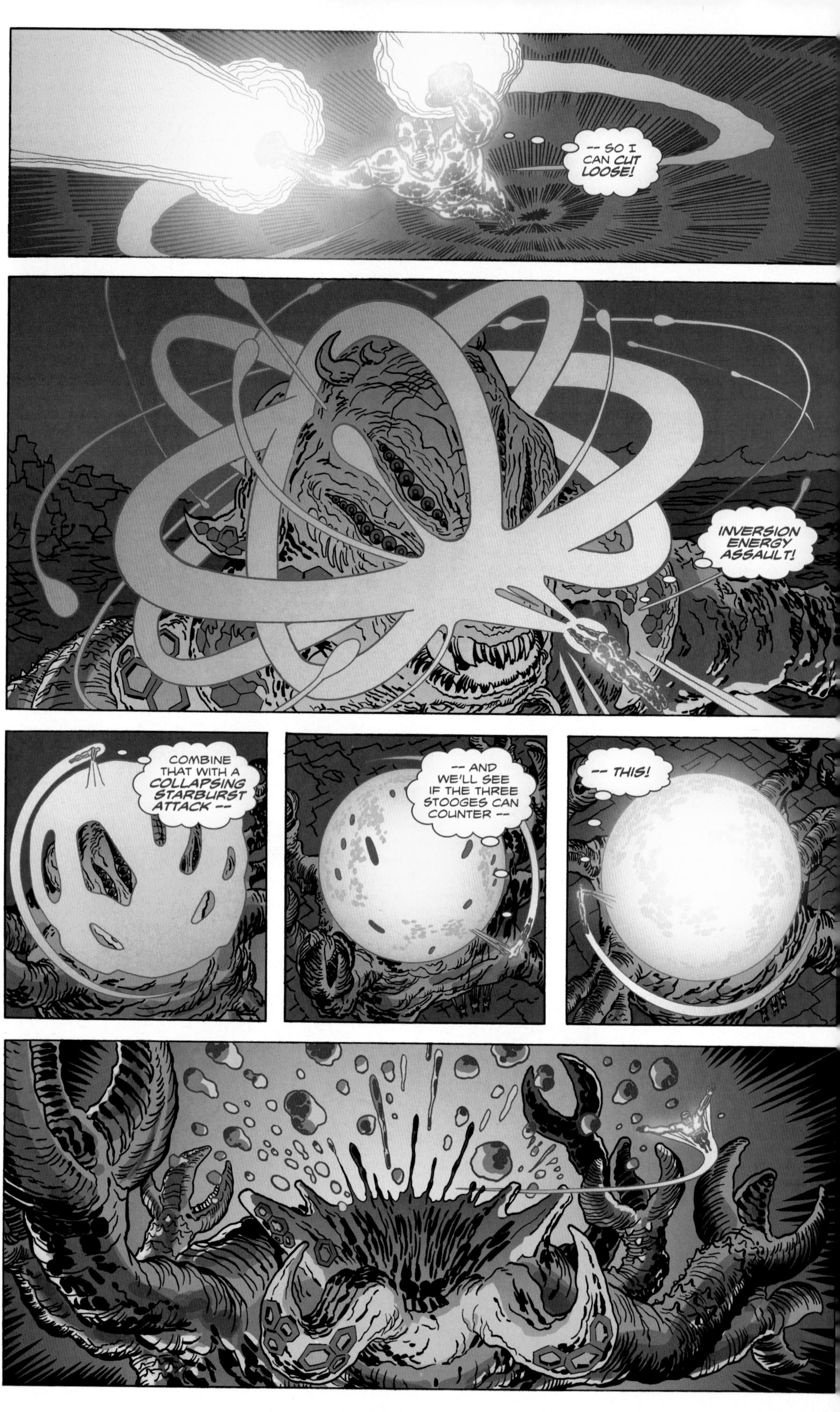
-- SO I CAN CUT LOOSE!
INVERSION ENERGY ASSAULT!
COMBINE THAT WITH A COLLAPSING STARBURST ATTACK --
-- AND WE'LL SEE IF THE THREE STOOGES CAN COUNTER --
-- THIS!

WHOA -- -- THIS DEBRIS IS TOXIC!

THAT MEANS I DID SOME DAMAGE!

TIME TO PRESS THE ADVANTAGE --

-- WITH A BUZZ BLAST MANEUVER!

RECALIBRATE YOUR FOCUS, TRIAD --

-- THE BEAST IS MOMENTARILY BLINDED!

SUCH CEREBRAL OBLITERATION... I AM IN MOURNING! ED... EEG-OH... TALK ME OFF THE LEDGE!

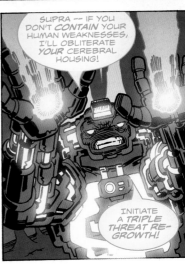

SUPRA -- IF YOU DON'T CONTAIN YOUR HUMAN WEAKNESSES, I'LL OBLITERATE YOUR CEREBRAL HOUSING!

INITIATE A TRIPLE THREAT RE-GROWTH!

I'M NOT SURE HOW TO *FIGHT* THIS THING --

-- CAN'T GET A SENSE OF ITS PHYSIOLOGY... IT'S POTENTIAL *WEAK SPOTS* --

-- IT'S ALMOST LIKE THEY'RE ADAPTING THIS CREATURE TO COUNTER EVERY ATTACK!

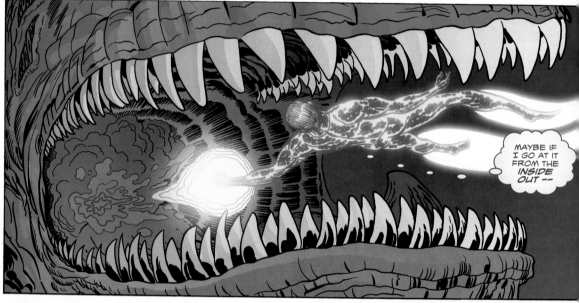

MAYBE IF I GO AT IT FROM THE *INSIDE OUT* --

A-HA!

WELL PLAYED!

THE TRIAD ABIDES -- AND SWALLOWS!

NOW, AS THE SIMULATED DIGESTION PROCESS BEGINS...

... WE CAN AWAIT THE TOTAL ANNIHILATION OF THIS PLANET! *DEATH FROM WITHIN!*

EN ROUTE TO THE EARTH'S CORE:

ALMOST... THERE...

THE *HEAT*... EVEN WITH MY GENETICALLY ENGINEERED HIDE... IT'S *UNBEARABLE*...

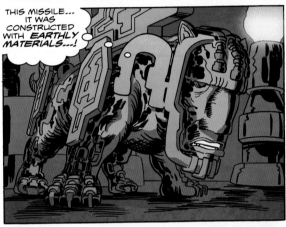

THIS MISSILE... IT WAS CONSTRUCTED WITH *EARTHLY MATERIALS*...!

THAT MEANS... I HAVE A CHANCE...

... JUST NEED TO... CONCENTRATE...

... FOCUS... OCULAR ENERGIES...

... TO FASHION... A WAY *INSIDE*...!

THIS... MAY NOT BE... *MY* WORLD...

... BUT I *REFUSE* TO ALLOW INNOCENTS... OF *ANY* SPECIES... TO *PERISH* ON MY WATCH...

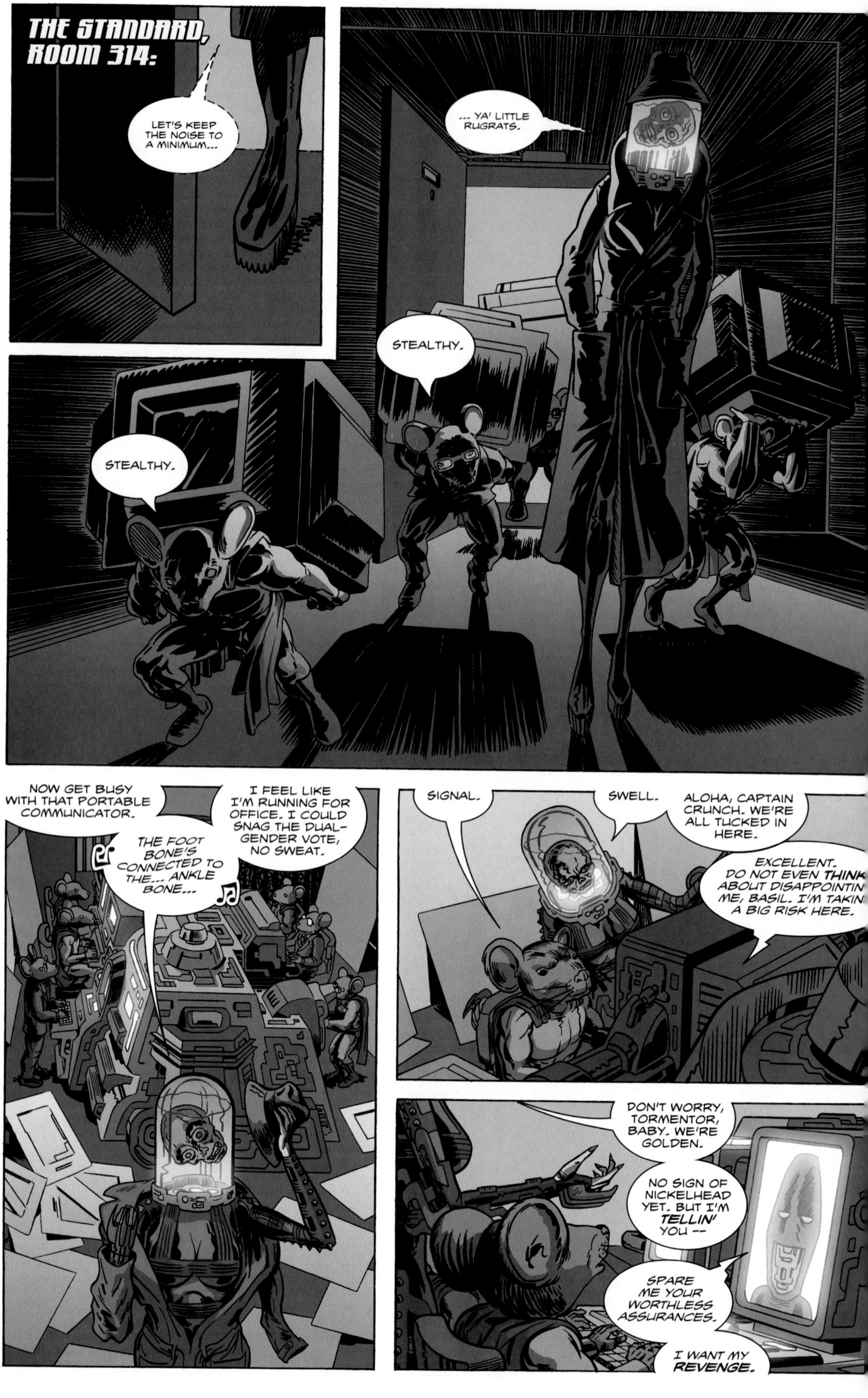
THE STANDARD, ROOM 314:
LET'S KEEP THE NOISE TO A MINIMUM...
... YA' LITTLE RUGRATS.
STEALTHY.
STEALTHY.
NOW GET BUSY WITH THAT PORTABLE COMMUNICATOR.
I FEEL LIKE I'M RUNNING FOR OFFICE. I COULD SNAG THE DUAL-GENDER VOTE, NO SWEAT.
THE FOOT BONE'S CONNECTED TO THE... ANKLE BONE...
SIGNAL.
SWELL.
ALOHA, CAPTAIN CRUNCH. WE'RE ALL TUCKED IN HERE.
EXCELLENT. DO NOT EVEN THINK ABOUT DISAPPOINTIN ME, BASIL. I'M TAKIN A BIG RISK HERE.
DON'T WORRY, TORMENTOR, BABY. WE'RE GOLDEN.
NO SIGN OF NICKELHEAD YET. BUT I'M TELLIN' YOU --
SPARE ME YOUR WORTHLESS ASSURANCES.
I WANT MY REVENGE.

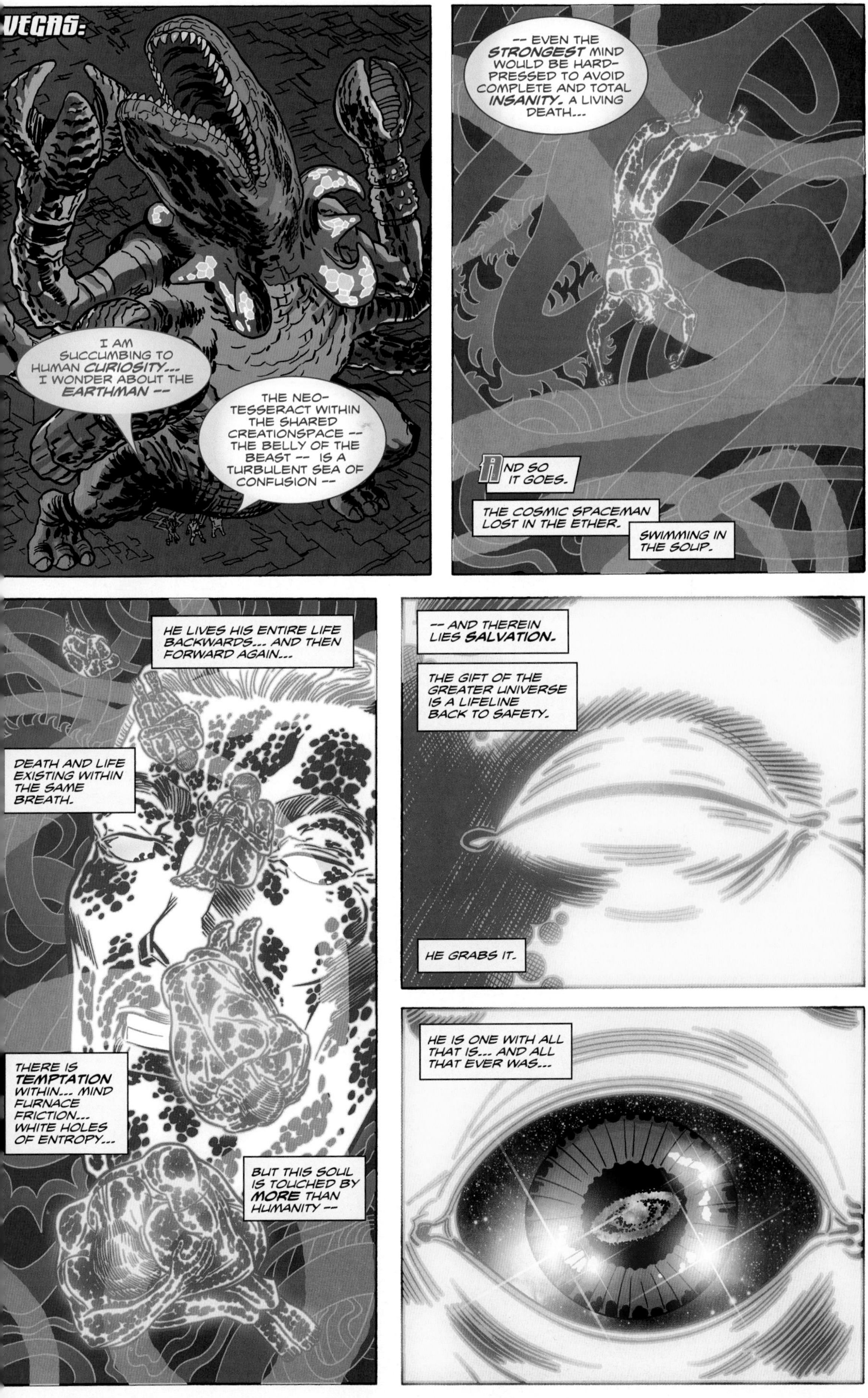
VEGAS:
I AM SUCCUMBING TO HUMAN CURIOSITY... I WONDER ABOUT THE EARTHMAN --
THE NEO-TESSERACT WITHIN THE SHARED CREATIONSPACE -- THE BELLY OF THE BEAST -- IS A TURBULENT SEA OF CONFUSION --
-- EVEN THE STRONGEST MIND WOULD BE HARD-PRESSED TO AVOID COMPLETE AND TOTAL INSANITY. A LIVING DEATH...
AND SO IT GOES.
THE COSMIC SPACEMAN LOST IN THE ETHER.
SWIMMING IN THE SOUP.
HE LIVES HIS ENTIRE LIFE BACKWARDS... AND THEN FORWARD AGAIN...
DEATH AND LIFE EXISTING WITHIN THE SAME BREATH.
THERE IS TEMPTATION WITHIN... MIND FURNACE FRICTION... WHITE HOLES OF ENTROPY...
BUT THIS SOUL IS TOUCHED BY MORE THAN HUMANITY --
-- AND THEREIN LIES SALVATION.
THE GIFT OF THE GREATER UNIVERSE IS A LIFELINE BACK TO SAFETY.
HE GRABS IT.
HE IS ONE WITH ALL THAT IS... AND ALL THAT EVER WAS...

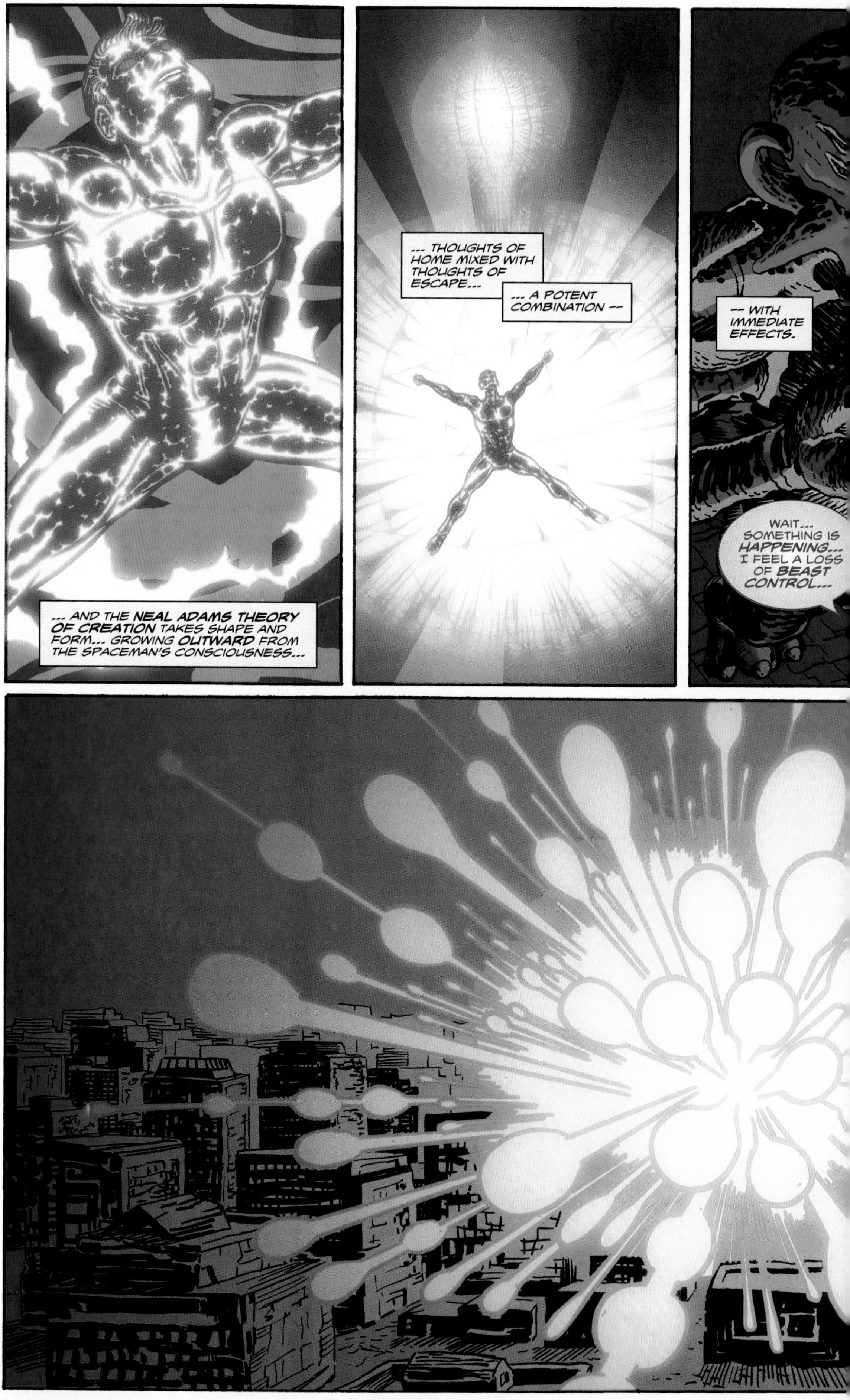
... AND THE NEAL ADAMS THEORY OF CREATION TAKES SHAPE AND FORM... GROWING OUTWARD FROM THE SPACEMAN'S CONSCIOUSNESS...
... THOUGHTS OF HOME MIXED WITH THOUGHTS OF ESCAPE...
... A POTENT COMBINATION --
-- WITH IMMEDIATE EFFECTS.
WAIT... SOMETHING IS HAPPENING... I FEEL A LOSS OF BEAST CONTROL...

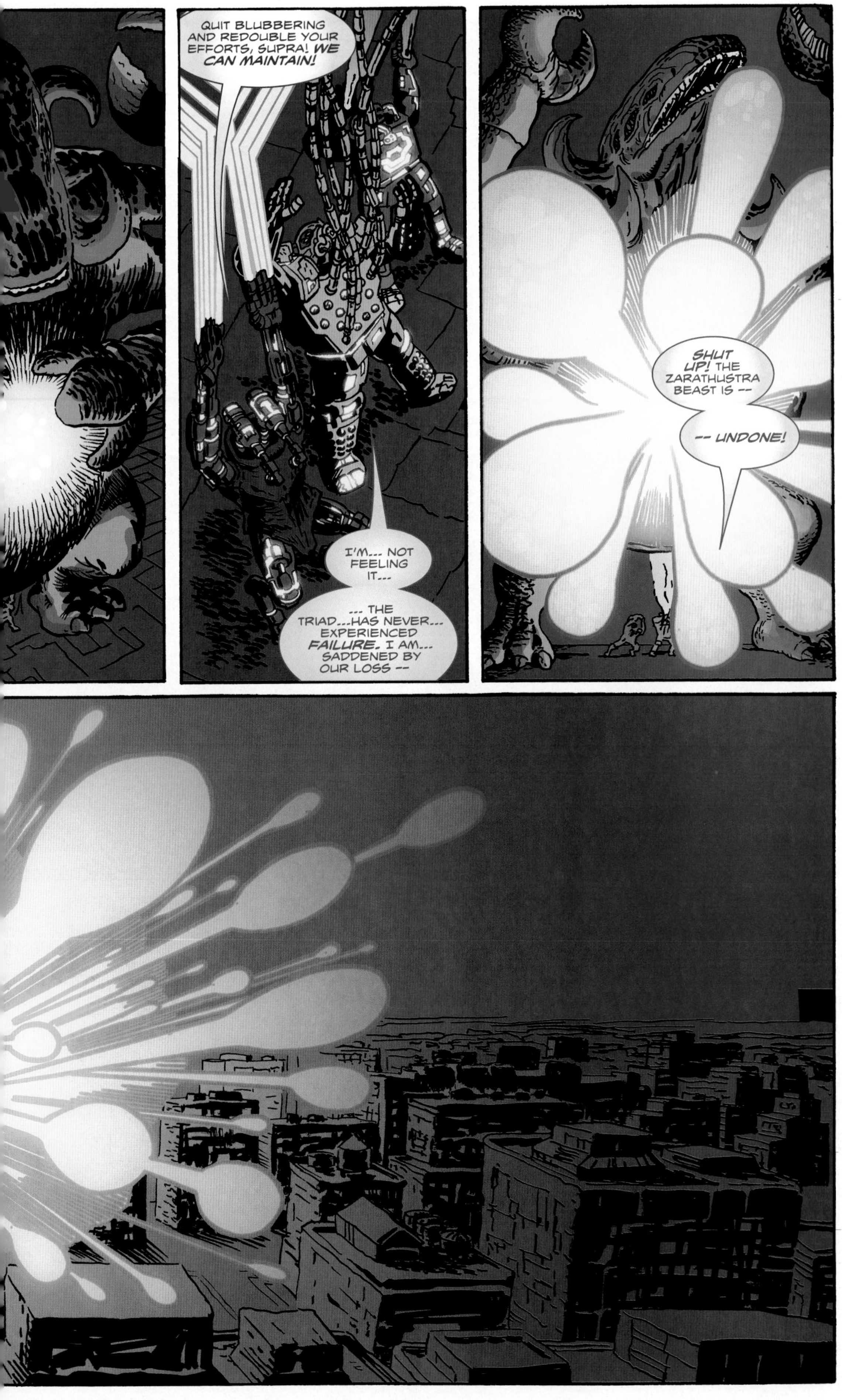
QUIT BLUBBERING AND REDOUBLE YOUR EFFORTS, SUPRA! WE CAN MAINTAIN!
I'M... NOT FEELING IT...
... THE TRIAD...HAS NEVER... EXPERIENCED FAILURE. I AM... SADDENED BY OUR LOSS --
SHUT UP! THE ZARATHUSTRA BEAST IS --
-- UNDONE!

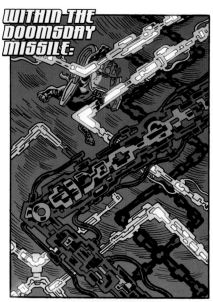

WITHIN THE DOOMSDAY MISSILE:
THERE MUST BE A PRIMARY WARHEAD OF SOME KIND...!
THE TECHNOLOGY HERE... IT BECOMES MORE AND MORE ALIEN IN NATURE, THE DEEPER I GO...
THIS MUST BE THE CORE --
BY ALL THAT IS SENTIENT --
-- I RECOGNIZE THIS DESIGN!
GALACTIC TERRORISM AT ITS MOST VILE!
PENETRATING THESE ACTIVE DEFENSES WILL BE PAINFUL AT BEST.
LET THE DANCE BEGIN --
HNNNGG--!

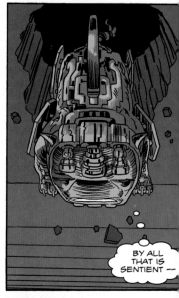

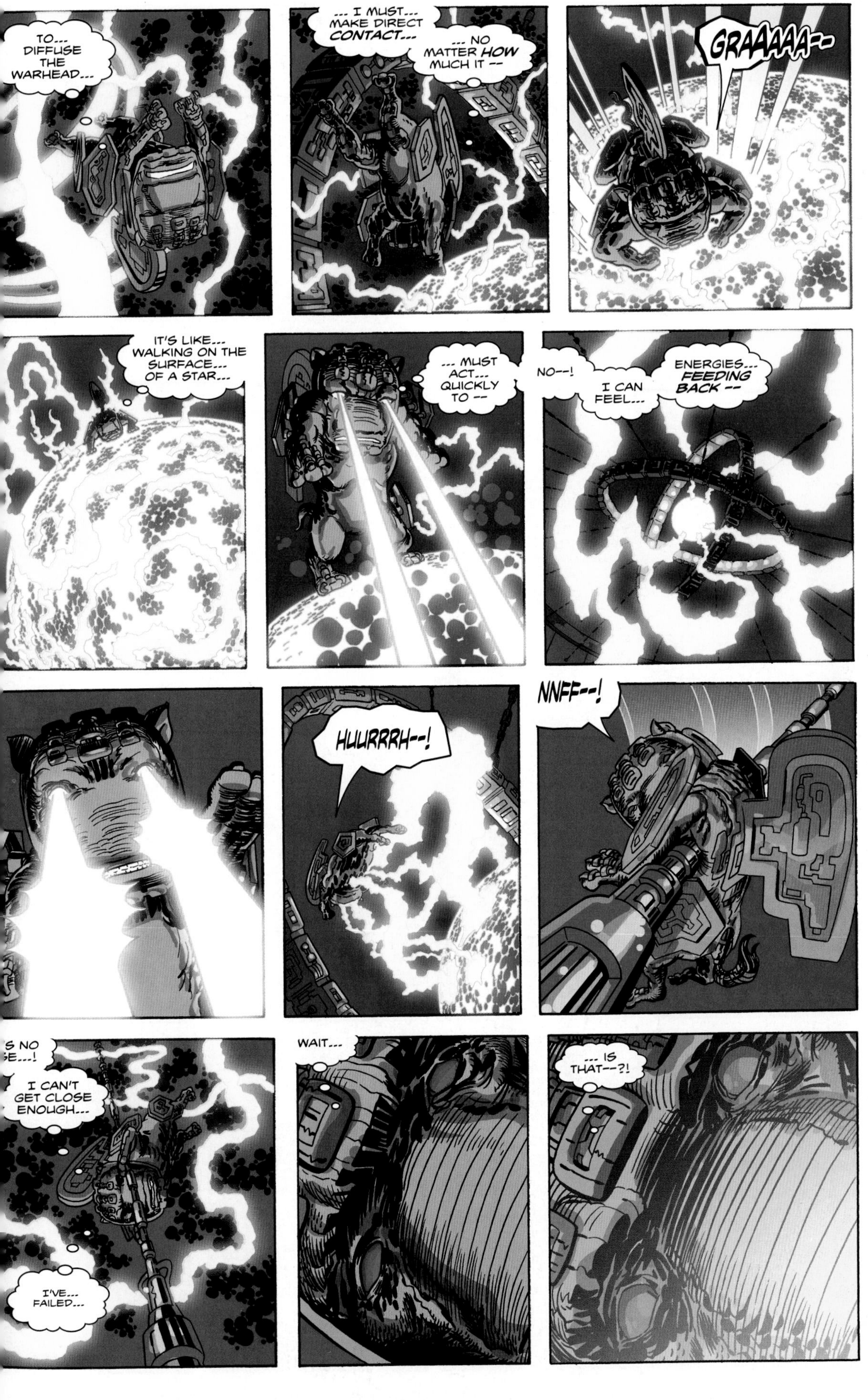
TO... DIFFUSE THE WARHEAD...
... I MUST... MAKE DIRECT CONTACT...
... NO MATTER HOW MUCH IT --
GRAAAAA--
IT'S LIKE... WALKING ON THE SURFACE... OF A STAR...
... MUST ACT... QUICKLY TO --
NO--!
I CAN FEEL...
ENERGIES... FEEDING BACK --
HUURRRH--!
NNFF--!
S NO GE...!
I CAN'T GET CLOSE ENOUGH...
I'VE... FAILED...
WAIT...
... IS THAT--?!

NEELA ARCHER?!

YES, IT'S ME. NICE THAT YOU REMEMBERED.

AND BEFORE YOU DO A GUT CHECK ON YOUR FACULTIES... I CAN HEAR YOUR THOUGHTS.

I THINK I CAN HEAR EVERYONE'S THOUGHTS.

I'M A LITTLE LATE FOR THE PARTY, BUT I'M QUICK ON THE UPTAKE.

AND I DON'T HAVE MUCH TIME.

YOU WERE ASSUMED DEAD BY SO MANY... ALMOST EVERYONE...

... EXCEPT...

I RECOGNIZE YOUR TRANSFORMATION... YOU HAVE BECOME --

IT'S BEAUTIFUL, ISN'T IT?

I REALLY HAD NO IDEA WHAT ADAM EXPERIENCES.

NOW I KNOW.

DON'T WORRY. THIS DEVICE IS A MINOR INCONVENIENCE.

I'LL DO WHAT NEEDS TO BE DONE HERE. ANY EXPLANATIONS WILL HAVE TO WAIT.

LIKE I SAID... I DON'T HAVE MUCH TIME.

WAIT--!

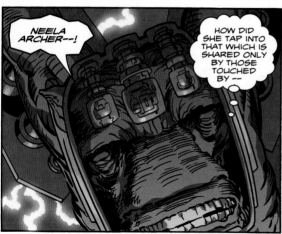

NEELA ARCHER--!

HOW DID SHE TAP INTO THAT WHICH IS SHARED ONLY BY THOSE TOUCHED BY --

NO...

THE WARHEAD --

-- IT'S BEGINNING TO --

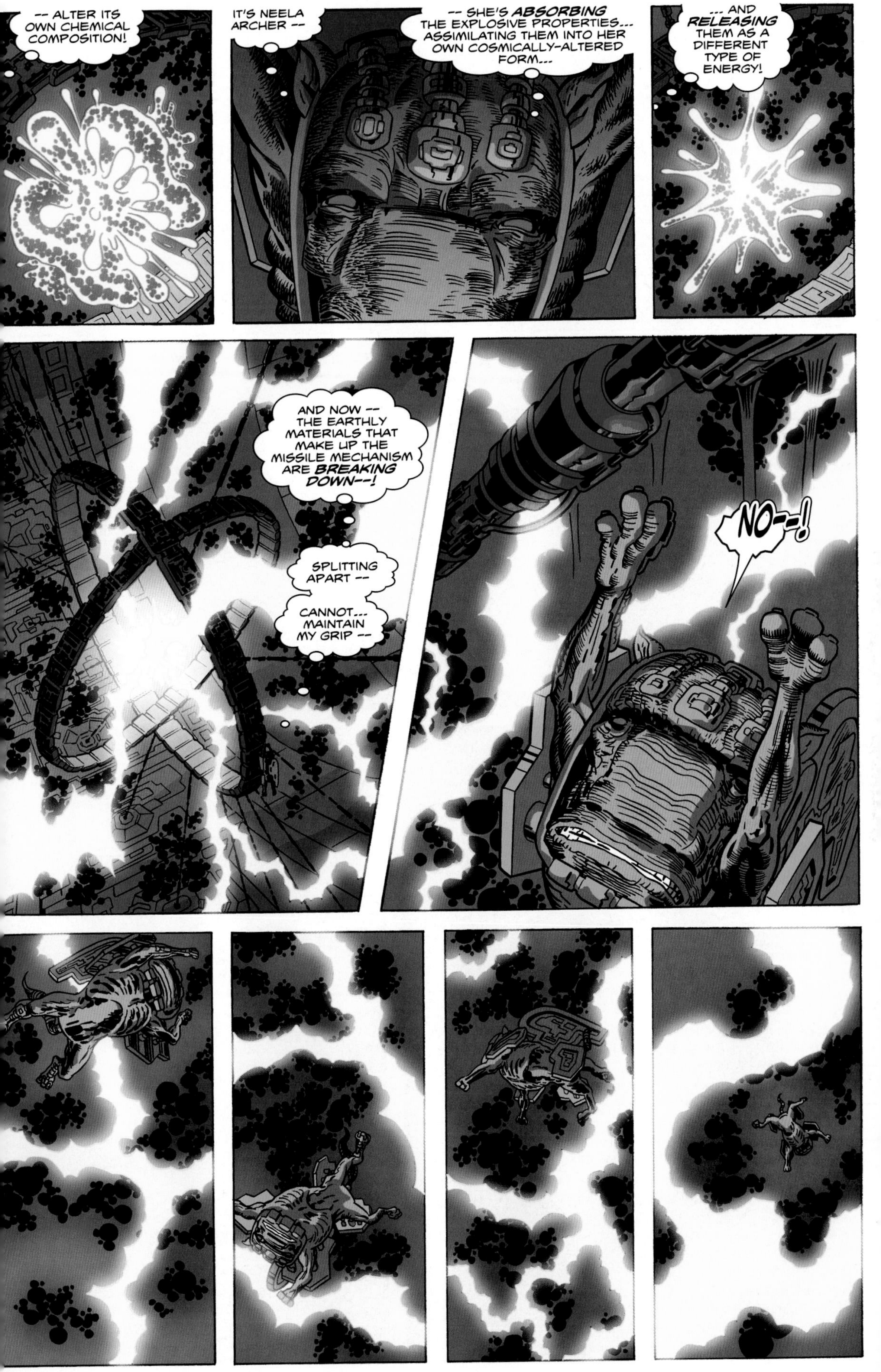
-- ALTER ITS OWN CHEMICAL COMPOSITION!
IT'S NEELA ARCHER --
-- SHE'S ABSORBING THE EXPLOSIVE PROPERTIES... ASSIMILATING THEM INTO HER OWN COSMICALLY-ALTERED FORM...
... AND RELEASING THEM AS A DIFFERENT TYPE OF ENERGY!
AND NOW -- THE EARTHLY MATERIALS THAT MAKE UP THE MISSILE MECHANISM ARE BREAKING DOWN--!
SPLITTING APART --
CANNOT... MAINTAIN MY GRIP --
NO--!

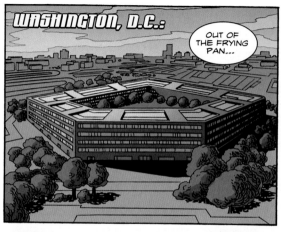

WASHINGTON, D.C.:

OUT OF THE FRYING PAN...

... INTO THE PENTAGON, RIGHT, SIS...?

NOW'S NOT THE TIME, ANGIE...

... I'M ACTUALLY GLAD THEY BROUGHT US HERE.

CONSIDERING WHAT WE'RE ALL JUST BEEN THROUGH, I'VE GOT A FEW THINGS I WANT TO SAY TO --

-- GENERAL BRIGG!

I HALF-EXPECTED YOU WOULDN'T HAVE THE NERVE TO DEAL WITH ME FACE-TO-FACE.

I'VE DEALT WITH MUCH WORSE, MISS ARCHER.

PARDON MY LANGUAGE, SIR -- BUT WHERE THE HELL DO YOU GET OFF TREATING NOT ONLY ADAM -- BUT MY ENTIRE FAMILY -- LIKE CRIMINALS THAT REQUIRE SOLITARY CONFINEMENT!

YOU BUILT THE INFINITY TOWER TO BE A PRISON!

A CONSPIRACY OF MASSIVE PROPORTIONS!

LET'S GET US A LAWYER, STELLA... WE'LL SUE THE RANK OFFA SGT. CARTER HERE --

ARE YOU DONE?

WE CAN HASH OUT YOUR CIVIL LIBERTIES LATER. I BROUGHT YOU HERE TO SHOW YOU SOME-THING...

... DO YOU RECOGNIZE THIS ENERGY WAVE PATTERN...?

WE'VE BEEN MONITORING THIS VIA SATELLITE FOR THE PAST FOUR HOURS...

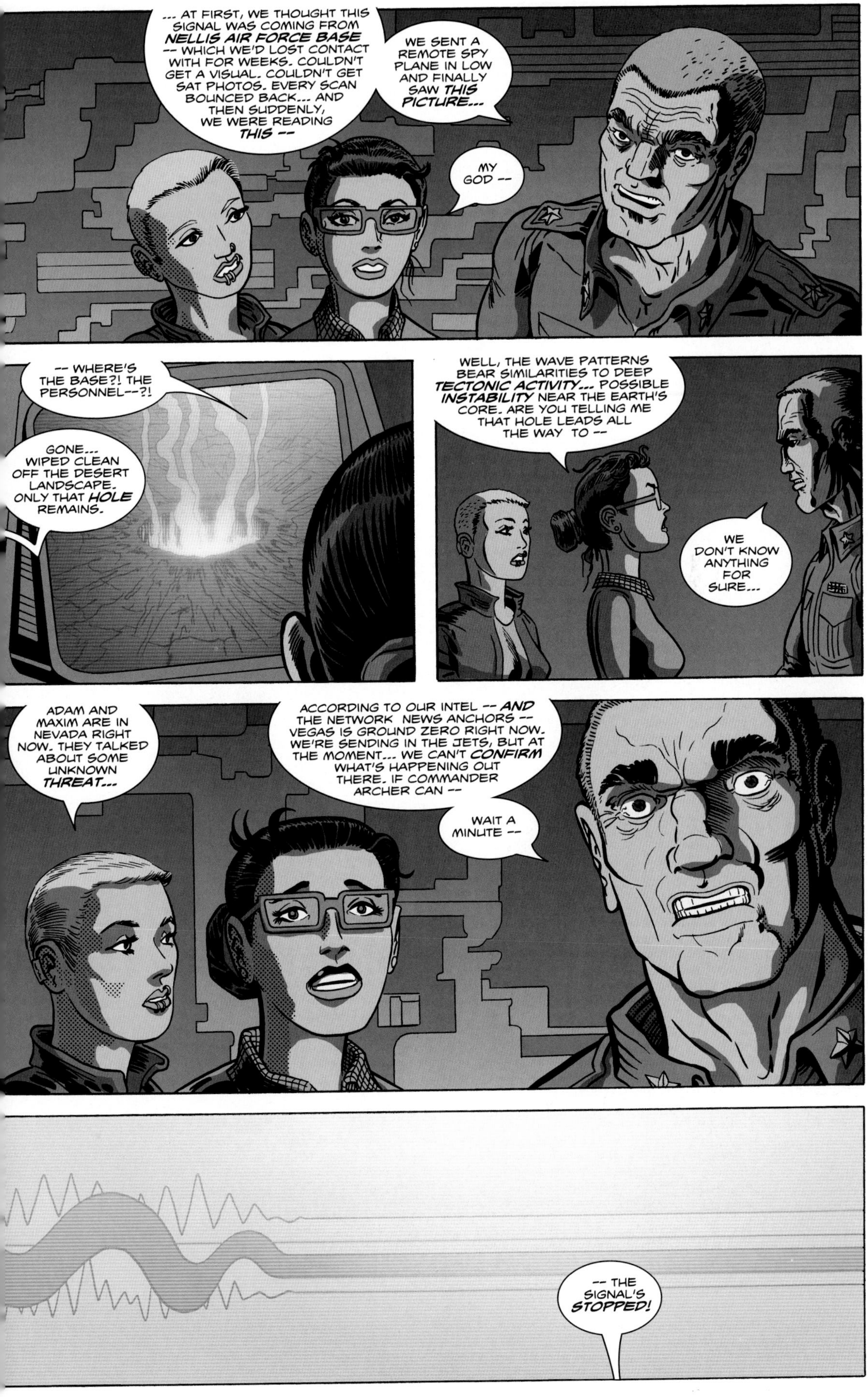

... AT FIRST, WE THOUGHT THIS SIGNAL WAS COMING FROM NELLIS AIR FORCE BASE -- WHICH WE'D LOST CONTACT WITH FOR WEEKS. COULDN'T GET A VISUAL. COULDN'T GET SAT PHOTOS. EVERY SCAN BOUNCED BACK... AND THEN SUDDENLY, WE WERE READING THIS --
WE SENT A REMOTE SPY PLANE IN LOW AND FINALLY SAW THIS PICTURE...
MY GOD --
-- WHERE'S THE BASE?! THE PERSONNEL--?!
GONE... WIPED CLEAN OFF THE DESERT LANDSCAPE. ONLY THAT HOLE REMAINS.
WELL, THE WAVE PATTERNS BEAR SIMILARITIES TO DEEP TECTONIC ACTIVITY... POSSIBLE INSTABILITY NEAR THE EARTH'S CORE. ARE YOU TELLING ME THAT HOLE LEADS ALL THE WAY TO --
WE DON'T KNOW ANYTHING FOR SURE...
ADAM AND MAXIM ARE IN NEVADA RIGHT NOW. THEY TALKED ABOUT SOME UNKNOWN THREAT...
ACCORDING TO OUR INTEL -- AND THE NETWORK NEWS ANCHORS -- VEGAS IS GROUND ZERO RIGHT NOW. WE'RE SENDING IN THE JETS, BUT AT THE MOMENT... WE CAN'T CONFIRM WHAT'S HAPPENING OUT THERE. IF COMMANDER ARCHER CAN --
WAIT A MINUTE --
-- THE SIGNAL'S STOPPED!

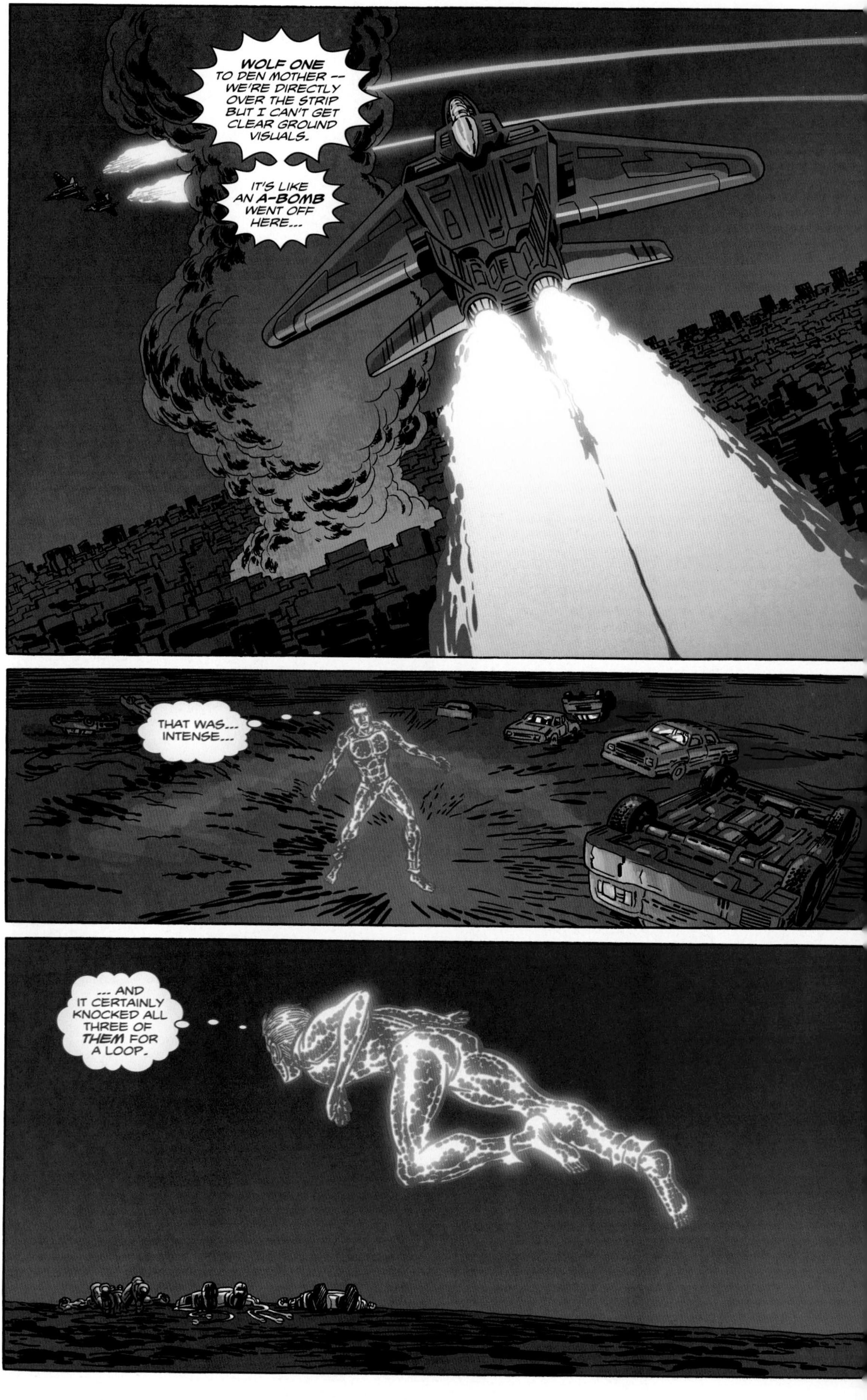
WOLF ONE TO DEN MOTHER -- WE'RE DIRECTLY OVER THE STRIP BUT I CAN'T GET CLEAR GROUND VISUALS.
IT'S LIKE AN A-BOMB WENT OFF HERE...
THAT WAS... INTENSE...
... AND IT CERTAINLY KNOCKED ALL THREE OF THEM FOR A LOOP.

PERFECT OPPORTUNITY FOR A LITTLE *INTERROGATION*--!

ONE OF YOU IS GOING TO SPILL HIS GUTS ABOUT WHATEVER THE HELL IT IS YOU'RE *DOING* HERE!

YOU --

-- TELL ME ABOUT THE WEAPON YOU TRIGGERED!

NNNN....

YOU HURT.... MY FEELINGS...

HE'S USELESS--!

HOLD UP...

... SOMETHING'S TELEPORTING IN!

ANOTHER ALIEN ASSASSIN?!

NO --

-- *MAXIM!*

BUT... THAT'S NOT HIS ENERGY SIGNATURE!

WHO HAS THE *POWER* TO TRANSPORT --

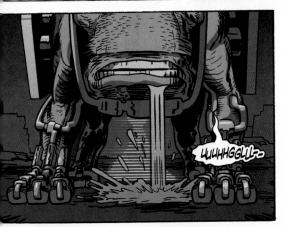

UUUHHGGUU--

MAXIM!

MY GOD--!

WHAT... HAPPENED TO HIM...?!

NNNNNNNN....

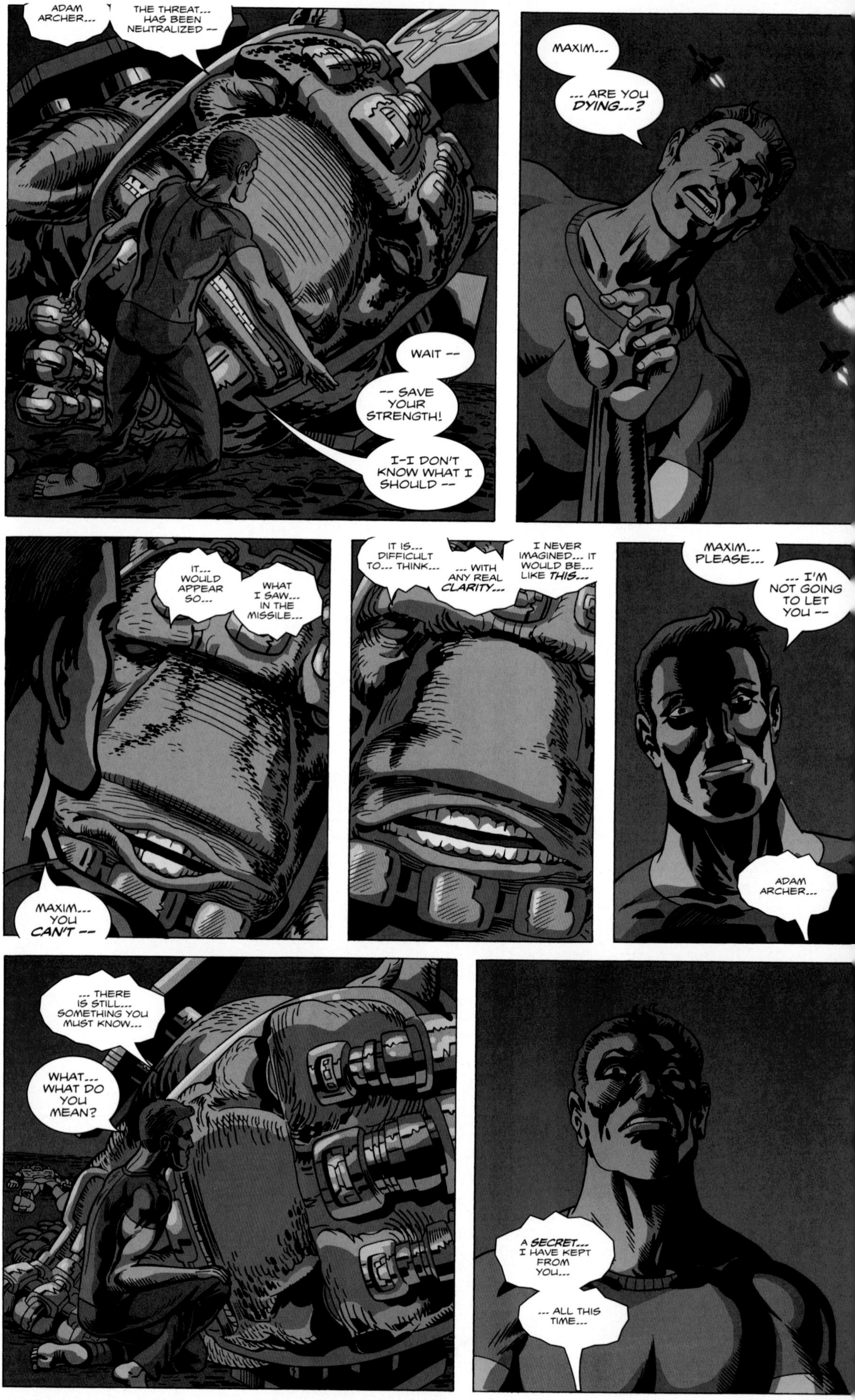
ADAM ARCHER...
THE THREAT... HAS BEEN NEUTRALIZED --
WAIT --
-- SAVE YOUR STRENGTH!
I-I DON'T KNOW WHAT I SHOULD --
MAXIM...
... ARE YOU DYING...?
IT... WOULD APPEAR SO...
WHAT I SAW... IN THE MISSILE...
MAXIM... YOU CAN'T --
IT IS... DIFFICULT TO... THINK...
... WITH ANY REAL CLARITY...
I NEVER IMAGINED... IT WOULD BE... LIKE THIS...
MAXIM... PLEASE...
... I'M NOT GOING TO LET YOU --
ADAM ARCHER...
... THERE IS STILL... SOMETHING YOU MUST KNOW...
WHAT... WHAT DO YOU MEAN?
A SECRET... I HAVE KEPT FROM YOU...
... ALL THIS TIME...

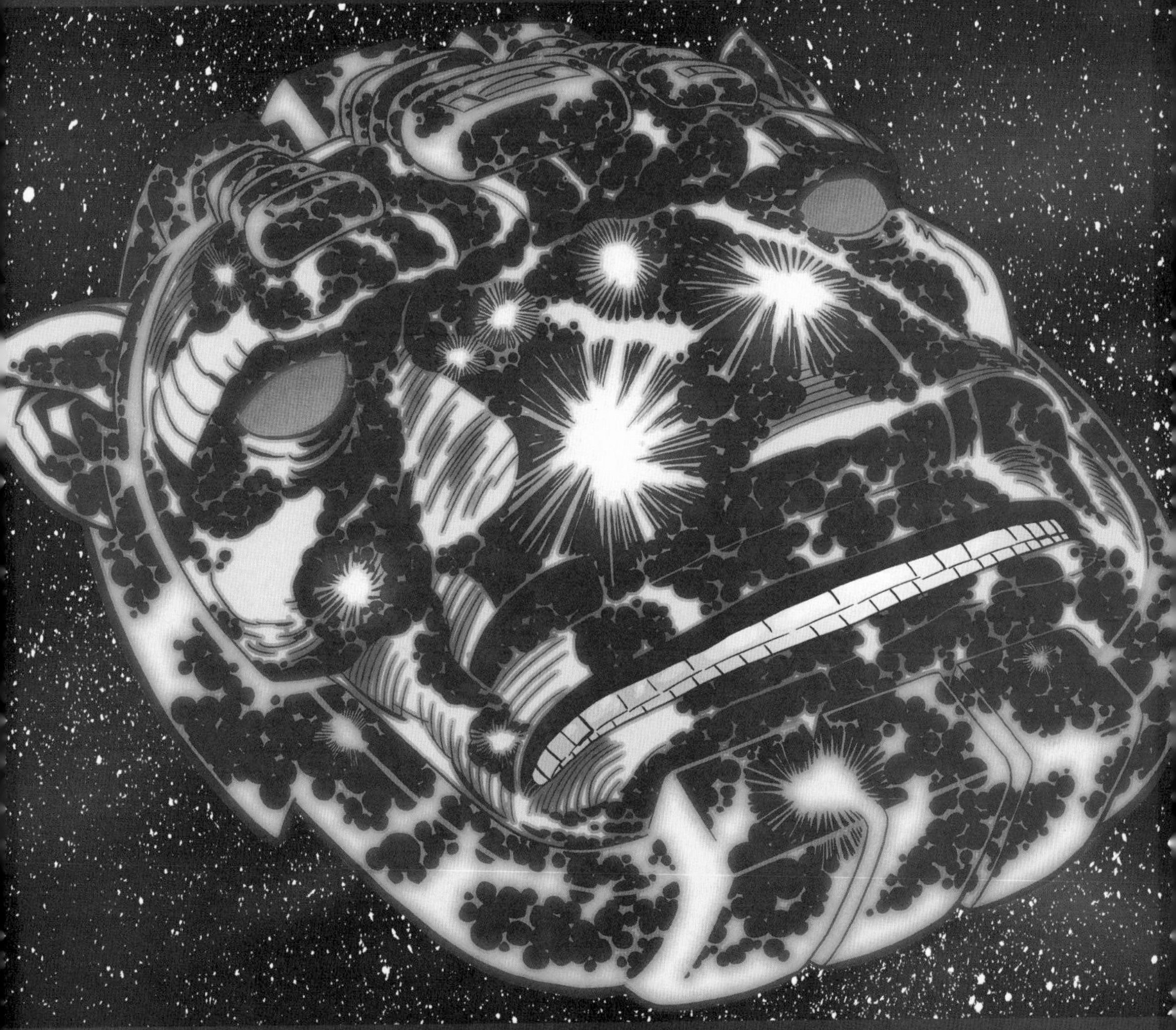

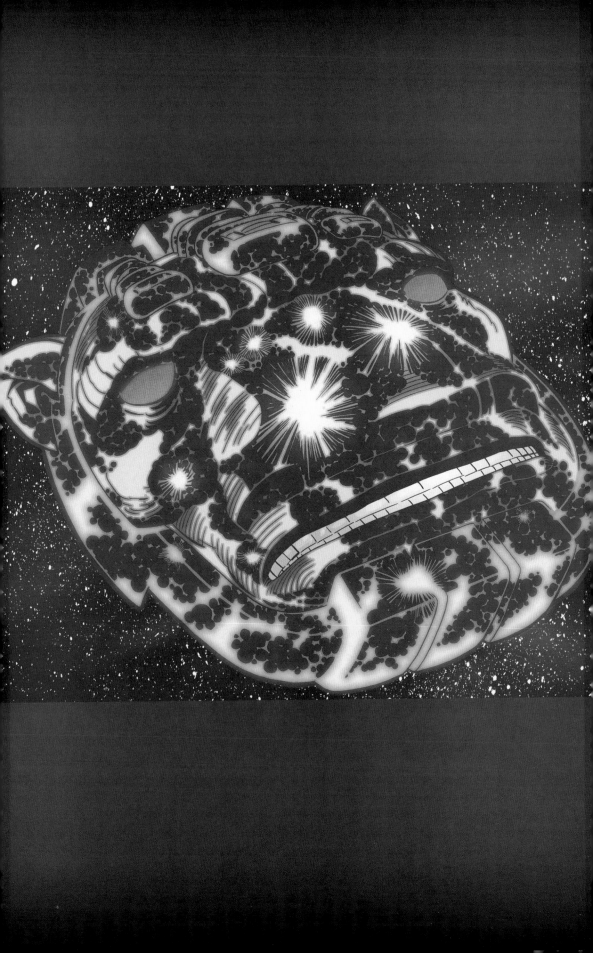

DETONATE REALITY SAGA

BOOK TWENTY-TWO

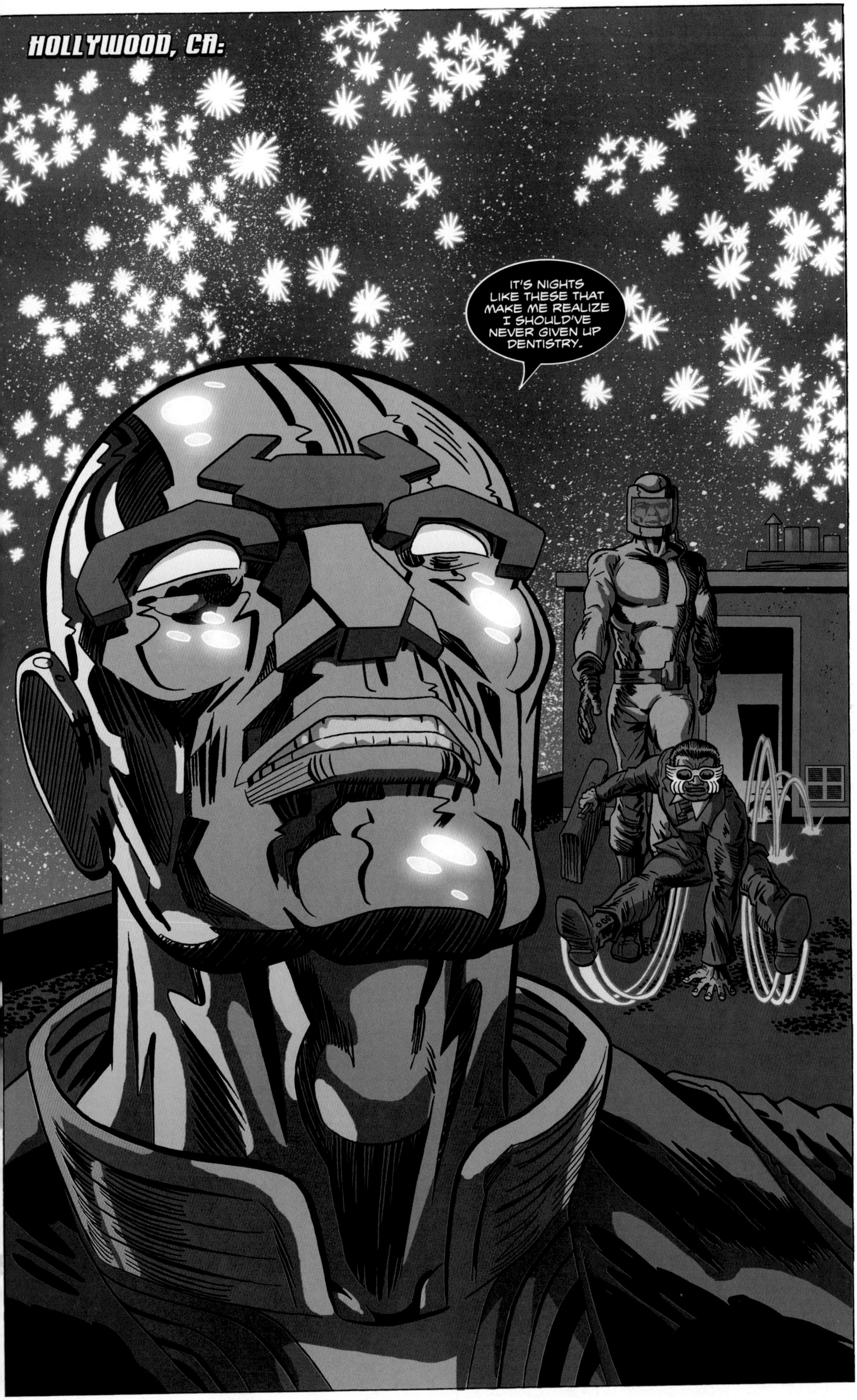
HOLLYWOOD, CA:
IT'S NIGHTS LIKE THESE THAT MAKE ME REALIZE I SHOULD'VE NEVER GIVEN UP DENTISTRY.

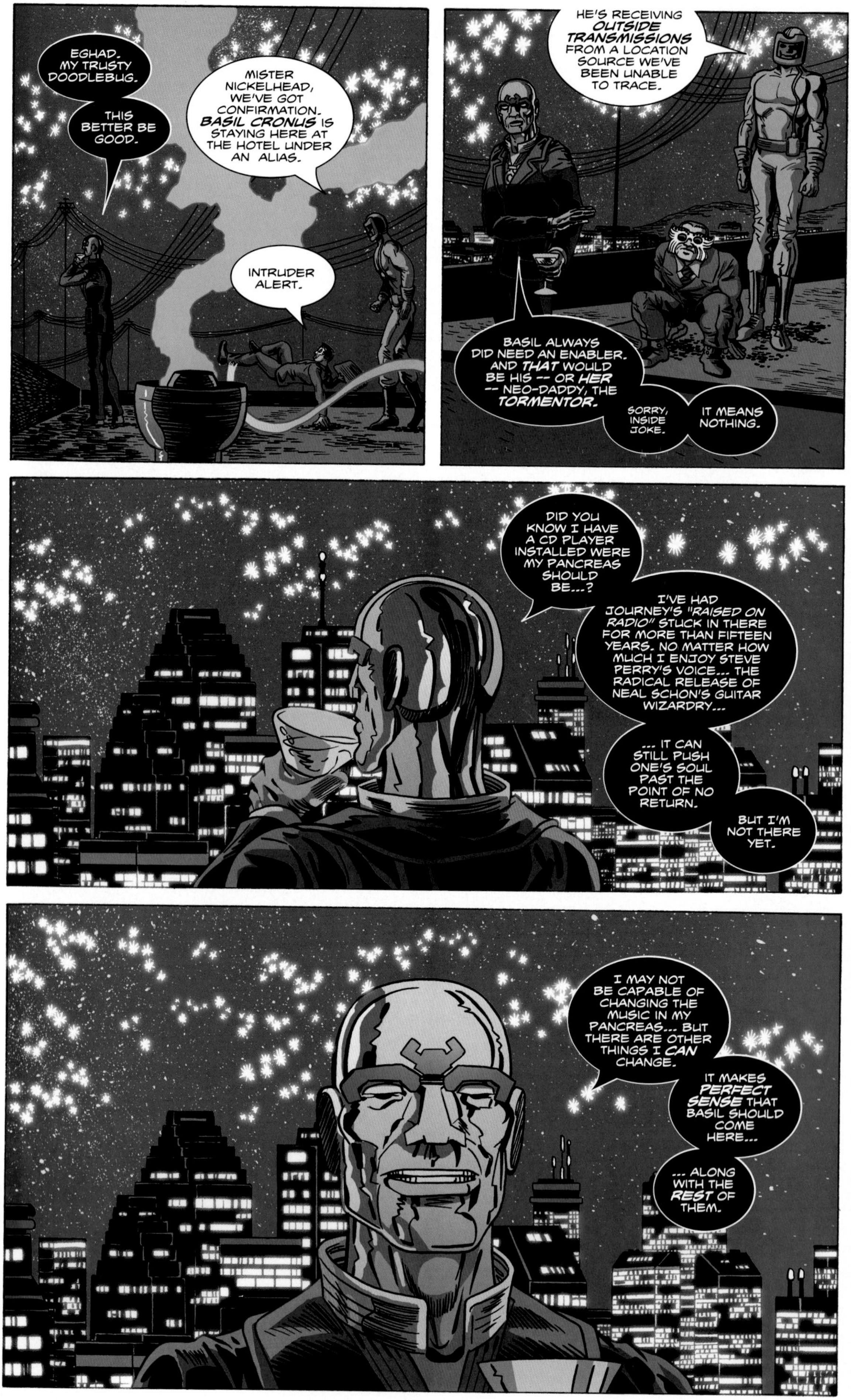
EGHAD. MY TRUSTY DOODLEBUG.
THIS BETTER BE GOOD.
MISTER NICKELHEAD, WE'VE GOT CONFIRMATION. BASIL CRONUS IS STAYING HERE AT THE HOTEL UNDER AN ALIAS.
INTRUDER ALERT.
HE'S RECEIVING OUTSIDE TRANSMISSIONS FROM A LOCATION SOURCE WE'VE BEEN UNABLE TO TRACE.
BASIL ALWAYS DID NEED AN ENABLER. AND THAT WOULD BE HIS -- OR HER -- NEO-DADDY, THE TORMENTOR.
SORRY, INSIDE JOKE.
IT MEANS NOTHING.
DID YOU KNOW I HAVE A CD PLAYER INSTALLED WERE MY PANCREAS SHOULD BE...?
I'VE HAD JOURNEY'S "RAISED ON RADIO" STUCK IN THERE FOR MORE THAN FIFTEEN YEARS. NO MATTER HOW MUCH I ENJOY STEVE PERRY'S VOICE... THE RADICAL RELEASE OF NEAL SCHON'S GUITAR WIZARDRY...
... IT CAN STILL PUSH ONE'S SOUL PAST THE POINT OF NO RETURN.
BUT I'M NOT THERE YET.
I MAY NOT BE CAPABLE OF CHANGING THE MUSIC IN MY PANCREAS... BUT THERE ARE OTHER THINGS I CAN CHANGE.
IT MAKES PERFECT SENSE THAT BASIL SHOULD COME HERE...
... ALONG WITH THE REST OF THEM.

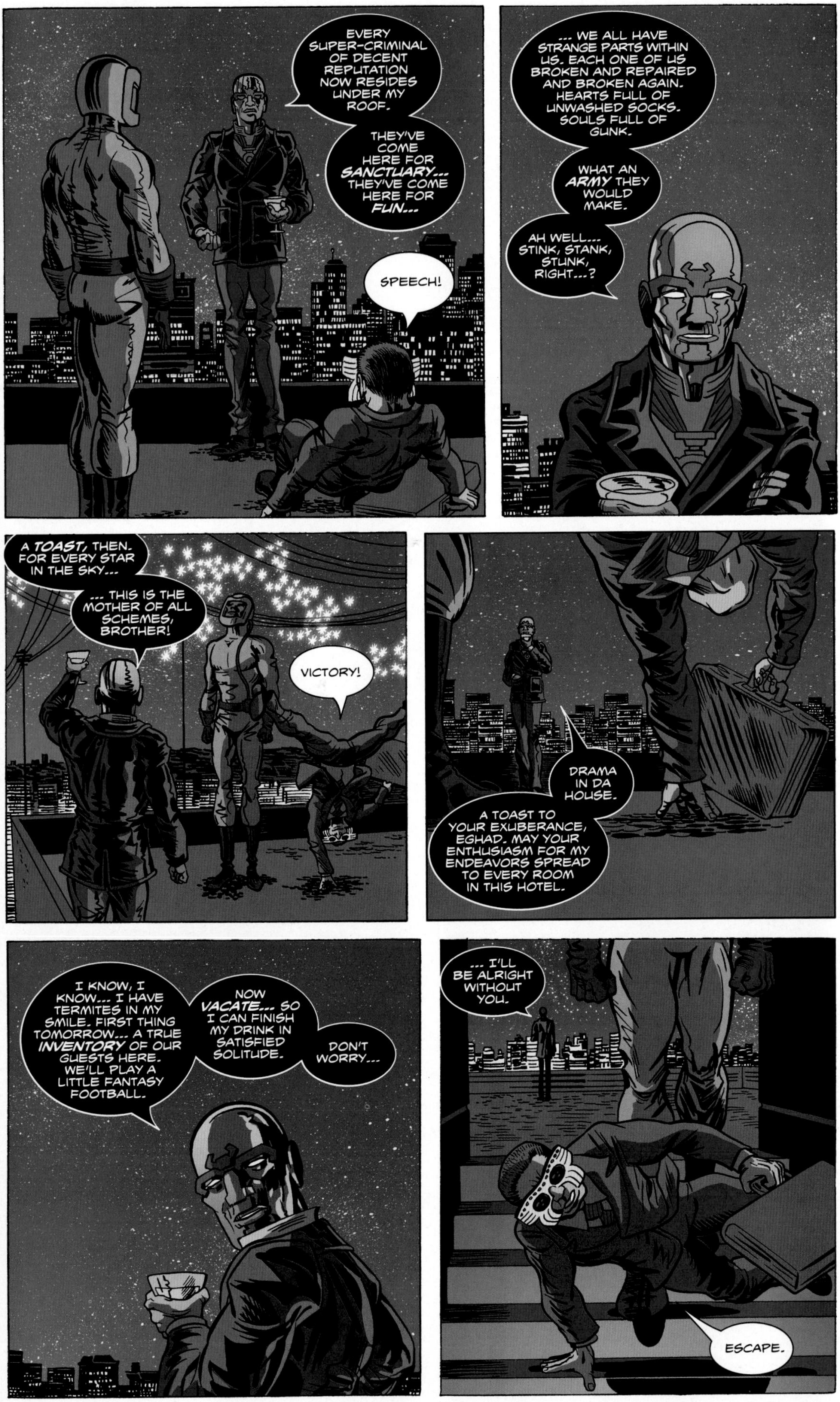
EVERY SUPER-CRIMINAL OF DECENT REPUTATION NOW RESIDES UNDER MY ROOF.
THEY'VE COME HERE FOR SANCTUARY... THEY'VE COME HERE FOR FUN...
SPEECH!
... WE ALL HAVE STRANGE PARTS WITHIN US. EACH ONE OF US BROKEN AND REPAIRED AND BROKEN AGAIN. HEARTS FULL OF UNWASHED SOCKS. SOULS FULL OF GUNK.
WHAT AN ARMY THEY WOULD MAKE.
AH WELL... STINK, STANK, STUNK, RIGHT...?
A TOAST, THEN. FOR EVERY STAR IN THE SKY...
... THIS IS THE MOTHER OF ALL SCHEMES, BROTHER!
VICTORY!
DRAMA IN DA HOUSE.
A TOAST TO YOUR EXUBERANCE, EGHAD. MAY YOUR ENTHUSIASM FOR MY ENDEAVORS SPREAD TO EVERY ROOM IN THIS HOTEL.
I KNOW, I KNOW... I HAVE TERMITES IN MY SMILE. FIRST THING TOMORROW... A TRUE INVENTORY OF OUR GUESTS HERE. WE'LL PLAY A LITTLE FANTASY FOOTBALL.
NOW VACATE... SO I CAN FINISH MY DRINK IN SATISFIED SOLITUDE.
DON'T WORRY...
... I'LL BE ALRIGHT WITHOUT YOU.
ESCAPE.

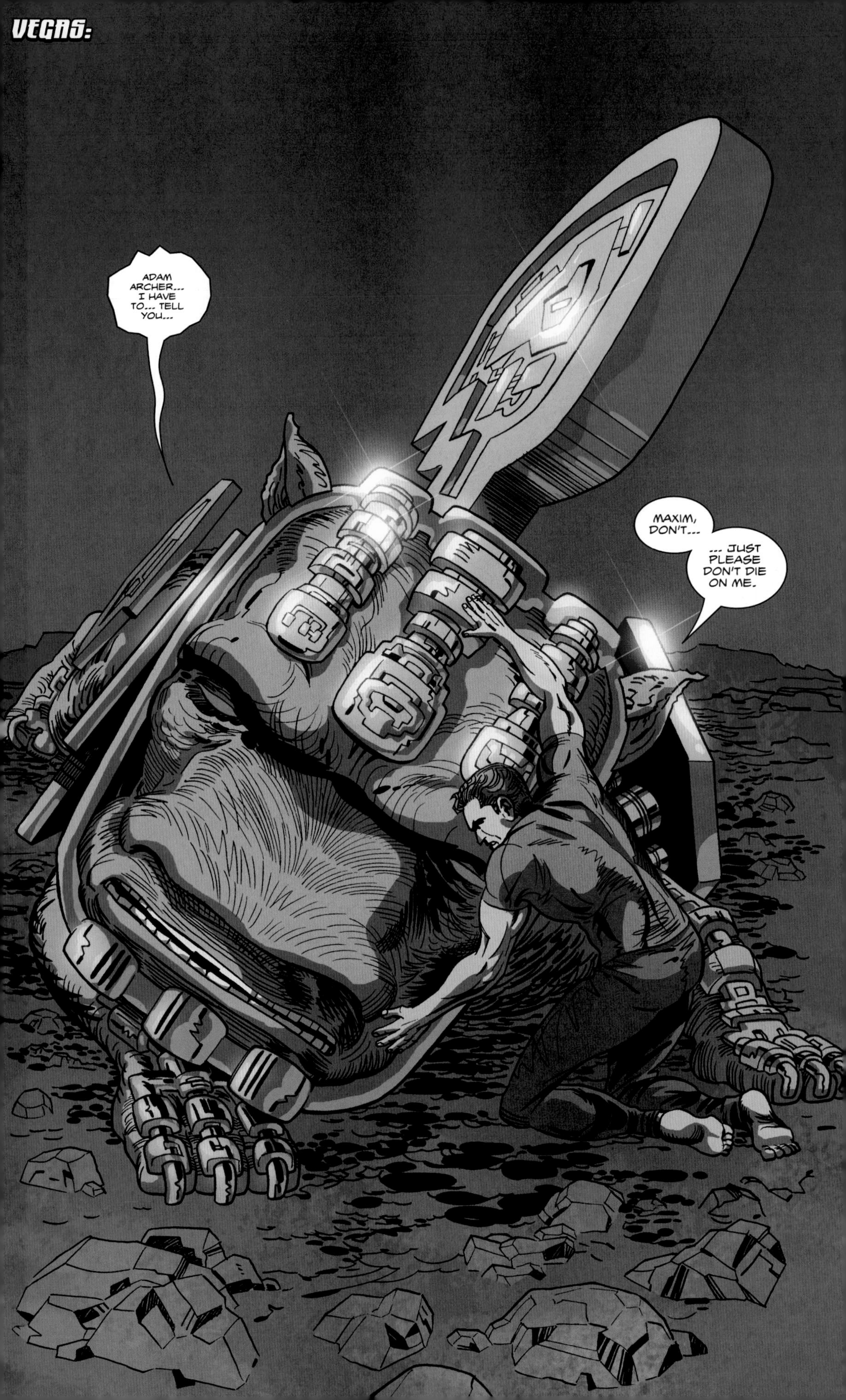
VEGAS:
ADAM ARCHER... I HAVE TO... TELL YOU...
MAXIM, DON'T...
... JUST PLEASE DON'T DIE ON ME.

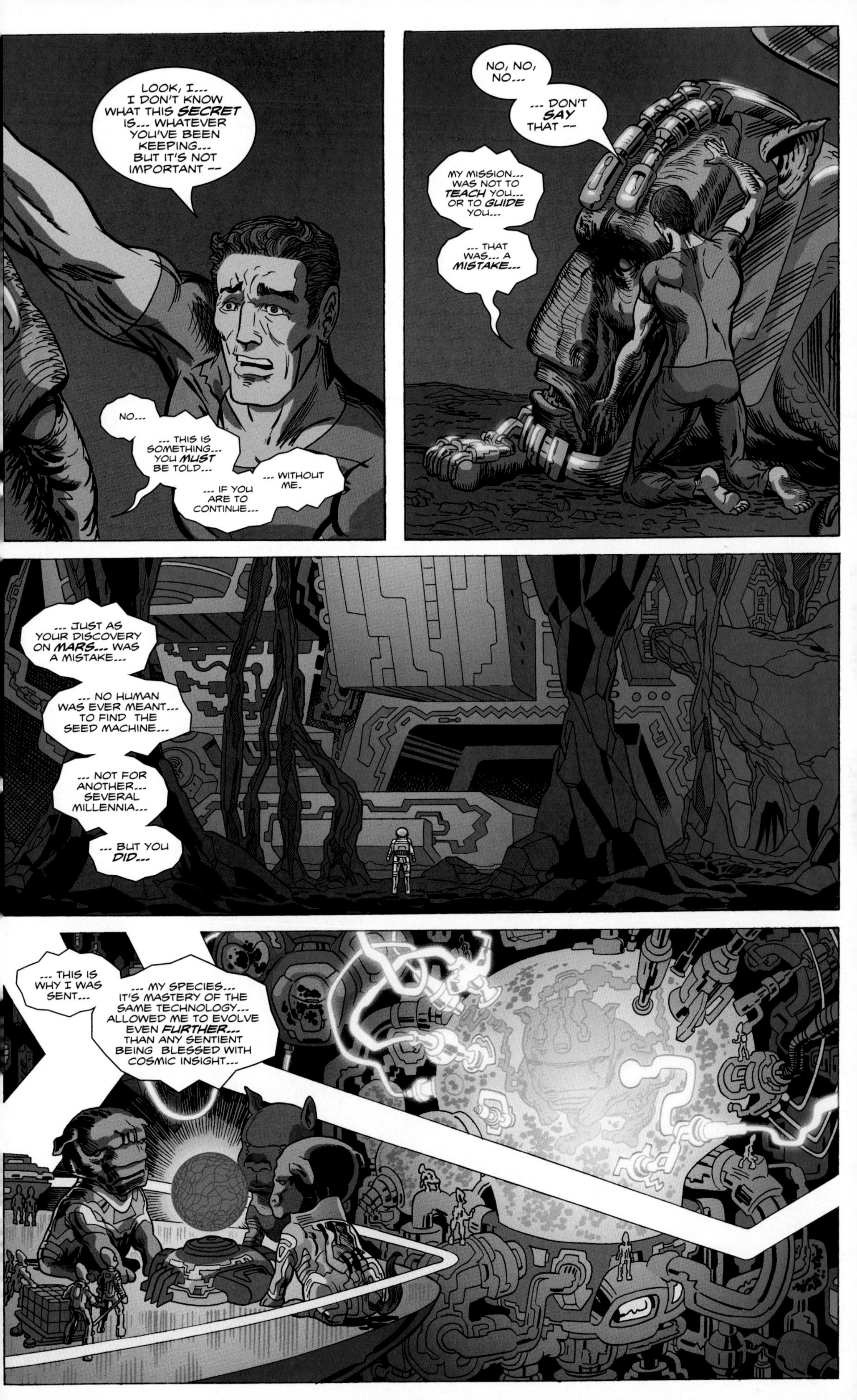
LOOK, I... I DON'T KNOW WHAT THIS SECRET IS... WHATEVER YOU'VE BEEN KEEPING... BUT IT'S NOT IMPORTANT --
NO...
... THIS IS SOMETHING... YOU MUST BE TOLD...
... IF YOU ARE TO CONTINUE...
... WITHOUT ME.
NO, NO, NO...
... DON'T SAY THAT --
MY MISSION... WAS NOT TO TEACH YOU... OR TO GUIDE YOU...
... THAT WAS... A MISTAKE...
... JUST AS YOUR DISCOVERY ON MARS... WAS A MISTAKE...
... NO HUMAN WAS EVER MEANT... TO FIND THE SEED MACHINE...
... NOT FOR ANOTHER... SEVERAL MILLENNIA...
... BUT YOU DID...
... THIS IS WHY I WAS SENT...
... MY SPECIES... IT'S MASTERY OF THE SAME TECHNOLOGY... ALLOWED ME TO EVOLVE EVEN FURTHER... THAN ANY SENTIENT BEING BLESSED WITH COSMIC INSIGHT...

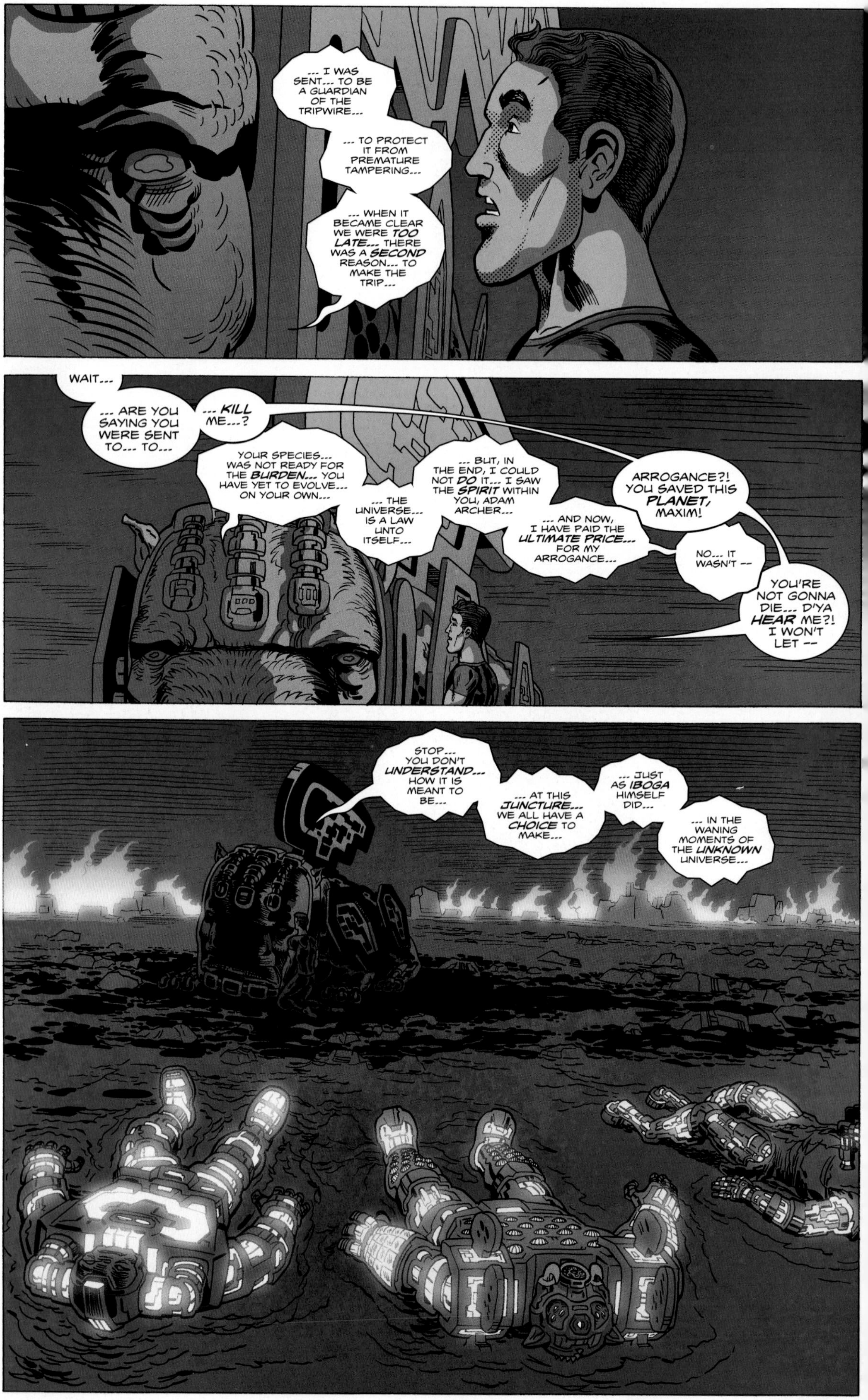
... I WAS SENT... TO BE A GUARDIAN OF THE TRIPWIRE...
... TO PROTECT IT FROM PREMATURE TAMPERING...
... WHEN IT BECAME CLEAR WE WERE TOO LATE... THERE WAS A SECOND REASON... TO MAKE THE TRIP...
WAIT...
... ARE YOU SAYING YOU WERE SENT TO... TO...
... KILL ME...?
YOUR SPECIES... WAS NOT READY FOR THE BURDEN... YOU HAVE YET TO EVOLVE... ON YOUR OWN...
... THE UNIVERSE... IS A LAW UNTO ITSELF...
... BUT, IN THE END, I COULD NOT DO IT... I SAW THE SPIRIT WITHIN YOU, ADAM ARCHER...
... AND NOW, I HAVE PAID THE ULTIMATE PRICE... FOR MY ARROGANCE...
ARROGANCE?! YOU SAVED THIS PLANET, MAXIM!
NO... IT WASN'T --
YOU'RE NOT GONNA DIE... D'YA HEAR ME?! I WON'T LET --
STOP... YOU DON'T UNDERSTAND... HOW IT IS MEANT TO BE...
... AT THIS JUNCTURE... WE ALL HAVE A CHOICE TO MAKE...
... JUST AS IBOGA HIMSELF DID...
... IN THE WANING MOMENTS OF THE UNKNOWN UNIVERSE...

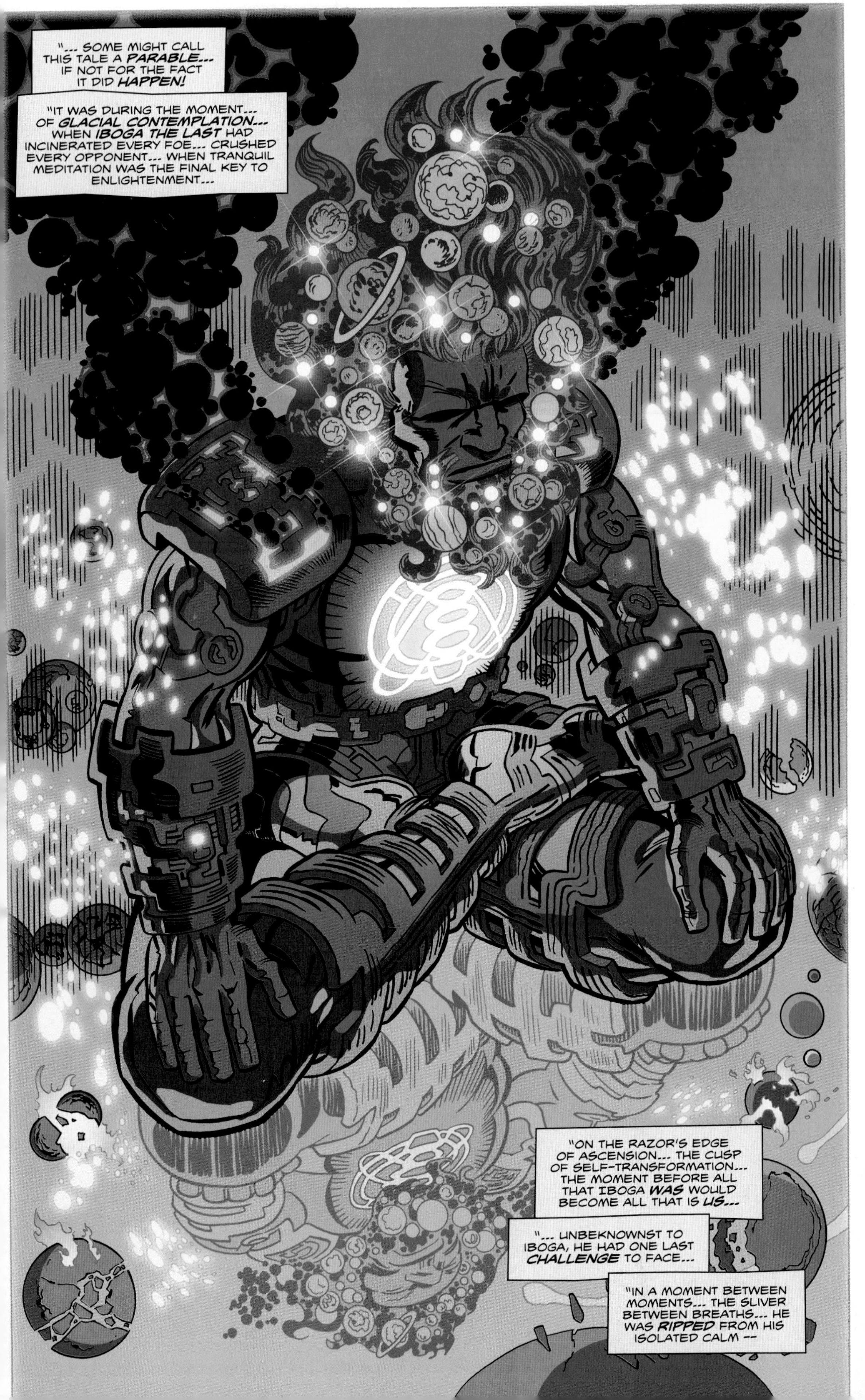
"... SOME MIGHT CALL THIS TALE A *PARABLE*... IF NOT FOR THE FACT IT DID *HAPPEN!*
"IT WAS DURING THE MOMENT... OF *GLACIAL CONTEMPLATION*... WHEN *IBOGA THE LAST* HAD INCINERATED EVERY FOE... CRUSHED EVERY OPPONENT... WHEN TRANQUIL MEDITATION WAS THE FINAL KEY TO ENLIGHTENMENT...
"ON THE RAZOR'S EDGE OF ASCENSION... THE CUSP OF SELF-TRANSFORMATION... THE MOMENT BEFORE ALL THAT IBOGA *WAS* WOULD BECOME ALL THAT IS *US*...
"... UNBEKNOWNST TO IBOGA, HE HAD ONE LAST *CHALLENGE* TO FACE...
"IN A MOMENT BETWEEN MOMENTS... THE SLIVER BETWEEN BREATHS... HE WAS *RIPPED* FROM HIS ISOLATED CALM --

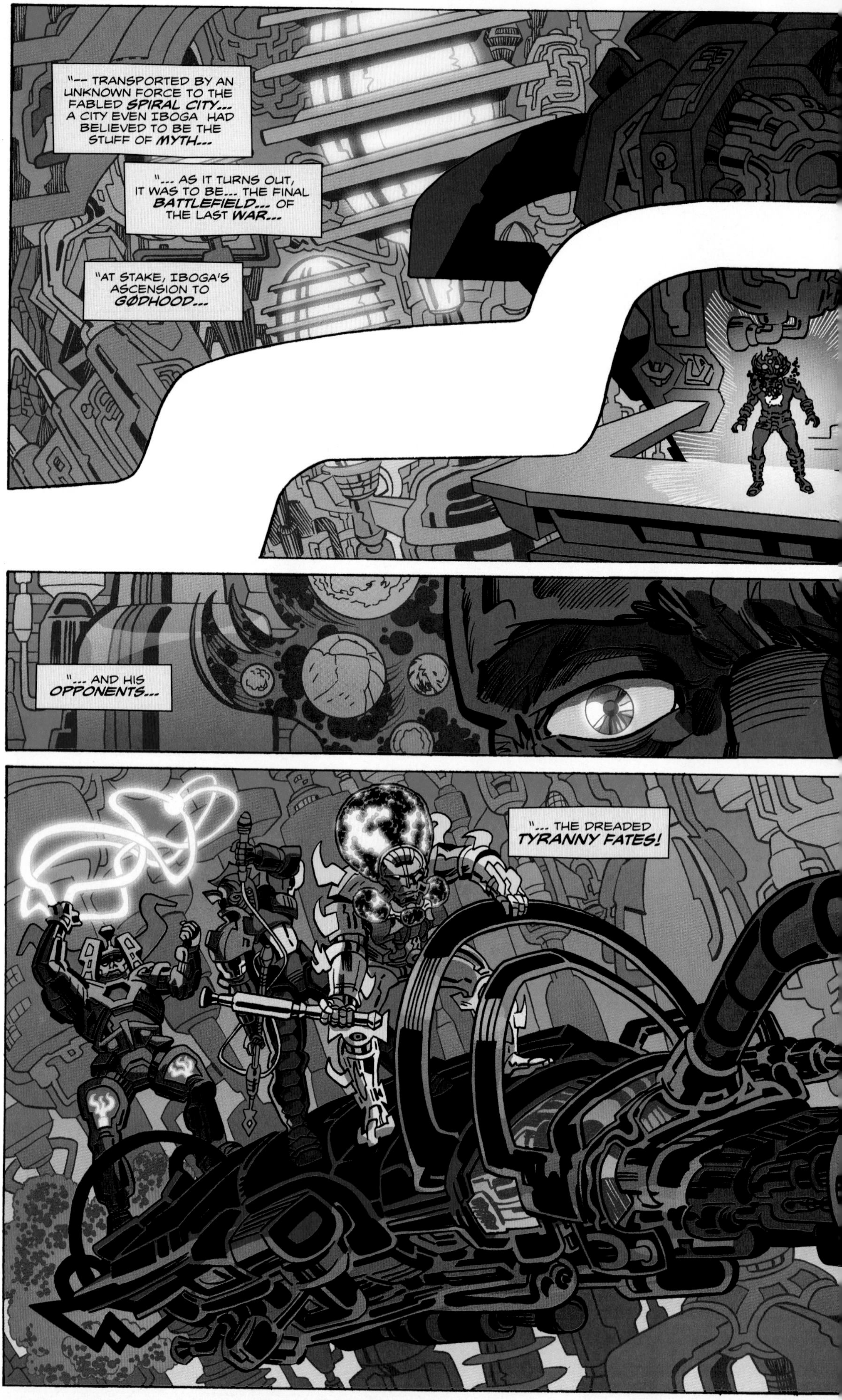
"-- TRANSPORTED BY AN UNKNOWN FORCE TO THE FABLED SPIRAL CITY... A CITY EVEN IBOGA HAD BELIEVED TO BE THE STUFF OF MYTH...
"... AS IT TURNS OUT, IT WAS TO BE... THE FINAL BATTLEFIELD... OF THE LAST WAR...
"AT STAKE, IBOGA'S ASCENSION TO GØDHOOD...
"... AND HIS OPPONENTS...
"... THE DREADED TYRANNY FATES!

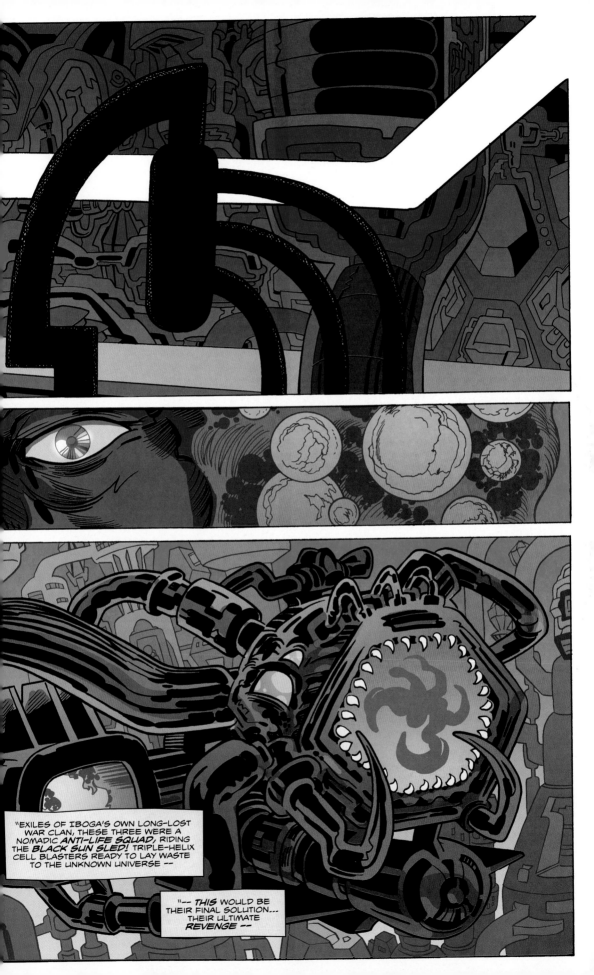

"EXILES OF IBOGA'S OWN LONG-LOST WAR CLAN, THESE THREE WERE A NOMADIC *ANTI-LIFE SQUAD*, RIDING THE *BLACK SUN SLED!* TRIPLE-HELIX CELL BLASTERS READY TO LAY WASTE TO THE UNKNOWN UNIVERSE --

"-- *THIS* WOULD BE THEIR FINAL SOLUTION... THEIR ULTIMATE *REVENGE* --

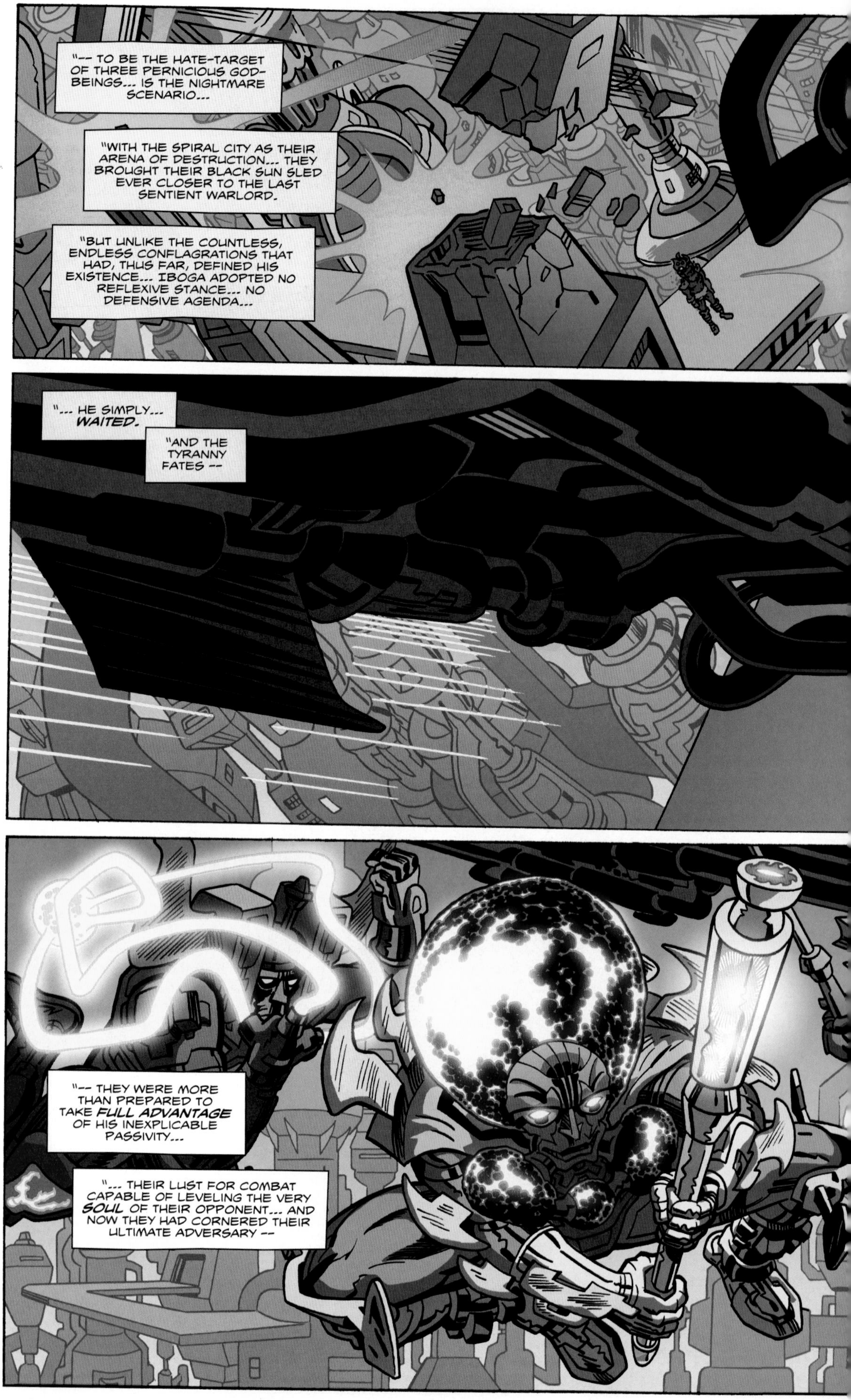
"-- TO BE THE HATE-TARGET OF THREE PERNICIOUS GOD-BEINGS... IS THE NIGHTMARE SCENARIO...
"WITH THE SPIRAL CITY AS THEIR ARENA OF DESTRUCTION... THEY BROUGHT THEIR BLACK SUN SLED EVER CLOSER TO THE LAST SENTIENT WARLORD.
"BUT UNLIKE THE COUNTLESS, ENDLESS CONFLAGRATIONS THAT HAD, THUS FAR, DEFINED HIS EXISTENCE... IBOGA ADOPTED NO REFLEXIVE STANCE... NO DEFENSIVE AGENDA...
"... HE SIMPLY... WAITED.
"AND THE TYRANNY FATES --
"-- THEY WERE MORE THAN PREPARED TO TAKE FULL ADVANTAGE OF HIS INEXPLICABLE PASSIVITY...
"... THEIR LUST FOR COMBAT CAPABLE OF LEVELING THE VERY SOUL OF THEIR OPPONENT... AND NOW THEY HAD CORNERED THEIR ULTIMATE ADVERSARY --

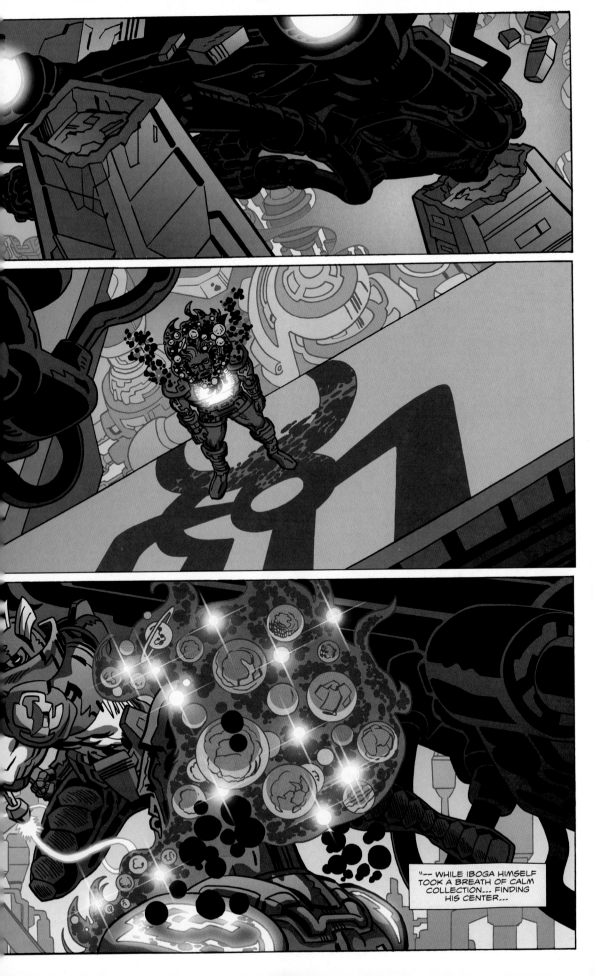

"-- WHILE IBOGA HIMSELF TOOK A BREATH OF CALM COLLECTION... FINDING HIS CENTER..."

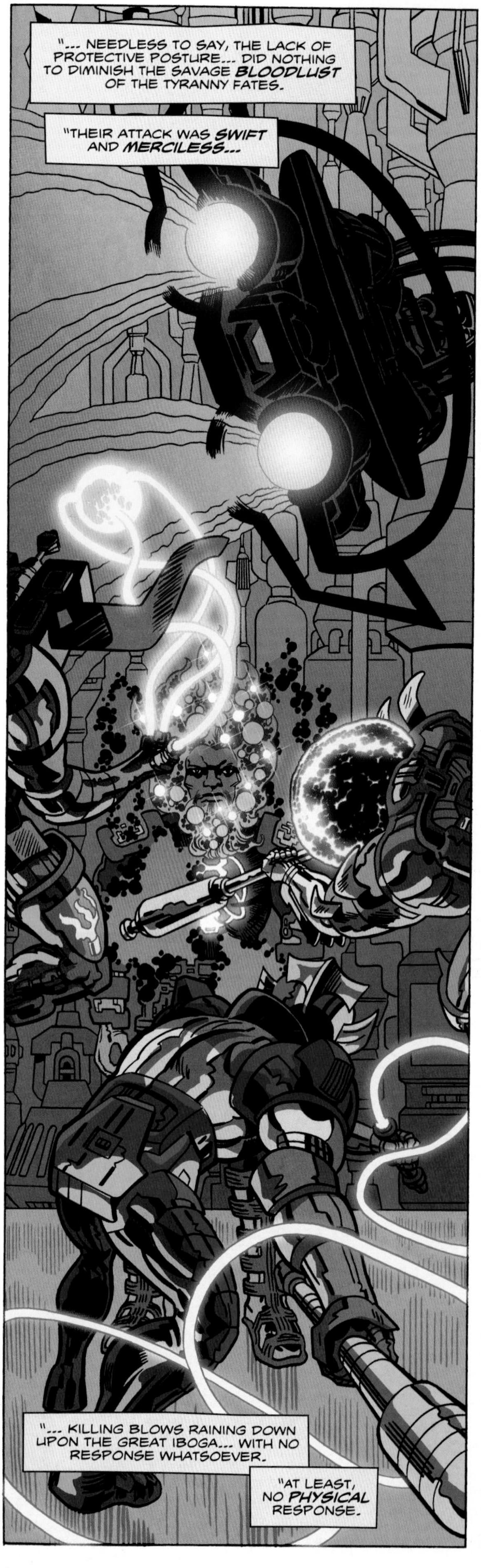
"... NEEDLESS TO SAY, THE LACK OF PROTECTIVE POSTURE... DID NOTHING TO DIMINISH THE SAVAGE BLOODLUST OF THE TYRANNY FATES.
"THEIR ATTACK WAS SWIFT AND MERCILESS...
"... KILLING BLOWS RAINING DOWN UPON THE GREAT IBOGA... WITH NO RESPONSE WHATSOEVER.
"AT LEAST, NO PHYSICAL RESPONSE.

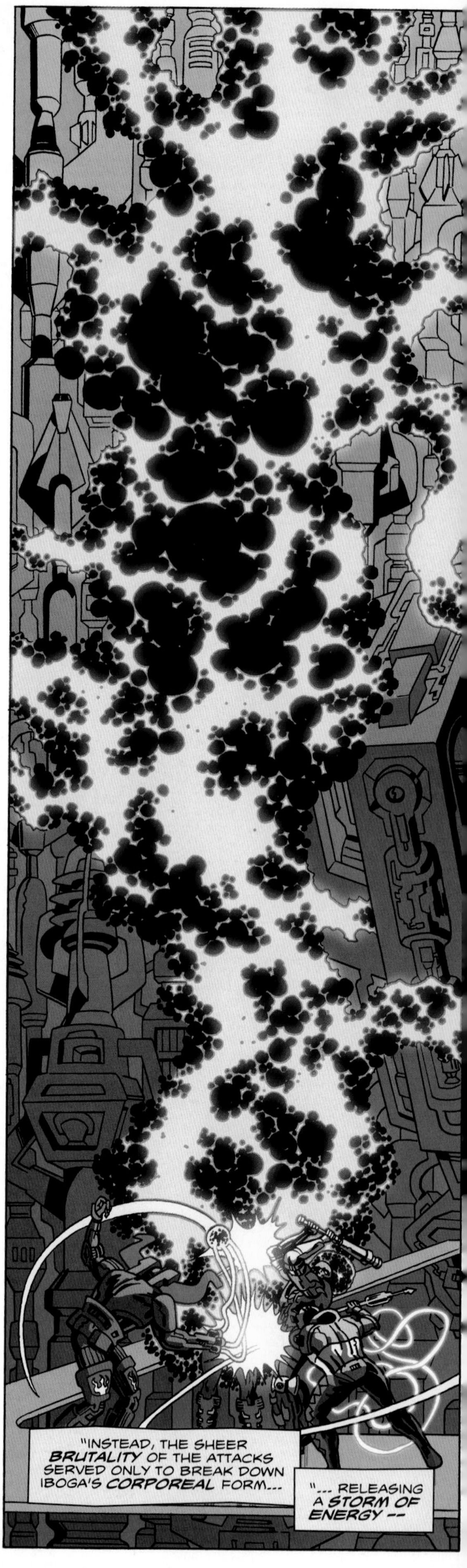
"INSTEAD, THE SHEER BRUTALITY OF THE ATTACKS SERVED ONLY TO BREAK DOWN IBOGA'S CORPOREAL FORM...
"... RELEASING A STORM OF ENERGY --

"AS A TANGENT OF HIS OUTWARD EXPANSION... THE SPIRAL CITY WAS *CONSUMED* TO HIS NEW *COMPLETENESS*...

"THE *TYRANNY FATES* WERE ALLOWED ONE LAST *NIGHTMARE* BEFORE THE *FINAL ABSORPTION* INTO THE FUTURE OF ALL THINGS.

"THERE IS A *LESSON* HERE... IBOGA CHOSE *NOT* TO FIGHT... TO ALLOW HIMSELF TO *EVOLVE*...

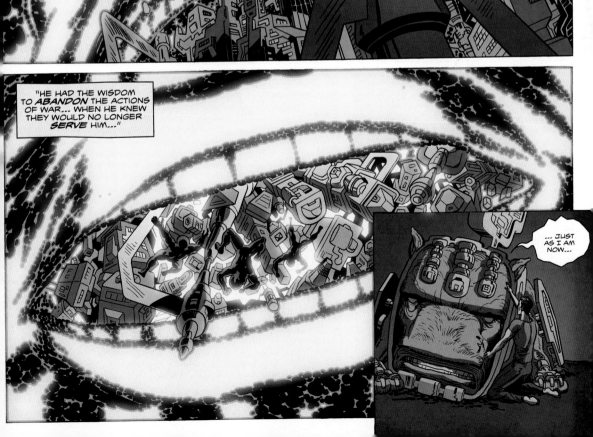

"HE HAD THE WISDOM TO *ABANDON* THE ACTIONS OF WAR... WHEN HE KNEW THEY WOULD NO LONGER *SERVE* HIM..."

... JUST AS I AM NOW...

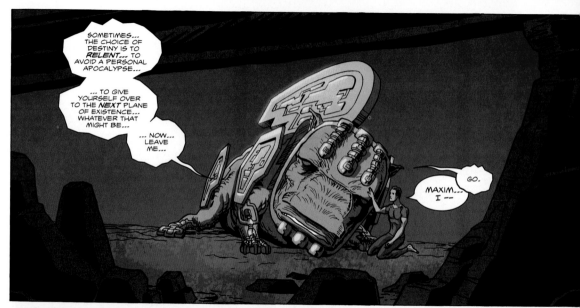

SOMETIMES... THE CHOICE OF DESTINY IS TO *RELENT*... TO AVOID A PERSONAL APOCALYPSE...

... TO GIVE YOURSELF OVER TO THE *NEXT* PLANE OF EXISTENCE... WHATEVER THAT MIGHT BE...

... NOW... LEAVE ME...

MAXIM... I --

GO.

GO.

HOLD IT.

NO.

I DON'T CARE *WHY* YOU WERE SENT HERE. I REALLY DON'T.

YOU'RE MY FRIEND. YOU HELPED ME *UNDERSTAND* THINGS... HELPED ME SEE THE BIGGER PICTURE... HELPED ME SEE THAT I MIGHT ACTUALLY HAVE A *PLACE* IN THE UNIVERSE...

YOU HELPED ME UNDERSTAND MY POWER...

... AT LEAST A LITTLE BIT...

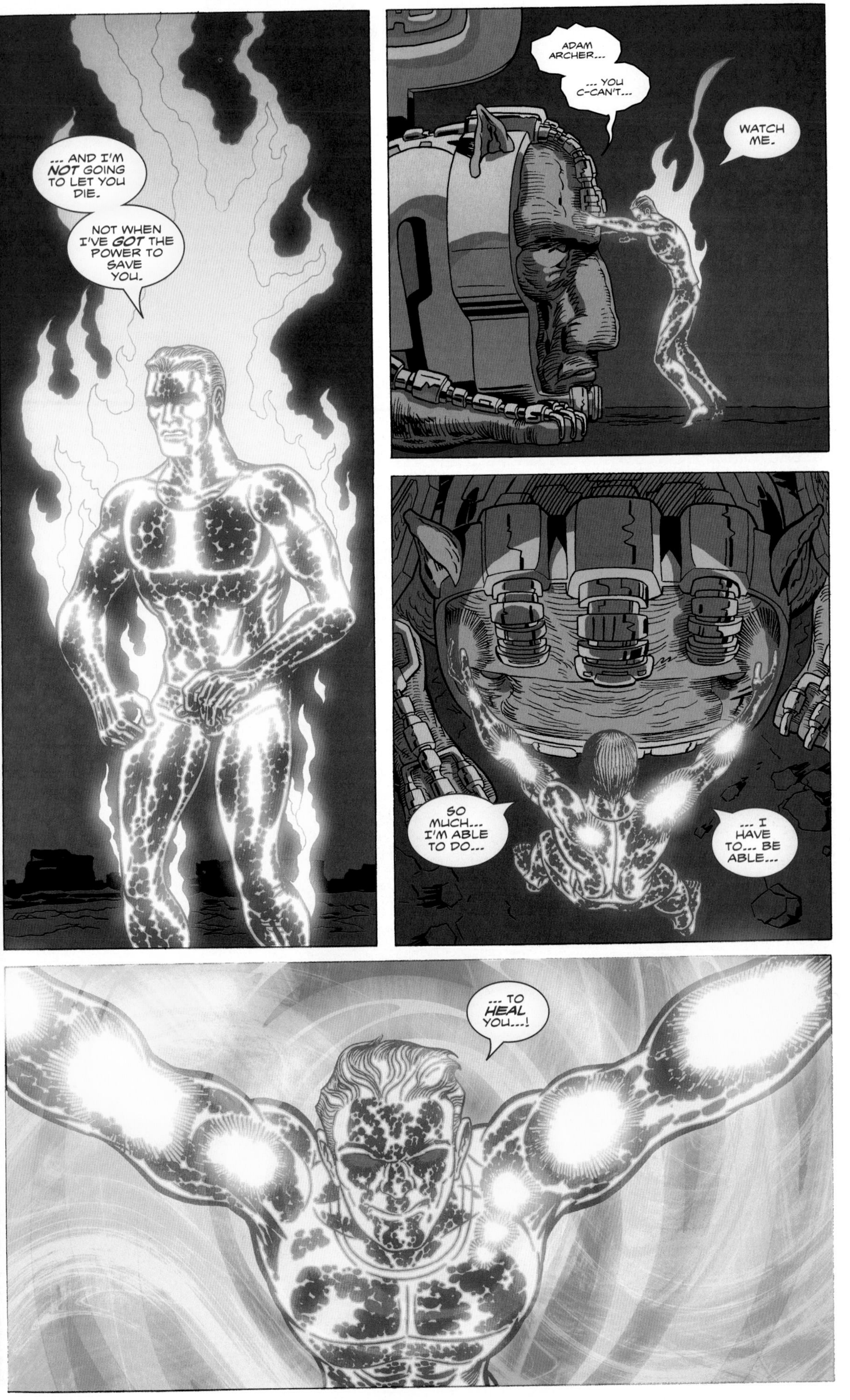
... AND I'M *NOT* GOING TO LET YOU DIE.
NOT WHEN I'VE *GOT* THE POWER TO SAVE YOU.
ADAM ARCHER...
... YOU C-CAN'T...
WATCH ME.
SO MUCH... I'M ABLE TO DO...
... I HAVE TO... BE ABLE...
... TO *HEAL* YOU...!

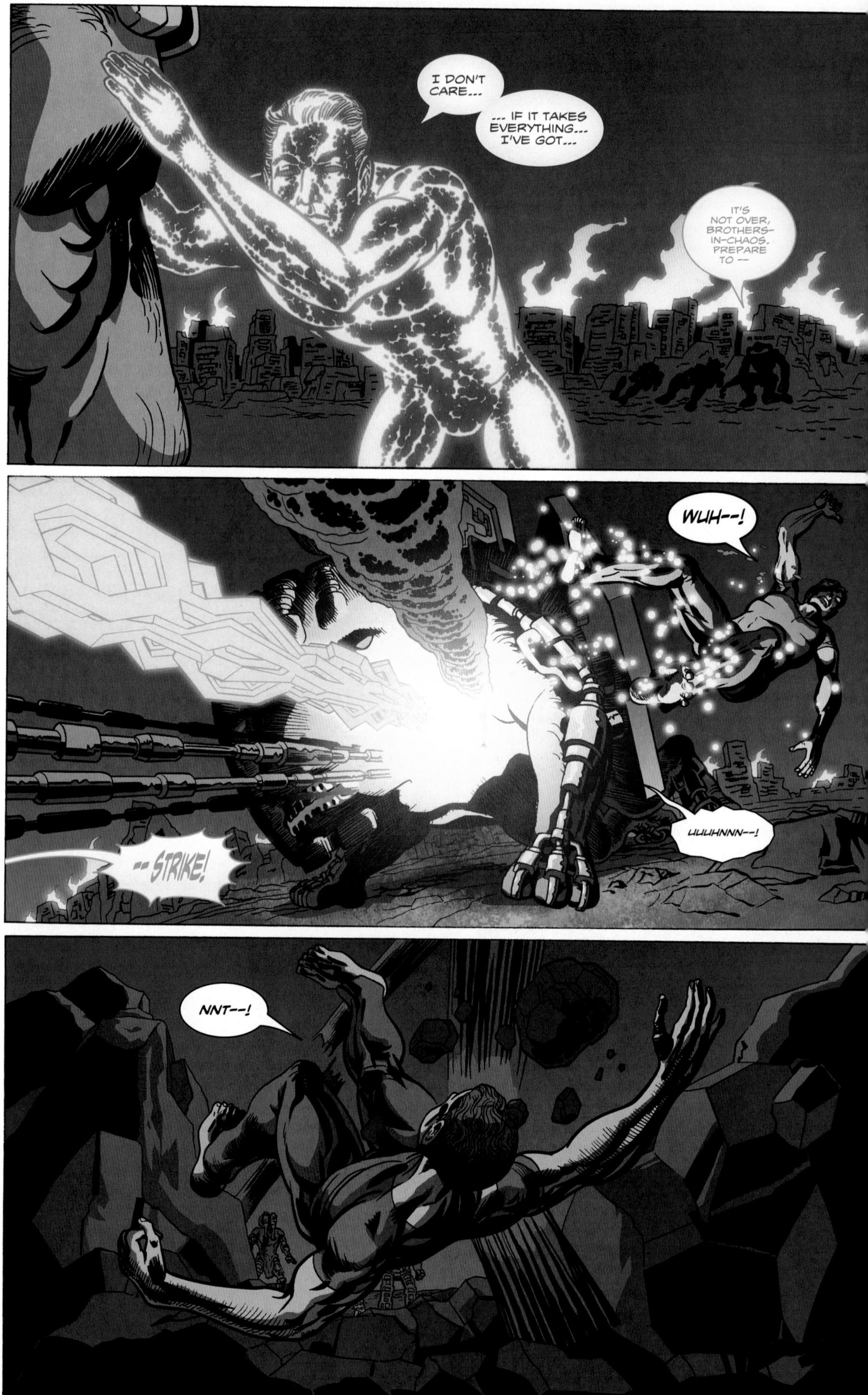
I DON'T CARE...
... IF IT TAKES EVERYTHING... I'VE GOT...
IT'S NOT OVER, BROTHERS-IN-CHAOS. PREPARE TO --
WUH--!
UUUHNNN--!
-- STRIKE!
NNT--!

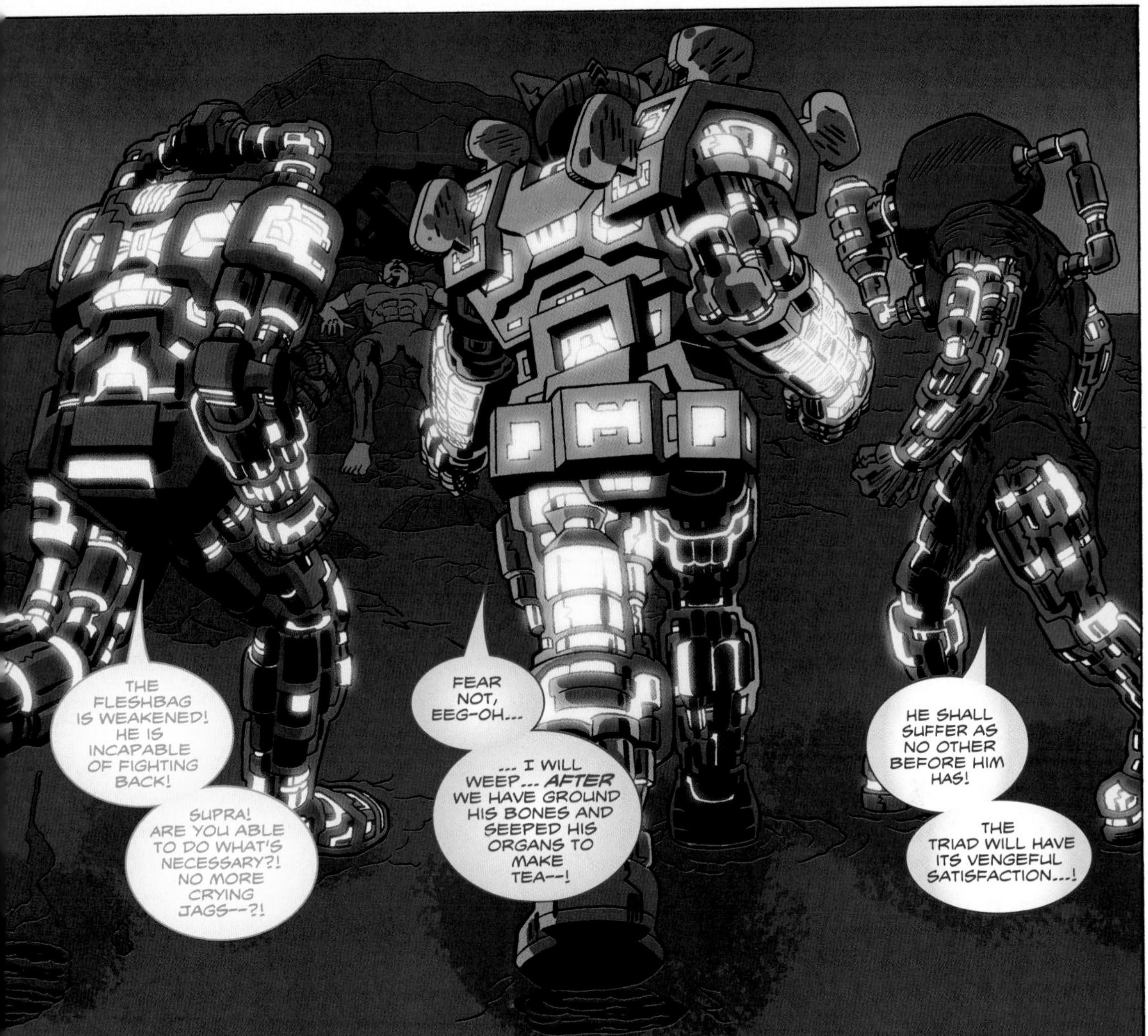
THE FLESHBAG IS WEAKENED! HE IS INCAPABLE OF FIGHTING BACK!
SUPRA! ARE YOU ABLE TO DO WHAT'S NECESSARY?! NO MORE CRYING JAGS--?!
FEAR NOT, EEG-OH...
... I WILL WEEP... AFTER WE HAVE GROUND HIS BONES AND SEEPED HIS ORGANS TO MAKE TEA--!
HE SHALL SUFFER AS NO OTHER BEFORE HIM HAS!
THE TRIAD WILL HAVE ITS VENGEFUL SATISFACTION...!

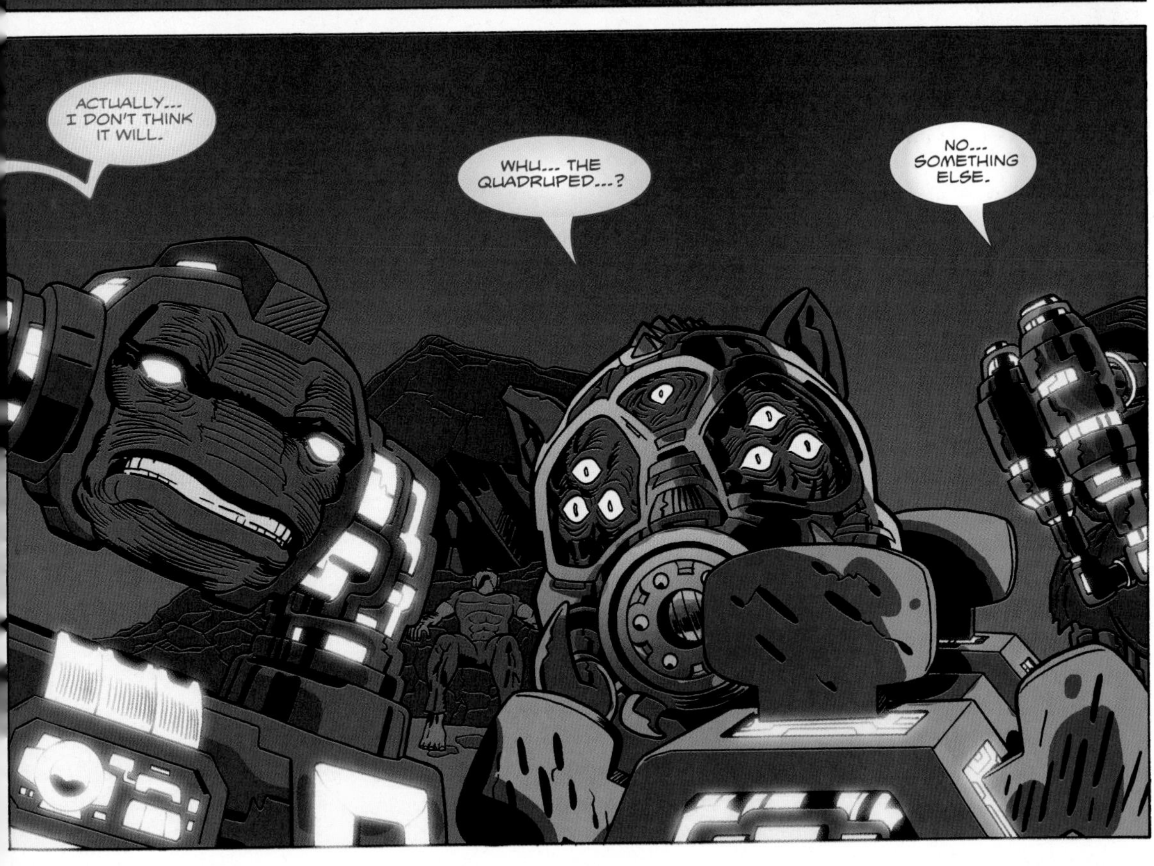
ACTUALLY... I DON'T THINK IT WILL.
WHU... THE QUADRUPED...?
NO... SOMETHING ELSE.

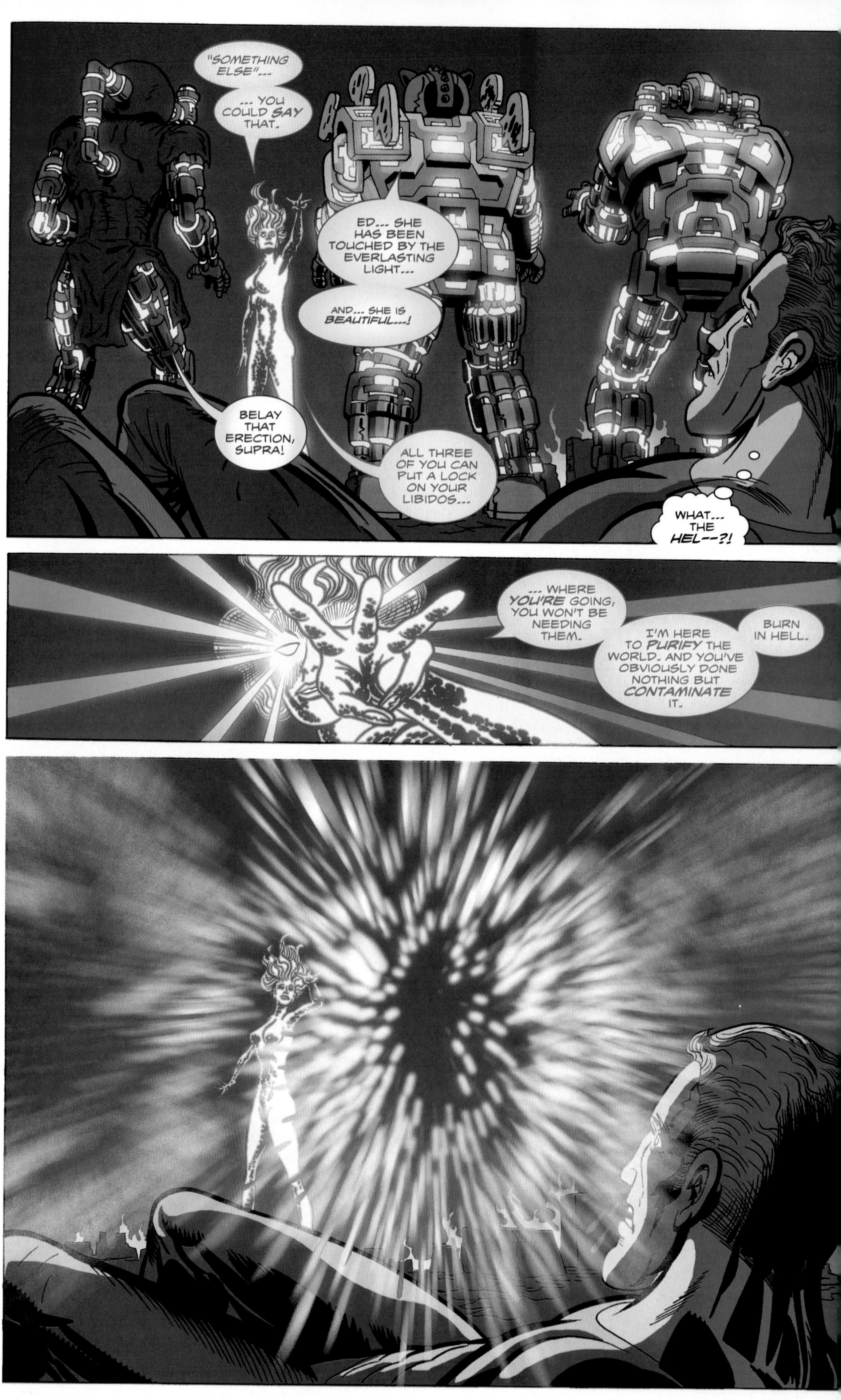
"SOMETHING ELSE"...
... YOU COULD SAY THAT.
ED... SHE HAS BEEN TOUCHED BY THE EVERLASTING LIGHT...
AND... SHE IS BEAUTIFUL...!
BELAY THAT ERECTION, SUPRA!
ALL THREE OF YOU CAN PUT A LOCK ON YOUR LIBIDOS...
WHAT... THE HEL--?!
... WHERE YOU'RE GOING, YOU WON'T BE NEEDING THEM.
I'M HERE TO PURIFY THE WORLD. AND YOU'VE OBVIOUSLY DONE NOTHING BUT CONTAMINATE IT.
BURN IN HELL.

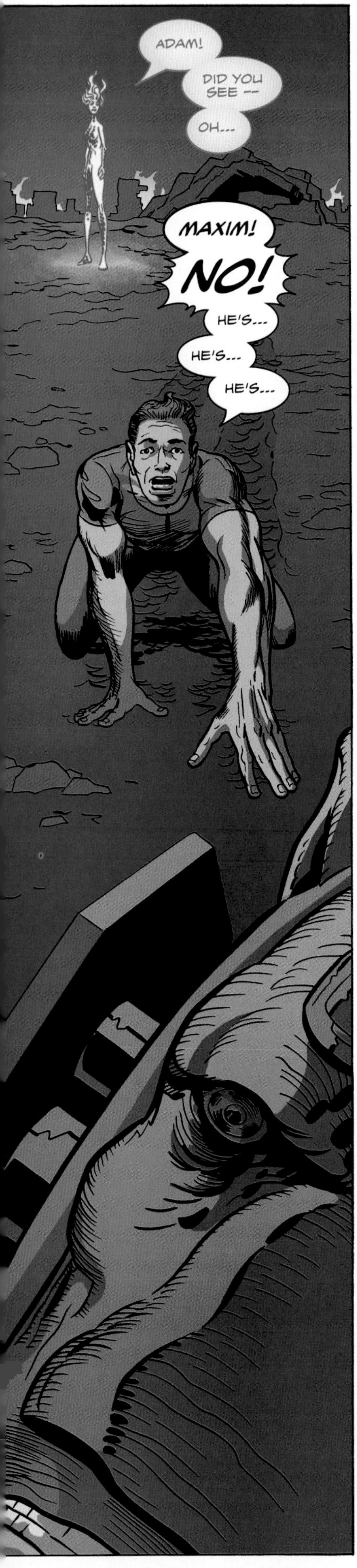
ADAM!
DID YOU SEE --
OH...
MAXIM!
NO!
HE'S...
HE'S...
HE'S...

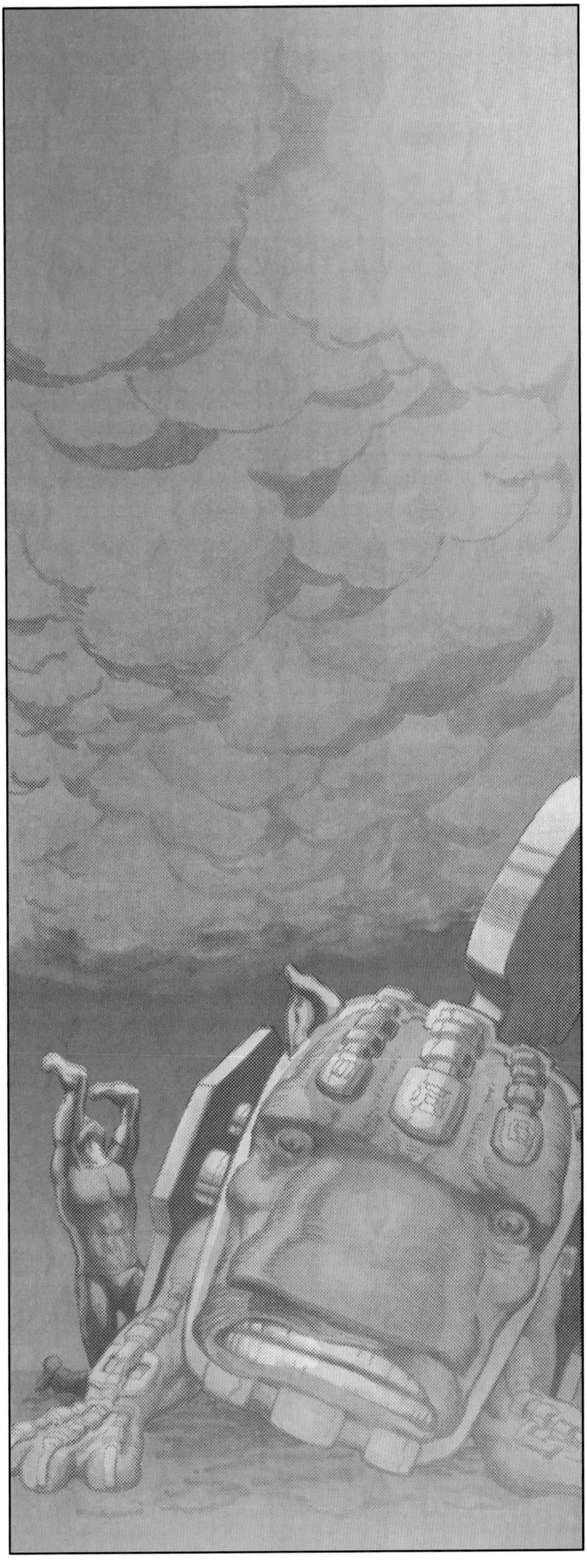

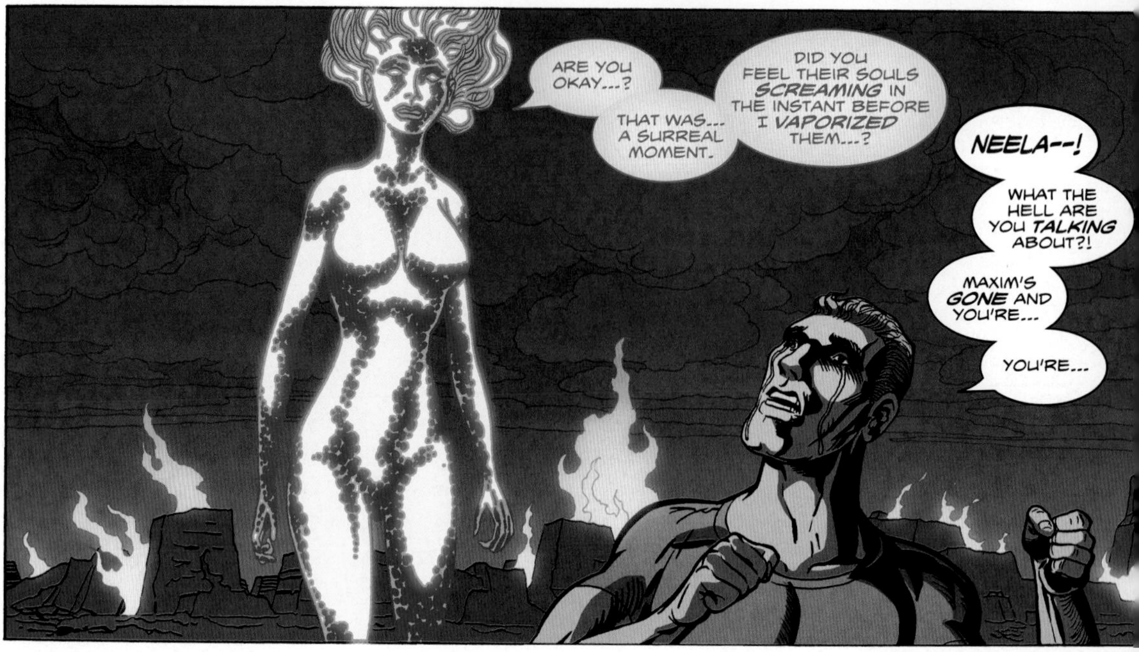
ARE YOU OKAY...?
THAT WAS... A SURREAL MOMENT.
DID YOU FEEL THEIR SOULS SCREAMING IN THE INSTANT BEFORE I VAPORIZED THEM...?
NEELA--!
WHAT THE HELL ARE YOU TALKING ABOUT?!
MAXIM'S GONE AND YOU'RE...
YOU'RE...

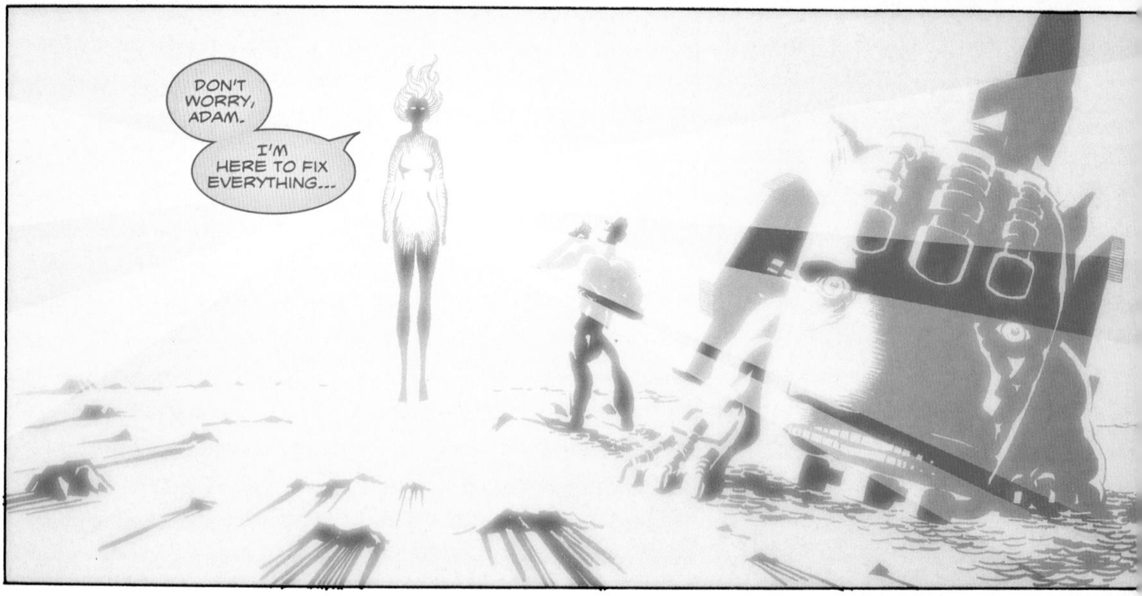
DON'T WORRY, ADAM.
I'M HERE TO FIX EVERYTHING...

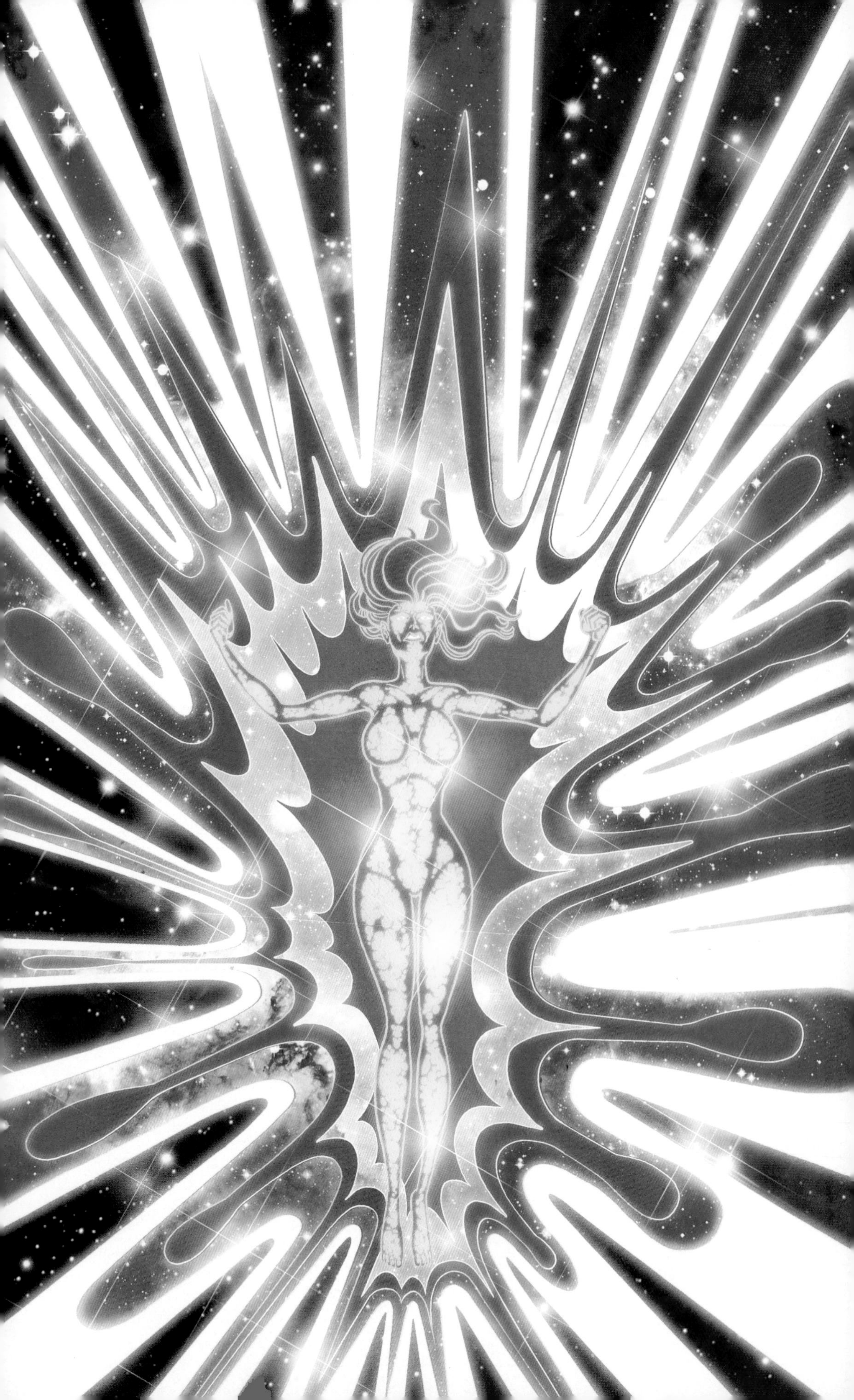

WORLDS APART

BOOK TWENTY-THREE

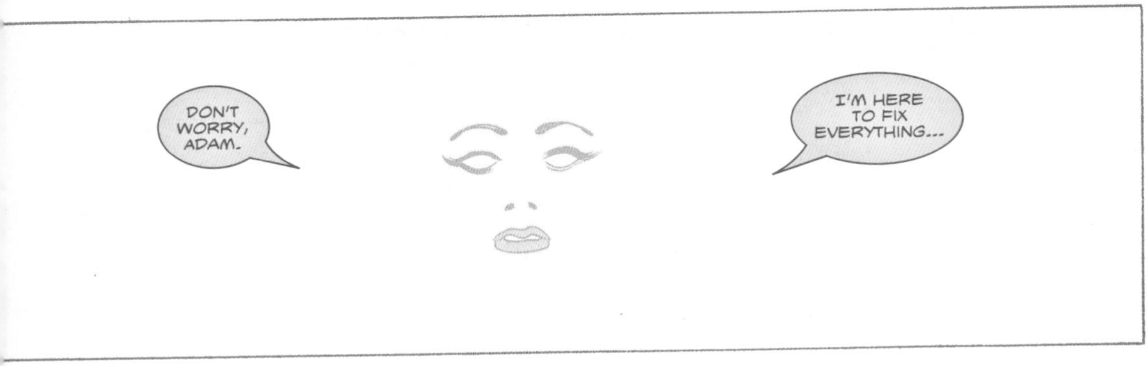
DON'T WORRY, ADAM.
I'M HERE TO FIX EVERYTHING...

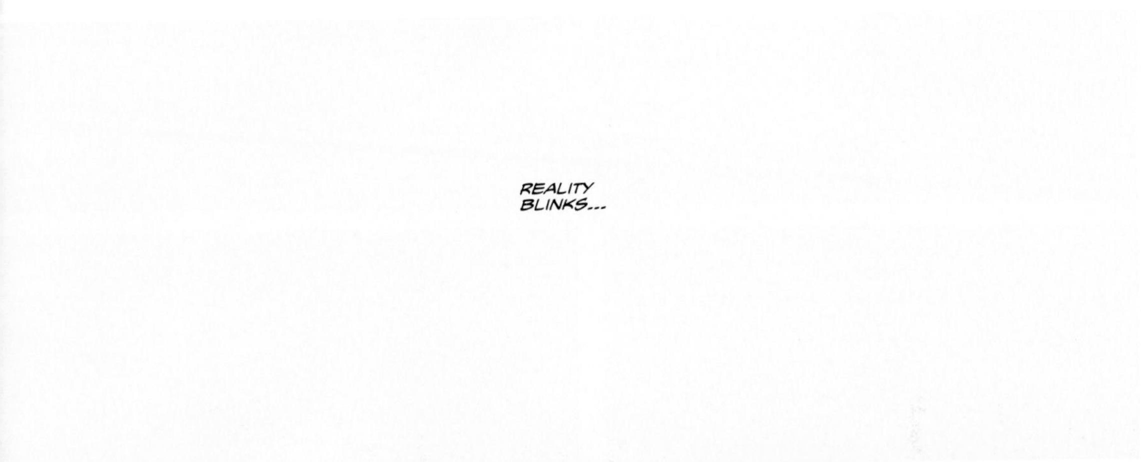
REALITY BLINKS...

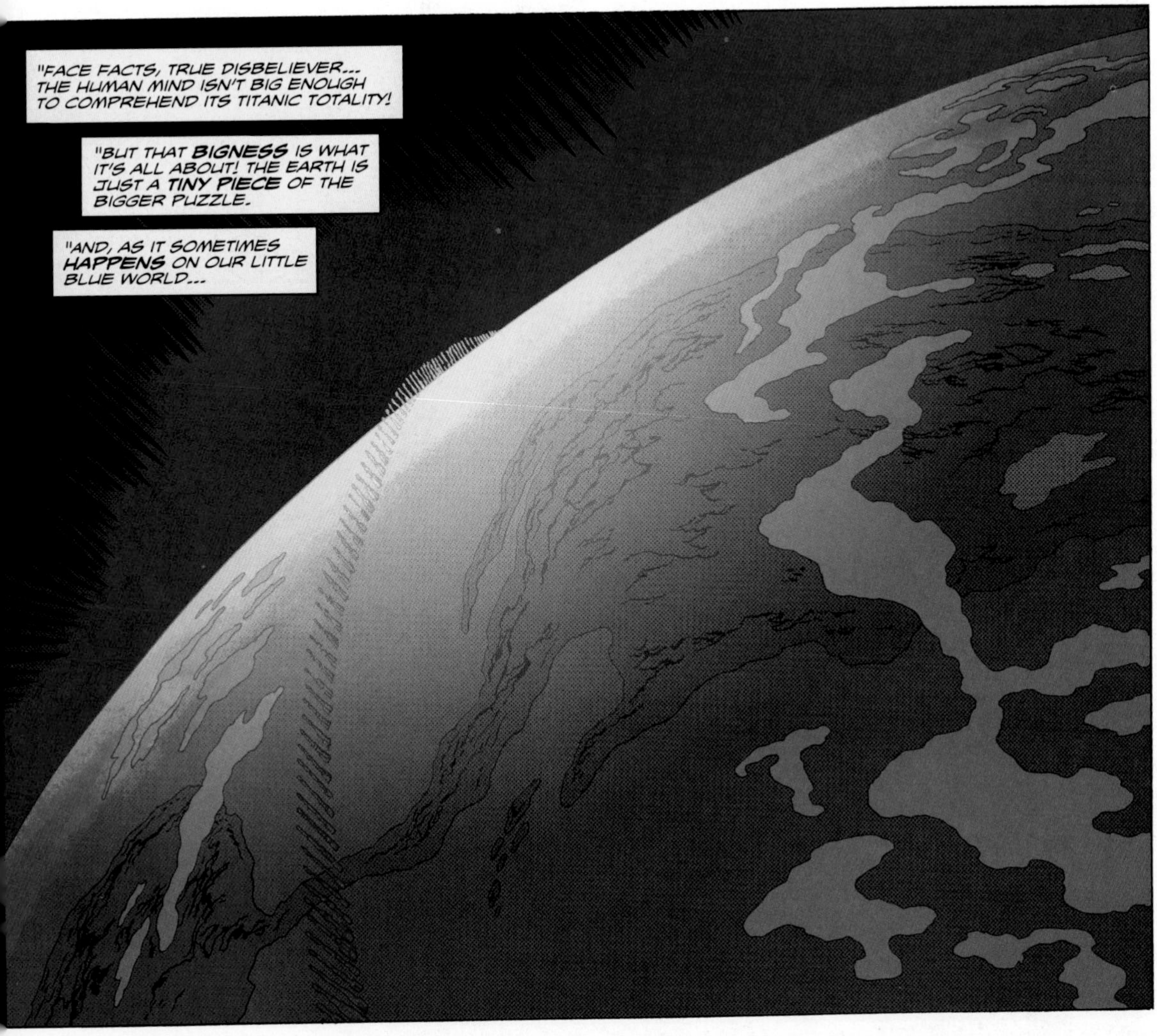
"FACE FACTS, TRUE DISBELIEVER... THE HUMAN MIND ISN'T BIG ENOUGH TO COMPREHEND ITS TITANIC TOTALITY!
"BUT THAT BIGNESS IS WHAT IT'S ALL ABOUT! THE EARTH IS JUST A TINY PIECE OF THE BIGGER PUZZLE.
"AND, AS IT SOMETIMES HAPPENS ON OUR LITTLE BLUE WORLD...

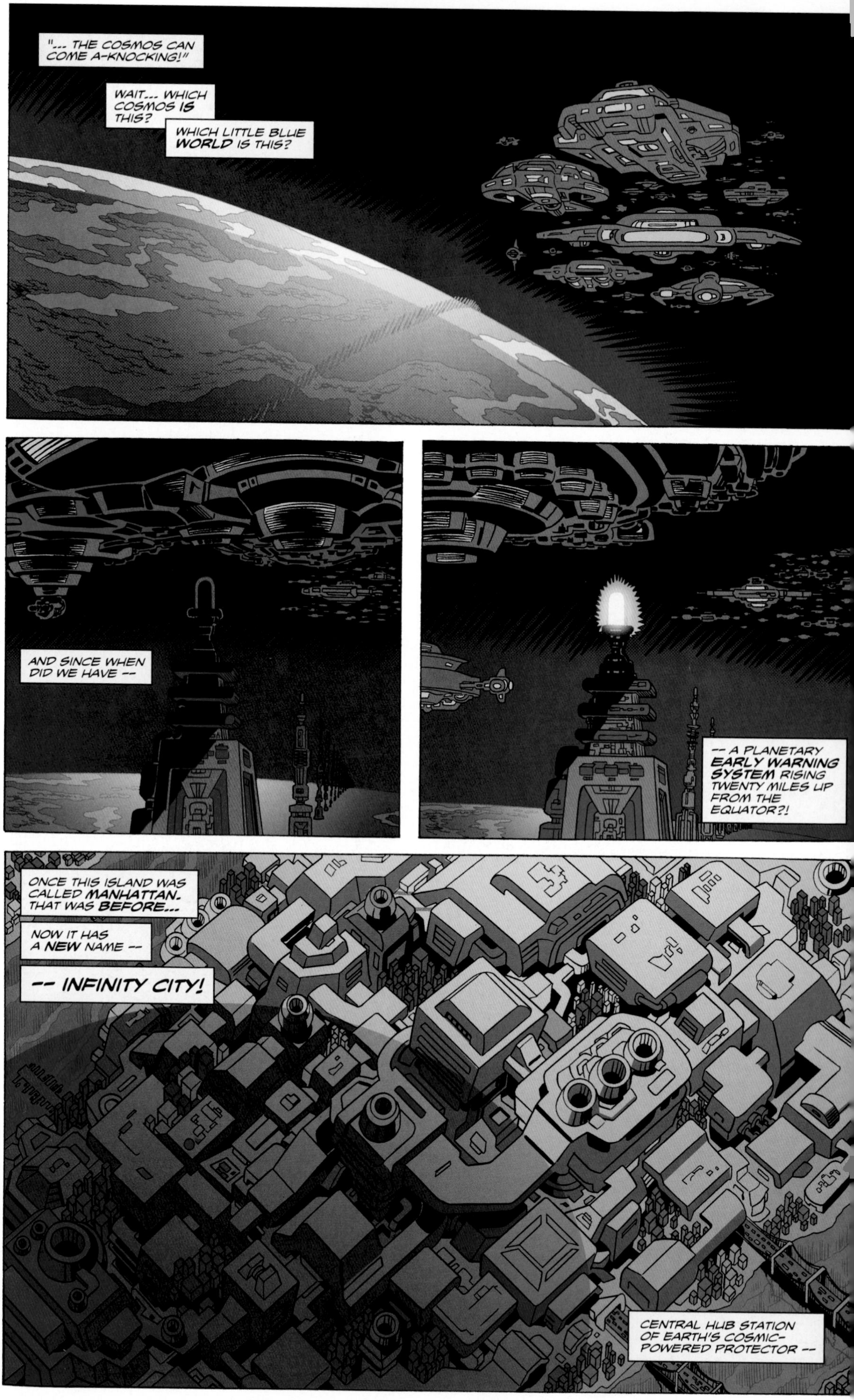
"... THE COSMOS CAN COME A-KNOCKING!"
WAIT... WHICH COSMOS IS THIS?
WHICH LITTLE BLUE WORLD IS THIS?
AND SINCE WHEN DID WE HAVE --
-- A PLANETARY EARLY WARNING SYSTEM RISING TWENTY MILES UP FROM THE EQUATOR?!
ONCE THIS ISLAND WAS CALLED MANHATTAN. THAT WAS BEFORE...
NOW IT HAS A NEW NAME --
-- INFINITY CITY!
CENTRAL HUB STATION OF EARTH'S COSMIC-POWERED PROTECTOR --

-- COMMANDER **NEELA ARCHER!**

-- YOUR ALERT ANTENNA PICKED THEM UP FIRST. TELEMETRY IS PROJECTING A WORLDWIDE **INVASION!**

I'VE ALREADY GOT THE SILO PREPPED, STELLA --

-- TELL BRIGG I'M ON MY WAY!

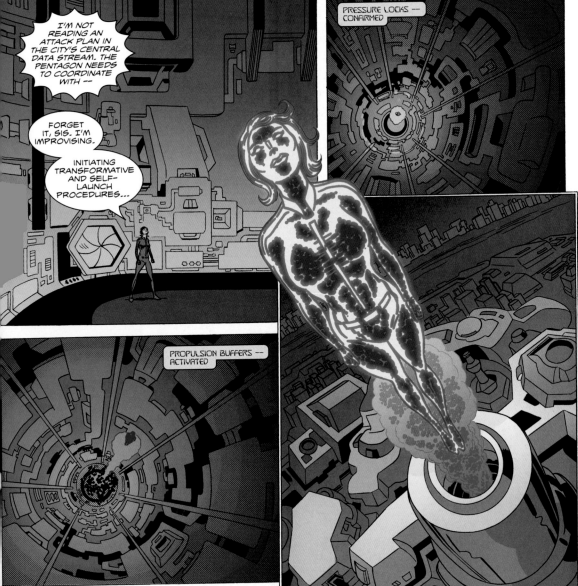

PRESSURE LOCKS -- CONFIRMED

I'M NOT READING AN ATTACK PLAN IN THE CITY'S CENTRAL DATA STREAM. THE PENTAGON NEEDS TO COORDINATE WITH --

FORGET IT, SIS. I'M IMPROVISING.

INITIATING TRANSFORMATIVE AND SELF-LAUNCH PROCEDURES...

PROPULSION BUFFERS -- ACTIVATED

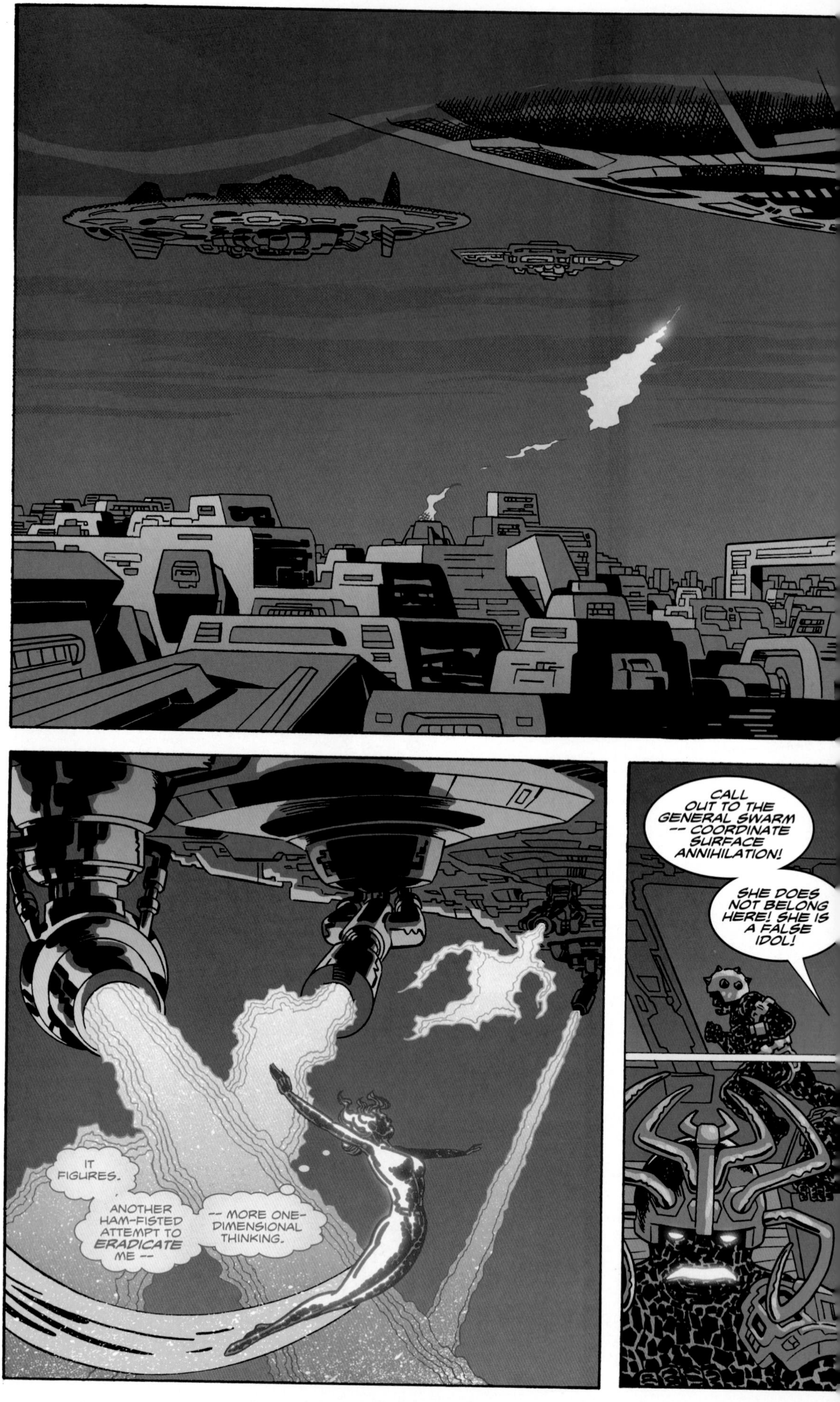
IT FIGURES.
ANOTHER HAM-FISTED ATTEMPT TO ERADICATE ME --
-- MORE ONE-DIMENSIONAL THINKING.
CALL OUT TO THE GENERAL SWARM -- COORDINATE SURFACE ANNIHILATION!
SHE DOES NOT BELONG HERE! SHE IS A FALSE IDOL!

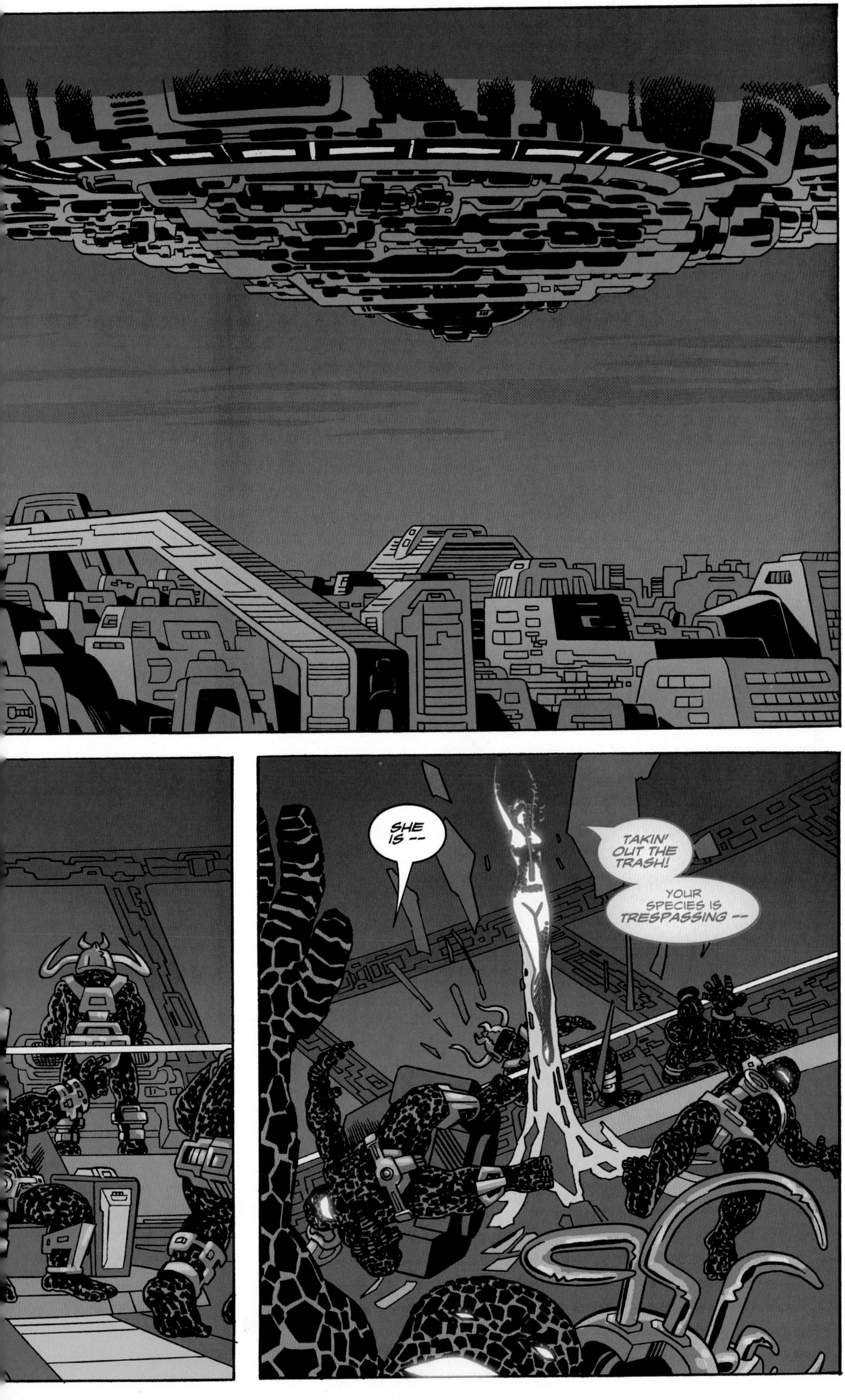
SHE IS --
TAKIN' OUT THE TRASH!
YOUR SPECIES IS TRESPASSING --

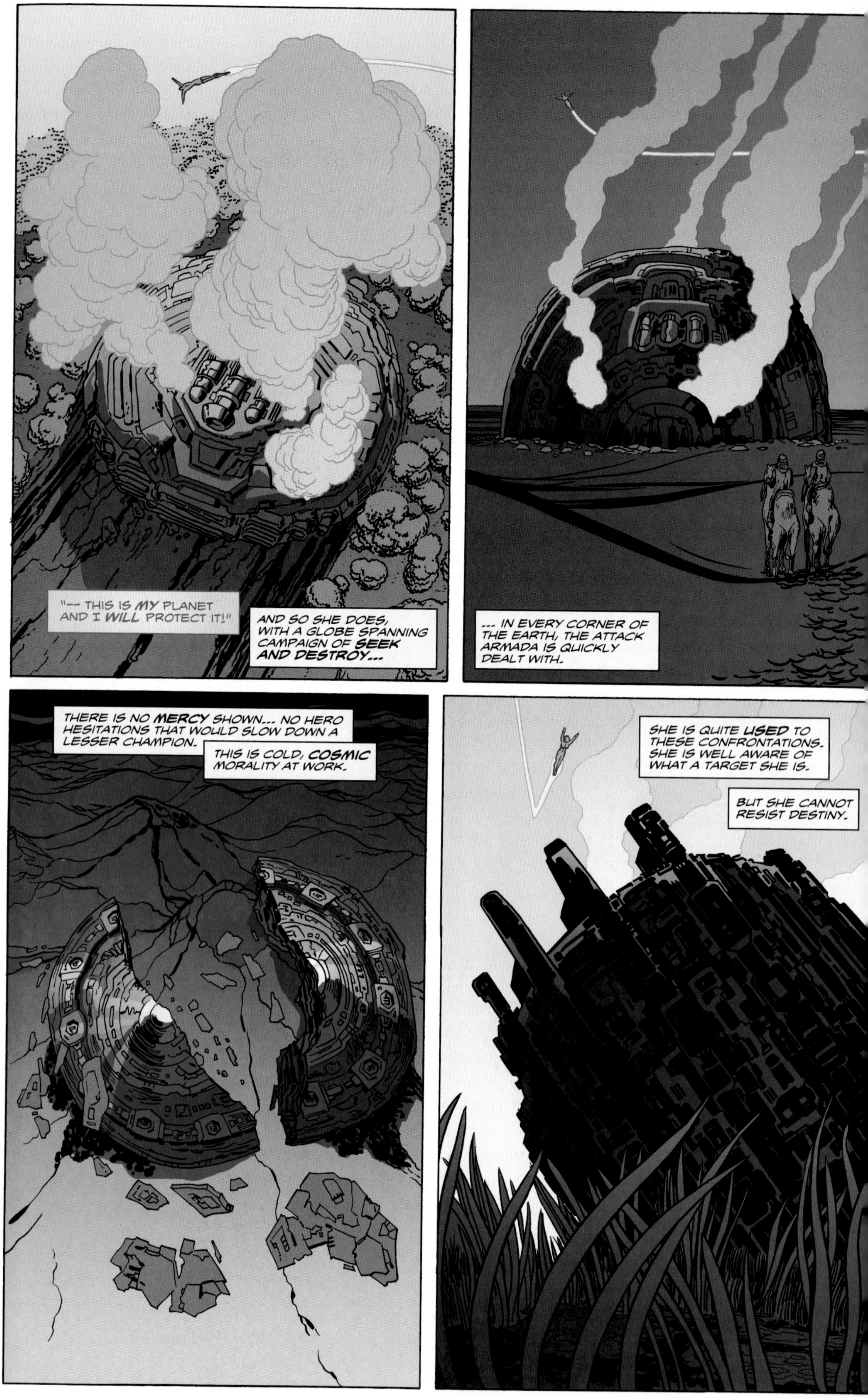
"-- THIS IS MY PLANET AND I WILL PROTECT IT!"
AND SO SHE DOES, WITH A GLOBE SPANNING CAMPAIGN OF SEEK AND DESTROY...
... IN EVERY CORNER OF THE EARTH, THE ATTACK ARMADA IS QUICKLY DEALT WITH.
THERE IS NO MERCY SHOWN... NO HERO HESITATIONS THAT WOULD SLOW DOWN A LESSER CHAMPION.
THIS IS COLD, COSMIC MORALITY AT WORK.
SHE IS QUITE USED TO THESE CONFRONTATIONS. SHE IS WELL AWARE OF WHAT A TARGET SHE IS.
BUT SHE CANNOT RESIST DESTINY.

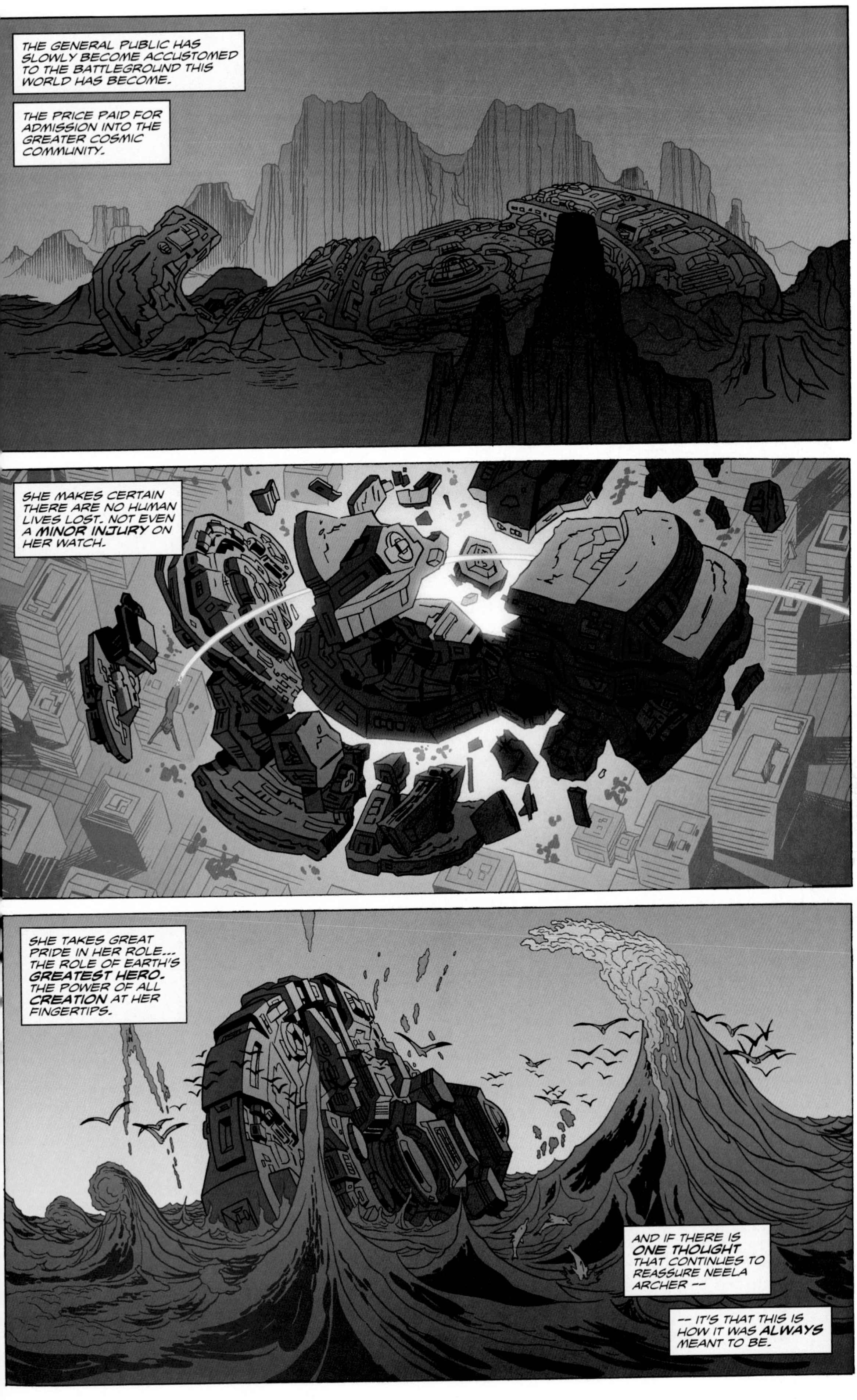
THE GENERAL PUBLIC HAS SLOWLY BECOME ACCUSTOMED TO THE BATTLEGROUND THIS WORLD HAS BECOME.
THE PRICE PAID FOR ADMISSION INTO THE GREATER COSMIC COMMUNITY.
SHE MAKES CERTAIN THERE ARE NO HUMAN LIVES LOST. NOT EVEN A **MINOR INJURY** ON HER WATCH.
SHE TAKES GREAT PRIDE IN HER ROLE... THE ROLE OF EARTH'S **GREATEST HERO.** THE POWER OF ALL **CREATION** AT HER FINGERTIPS.
AND IF THERE IS **ONE THOUGHT** THAT CONTINUES TO REASSURE NEELA ARCHER --
-- IT'S THAT THIS IS HOW IT WAS **ALWAYS** MEANT TO BE.

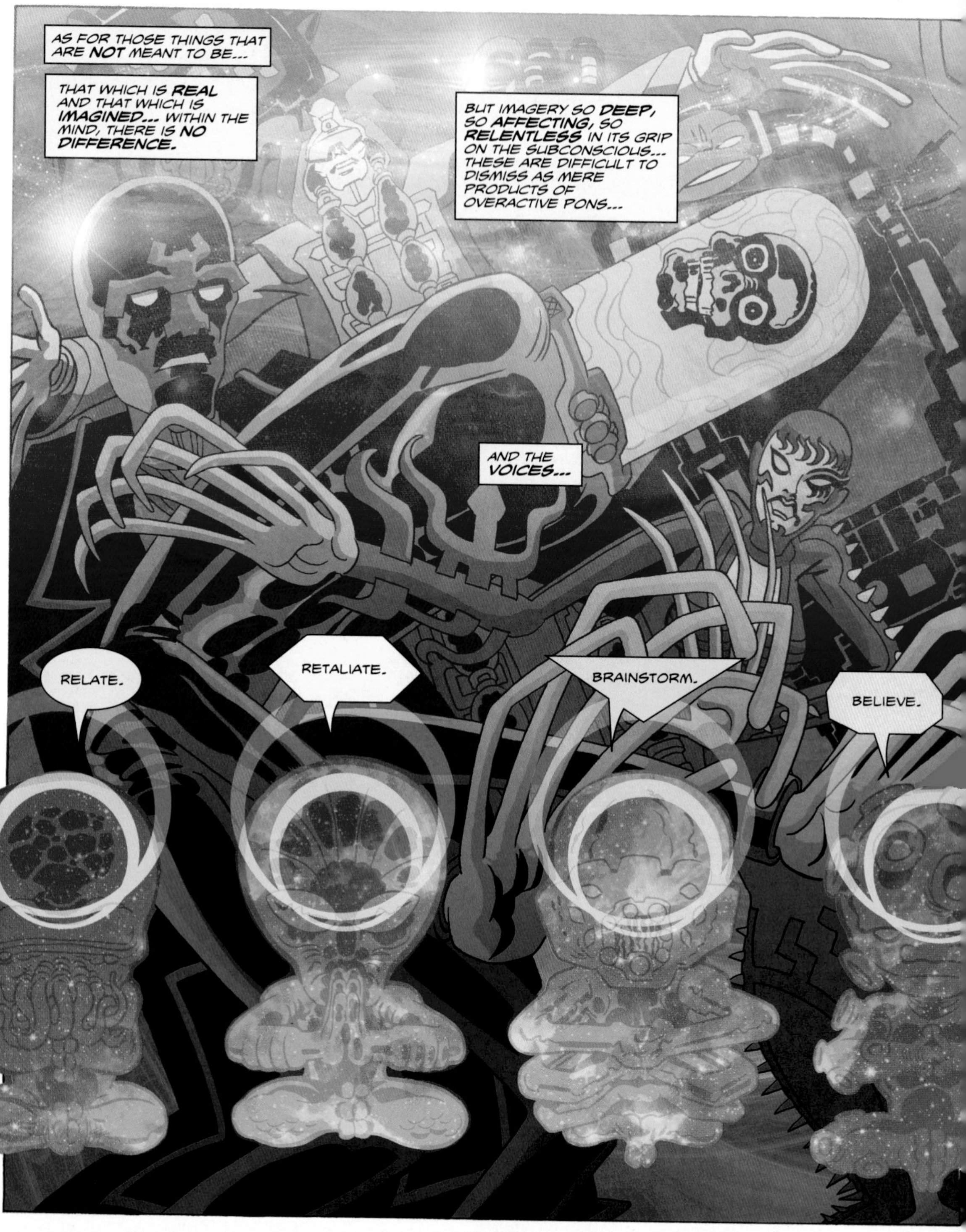
AS FOR THOSE THINGS THAT ARE NOT MEANT TO BE...
THAT WHICH IS REAL AND THAT WHICH IS IMAGINED... WITHIN THE MIND, THERE IS NO DIFFERENCE.
BUT IMAGERY SO DEEP, SO AFFECTING, SO RELENTLESS IN ITS GRIP ON THE SUBCONSCIOUS... THESE ARE DIFFICULT TO DISMISS AS MERE PRODUCTS OF OVERACTIVE PONS...
AND THE VOICES...
RELATE.
RETALIATE.
BRAINSTORM.
BELIEVE.
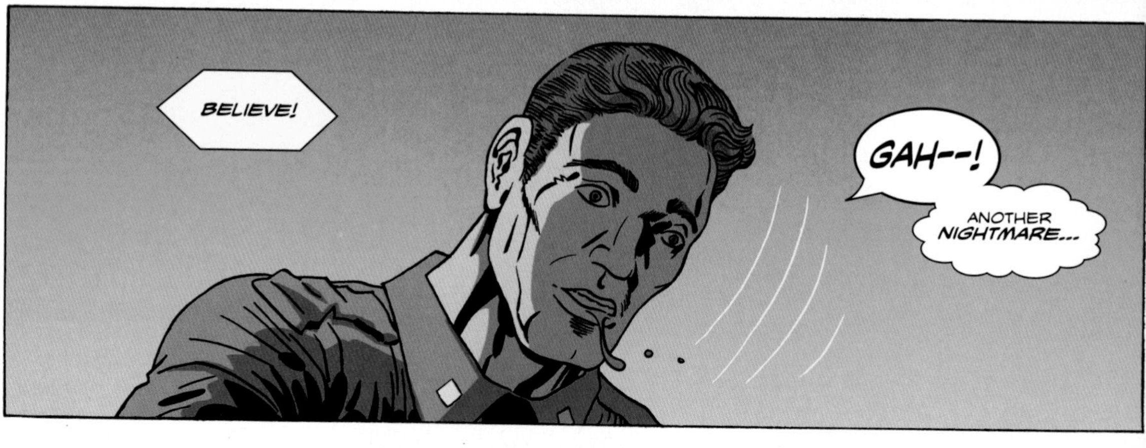
BELIEVE!
GAH--!
ANOTHER NIGHTMARE...

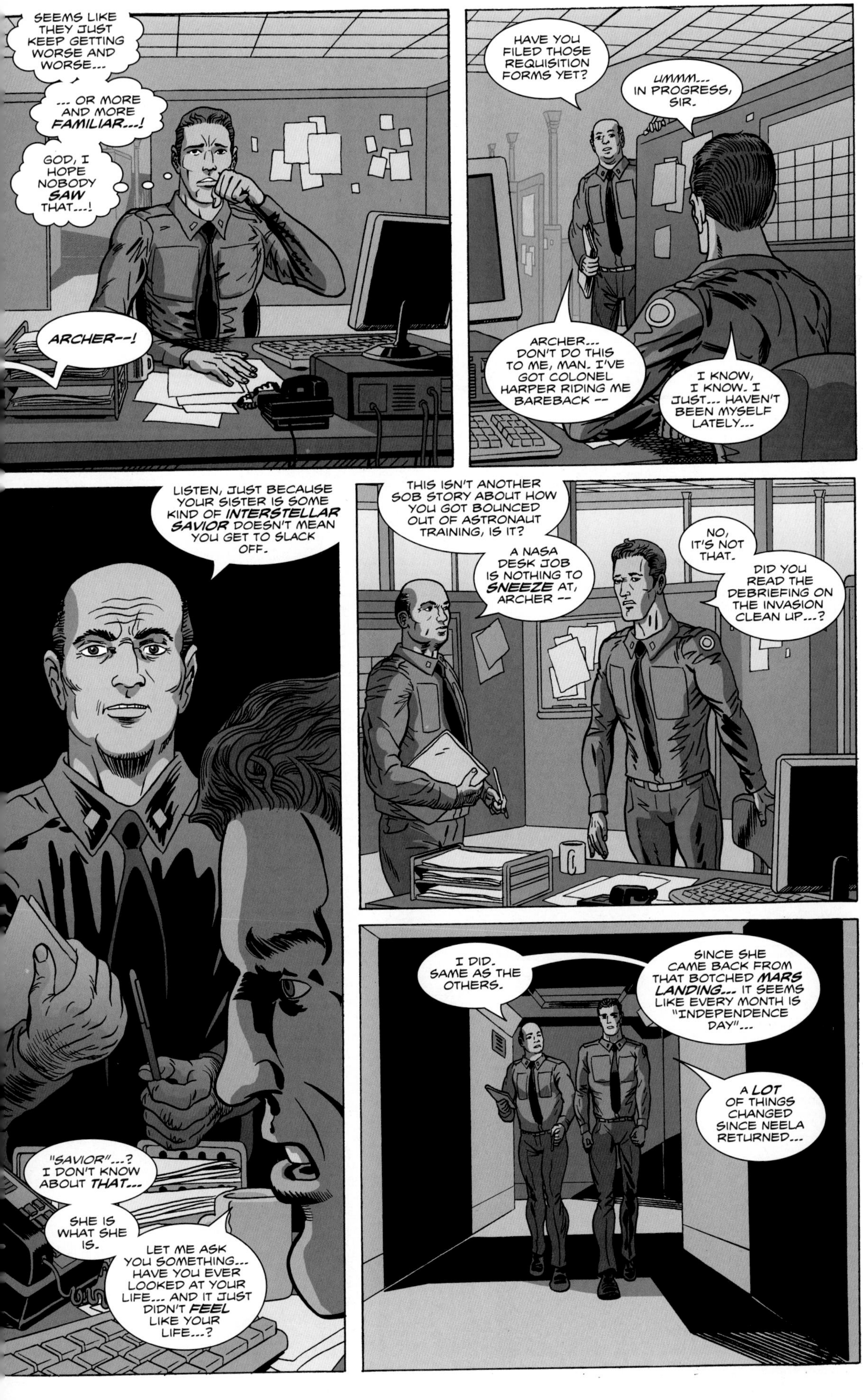
SEEMS LIKE THEY JUST KEEP GETTING WORSE AND WORSE...
... OR MORE AND MORE FAMILIAR...!
GOD, I HOPE NOBODY SAW THAT...!
ARCHER--!
HAVE YOU FILED THOSE REQUISITION FORMS YET?
UMMM... IN PROGRESS, SIR.
ARCHER... DON'T DO THIS TO ME, MAN. I'VE GOT COLONEL HARPER RIDING ME BAREBACK --
I KNOW, I KNOW. I JUST... HAVEN'T BEEN MYSELF LATELY...
LISTEN, JUST BECAUSE YOUR SISTER IS SOME KIND OF INTERSTELLAR SAVIOR DOESN'T MEAN YOU GET TO SLACK OFF.
"SAVIOR"...? I DON'T KNOW ABOUT THAT...
SHE IS WHAT SHE IS.
LET ME ASK YOU SOMETHING... HAVE YOU EVER LOOKED AT YOUR LIFE... AND IT JUST DIDN'T FEEL LIKE YOUR LIFE...?
THIS ISN'T ANOTHER SOB STORY ABOUT HOW YOU GOT BOUNCED OUT OF ASTRONAUT TRAINING, IS IT?
A NASA DESK JOB IS NOTHING TO SNEEZE AT, ARCHER --
NO, IT'S NOT THAT.
DID YOU READ THE DEBRIEFING ON THE INVASION CLEAN UP...?
I DID. SAME AS THE OTHERS.
SINCE SHE CAME BACK FROM THAT BOTCHED MARS LANDING... IT SEEMS LIKE EVERY MONTH IS "INDEPENDENCE DAY"...
A LOT OF THINGS CHANGED SINCE NEELA RETURNED...

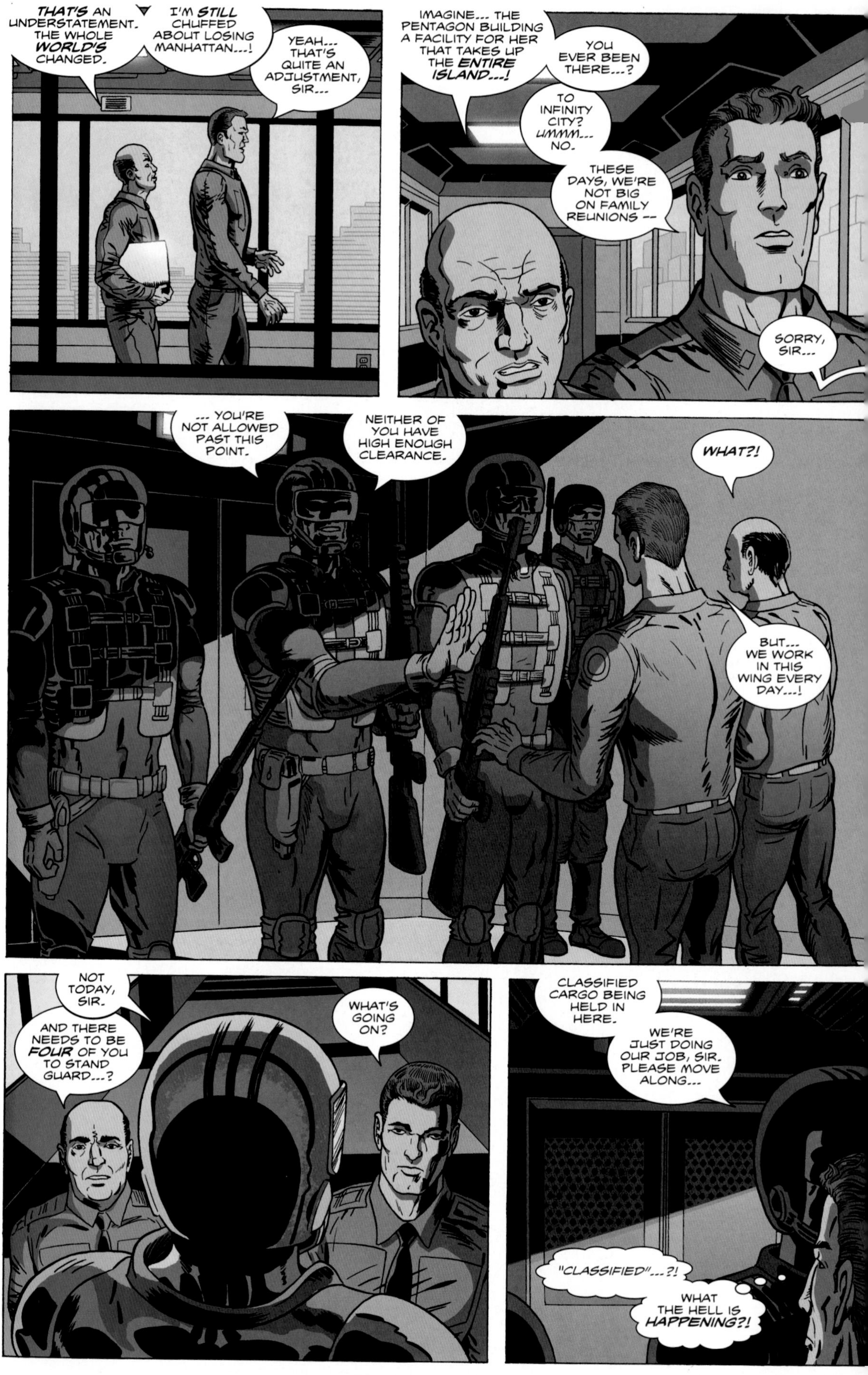
THAT'S AN UNDERSTATEMENT. THE WHOLE WORLD'S CHANGED.
I'M STILL CHUFFED ABOUT LOSING MANHATTAN...!
YEAH... THAT'S QUITE AN ADJUSTMENT, SIR...
IMAGINE... THE PENTAGON BUILDING A FACILITY FOR HER THAT TAKES UP THE ENTIRE ISLAND...!
YOU EVER BEEN THERE...?
TO INFINITY CITY? UMMM... NO.
THESE DAYS, WE'RE NOT BIG ON FAMILY REUNIONS --
SORRY, SIR...
... YOU'RE NOT ALLOWED PAST THIS POINT.
NEITHER OF YOU HAVE HIGH ENOUGH CLEARANCE.
WHAT?!
BUT... WE WORK IN THIS WING EVERY DAY...!
NOT TODAY, SIR.
AND THERE NEEDS TO BE FOUR OF YOU TO STAND GUARD...?
WHAT'S GOING ON?
CLASSIFIED CARGO BEING HELD IN HERE.
WE'RE JUST DOING OUR JOB, SIR. PLEASE MOVE ALONG...
"CLASSIFIED"...?!
WHAT THE HELL IS HAPPENING?!

WELL, THIS IS FANCY...

YOU KNOW MY WEAKNESS FOR PEOPLE WATCHING.

ANGIE, WOULD YOU JUST *LISTEN* TO ME? I'VE BEEN HAVING THESE *NIGHTMARES*...

... OKAY, MAYBE THEY'RE *NOT* NIGHTMARES. DREAMS... *VISIONS,* MAYBE.

YOU WOULDN'T BELIEVE ME IF I DESCRIBED THEM. BUT SOMETHING ABOUT THEM... IT'S NOTHING I COULD'VE IMAGINED ON MY *OWN*...

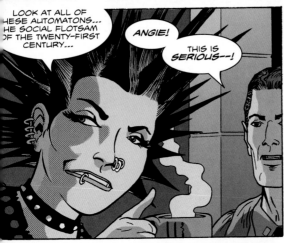

LOOK AT ALL OF THESE AUTOMATONS... THE SOCIAL FLOTSAM OF THE TWENTY-FIRST CENTURY...

ANGIE!

THIS IS *SERIOUS*--!

CHILL OUT, BRO. YOUR UNDERACHIEVEMENT INSECURITIES ARE WAY TIRED.

WE'VE *ALL* GOT WEIRD STUFF ROLLING AROUND IN OUR HEADS. IT'S JUST HOW THE BRAIN WORKS.

LAST NIGHT I DREAMT I HAD A FRENCH ACCENT AND WAS DATING ROBERT EVANS, CIRCA 1974 --

ALRIGHT, ALRIGHT...!

SHE'S NOT GOING TO *GET* IT...

IT'S MORE THAN THE *DREAMS.* IT'S THE WHOLE WORLD. EVERYTHING *AROUND* US...

... NONE OF IT *FEELS* RIGHT.

THINKING BACK ON MY ENTIRE LIFE SO FAR... THERE'S SOMETHING *WRONG* HERE.

I JUST... DON'T KNOW EXACTLY *WHAT'S* WRONG...!

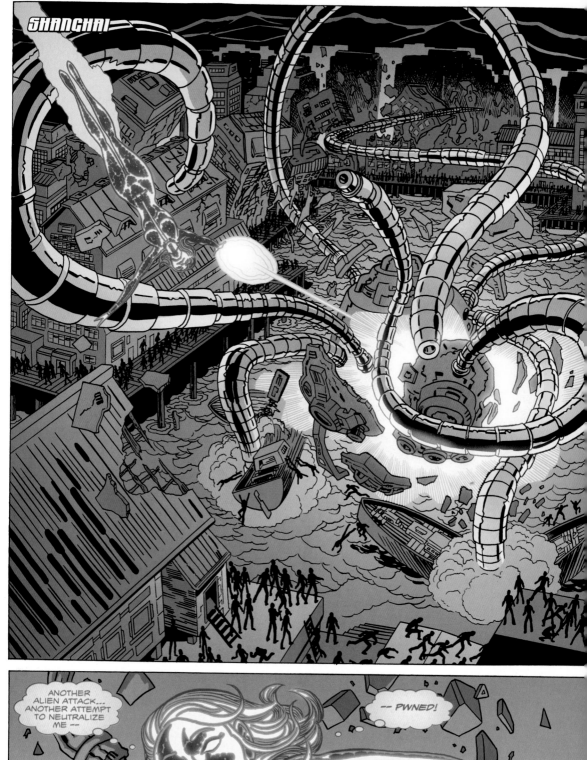

SHANGHAI

ANOTHER ALIEN ATTACK... ANOTHER ATTEMPT TO NEUTRALIZE ME --

-- PWNED!

FOR SOME, REALITY IS A **COMFORTABLE** STATE...

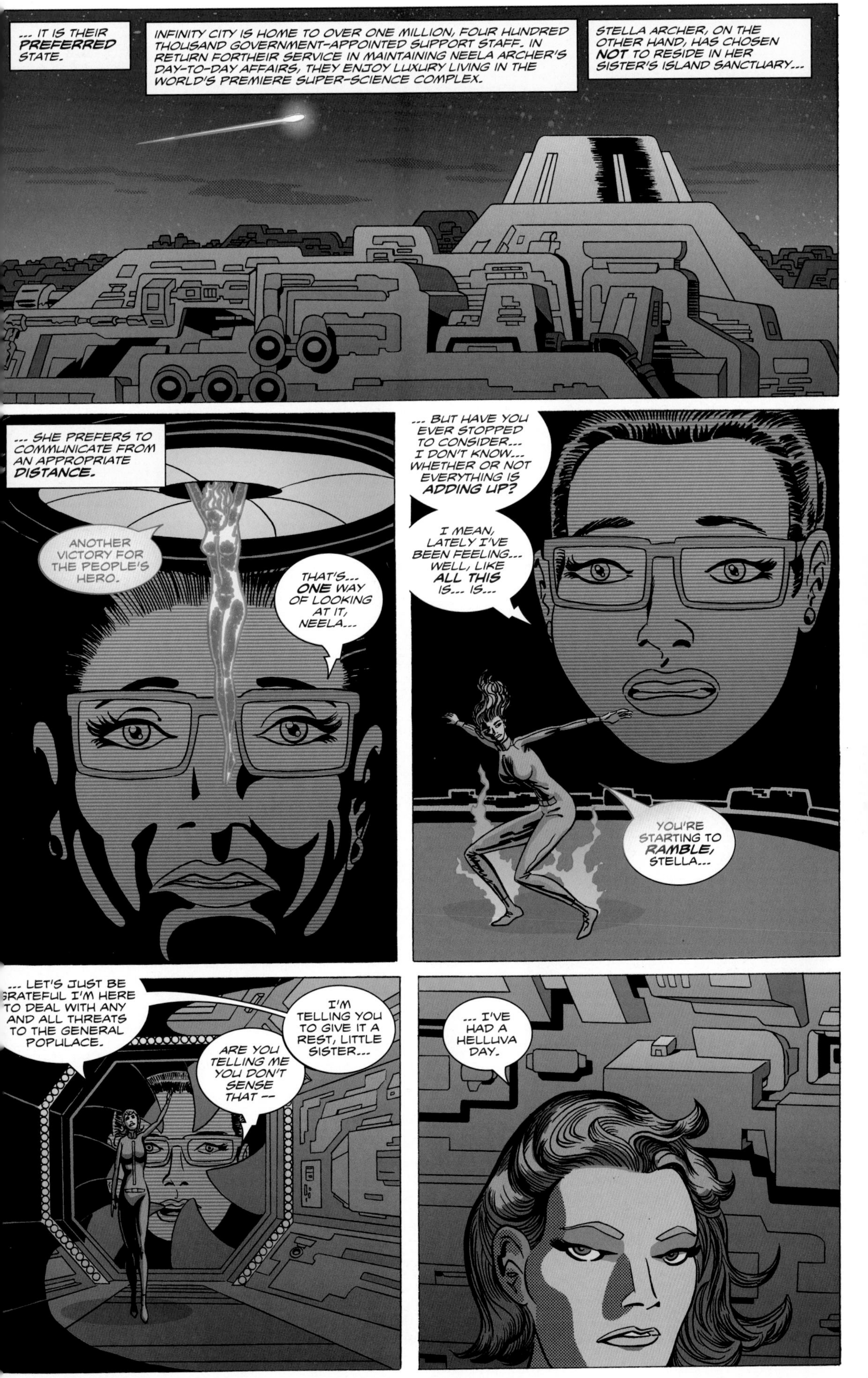

... IT IS THEIR PREFERRED STATE.
INFINITY CITY IS HOME TO OVER ONE MILLION, FOUR HUNDRED THOUSAND GOVERNMENT-APPOINTED SUPPORT STAFF. IN RETURN FORTHEIR SERVICE IN MAINTAINING NEELA ARCHER'S DAY-TO-DAY AFFAIRS, THEY ENJOY LUXURY LIVING IN THE WORLD'S PREMIERE SUPER-SCIENCE COMPLEX.
STELLA ARCHER, ON THE OTHER HAND, HAS CHOSEN NOT TO RESIDE IN HER SISTER'S ISLAND SANCTUARY...
... SHE PREFERS TO COMMUNICATE FROM AN APPROPRIATE DISTANCE.
ANOTHER VICTORY FOR THE PEOPLE'S HERO.
THAT'S... ONE WAY OF LOOKING AT IT, NEELA...
... BUT HAVE YOU EVER STOPPED TO CONSIDER... I DON'T KNOW... WHETHER OR NOT EVERYTHING IS ADDING UP?
I MEAN, LATELY I'VE BEEN FEELING... WELL, LIKE ALL THIS IS... IS...
YOU'RE STARTING TO RAMBLE, STELLA...
... LET'S JUST BE GRATEFUL I'M HERE TO DEAL WITH ANY AND ALL THREATS TO THE GENERAL POPULACE.
ARE YOU TELLING ME YOU DON'T SENSE THAT --
I'M TELLING YOU TO GIVE IT A REST, LITTLE SISTER...
... I'VE HAD A HELLUVA DAY.

... I'VE HAD A HELLUVA DAY.

NEELA -- -- NEELA!

DAMMIT... SHE ACTUALLY CUT ME OFF...!

VISITOR ARRIVAL. NASA PERSONNEL. CLEARANCE LEVEL CONFIRMED.

VERY WELL... ... BREAK STERILE SEALS. OPEN HATCH.

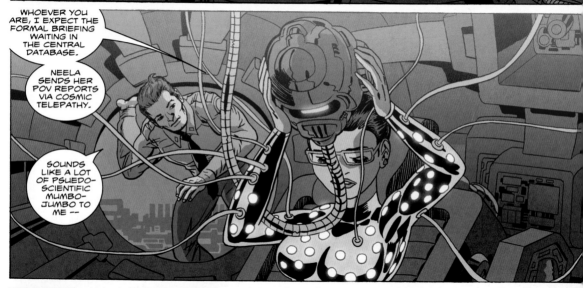

WHOEVER YOU ARE, I EXPECT THE FORMAL BRIEFING WAITING IN THE CENTRAL DATABASE.

NEELA SENDS HER POV REPORTS VIA COSMIC TELEPATHY.

SOUNDS LIKE A LOT OF PSUEDO-SCIENTIFIC MUMBO-JUMBO TO ME --

ADAM!

FOR GOD'S SAKE, YOU SCARED ME...!

DIDN'T MEAN TO.

YOU'RE NOT USUALLY SO ON EDGE, STELLA.

FREAK!

I OUT-RANK YOU, Y'KNOW!

I KNOW. IT'S WHY I'M HERE.

WHY? YOU WANT A TOUR OF INFINITY CITY...?

SORT OF.

COME WITH ME BACK TO NASA HEADQUARTERS. YOU'VE GOT CLEARANCE THAT I DON'T.

YOU'RE SERIOUS?

MORE THAN I'VE EVER BEEN.

PLEASE...

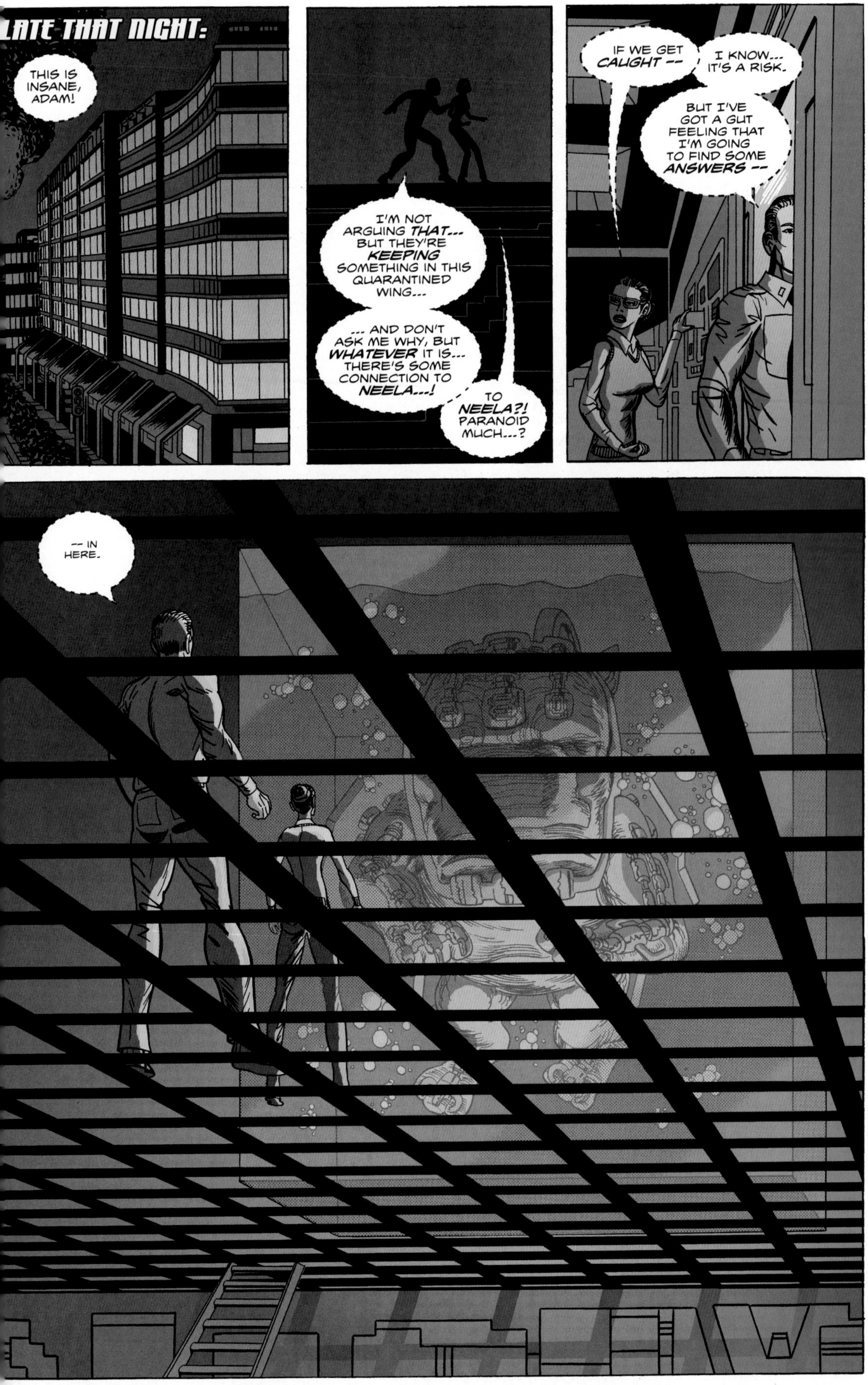
LATE THAT NIGHT:
THIS IS INSANE, ADAM!
I'M NOT ARGUING THAT... BUT THEY'RE KEEPING SOMETHING IN THIS QUARANTINED WING...
... AND DON'T ASK ME WHY, BUT WHATEVER IT IS... THERE'S SOME CONNECTION TO NEELA...!
TO NEELA?! PARANOID MUCH...?
IF WE GET CAUGHT --
I KNOW... IT'S A RISK.
BUT I'VE GOT A GUT FEELING THAT I'M GOING TO FIND SOME ANSWERS --
-- IN HERE.

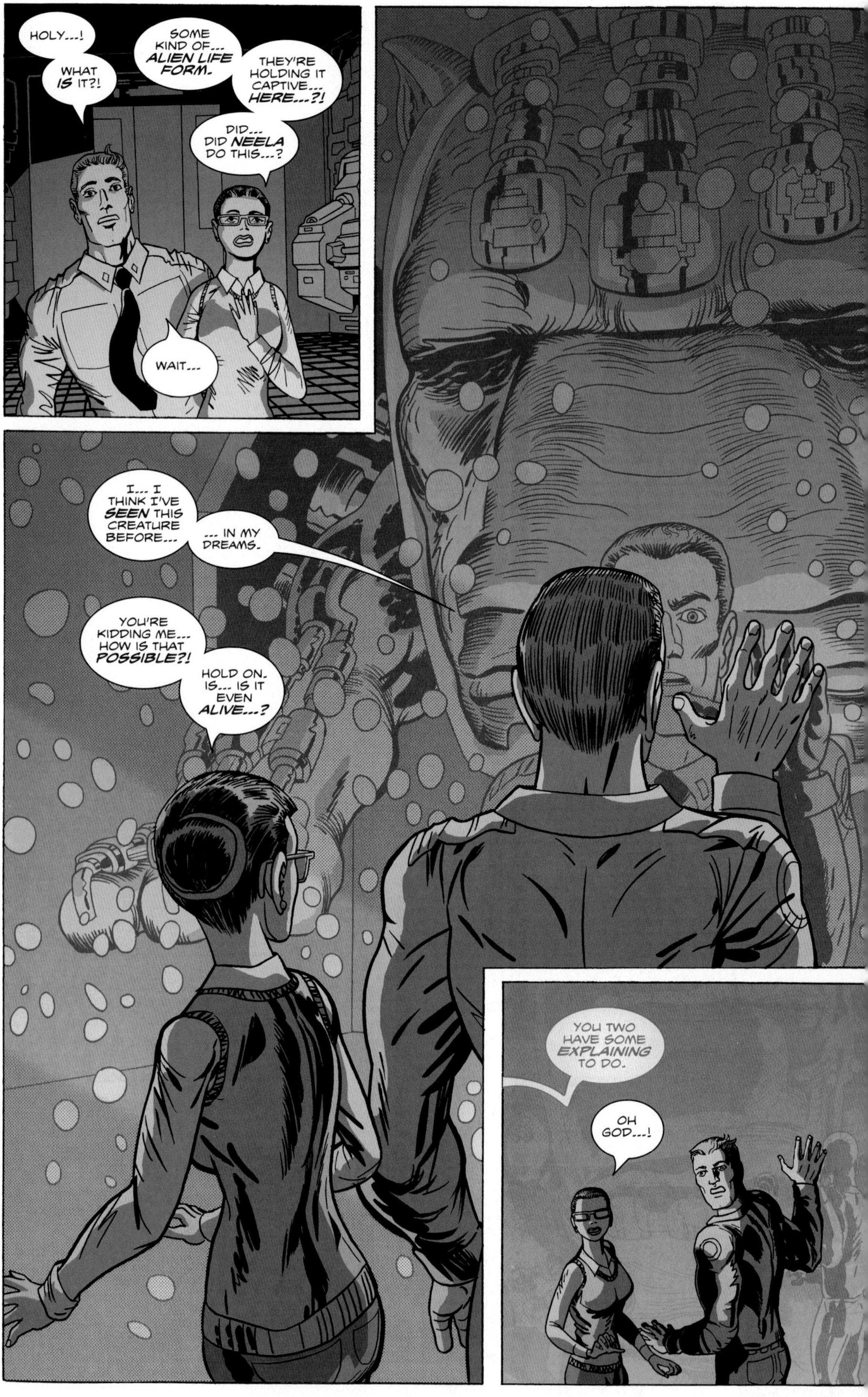
HOLY...!
WHAT IS IT?!
SOME KIND OF... ALIEN LIFE FORM.
THEY'RE HOLDING IT CAPTIVE... HERE...?!
DID... DID NEELA DO THIS...?
WAIT...
I... I THINK I'VE SEEN THIS CREATURE BEFORE...
... IN MY DREAMS.
YOU'RE KIDDING ME... HOW IS THAT POSSIBLE?!
HOLD ON. IS... IS IT EVEN ALIVE...?
YOU TWO HAVE SOME EXPLAINING TO DO.
OH GOD...!

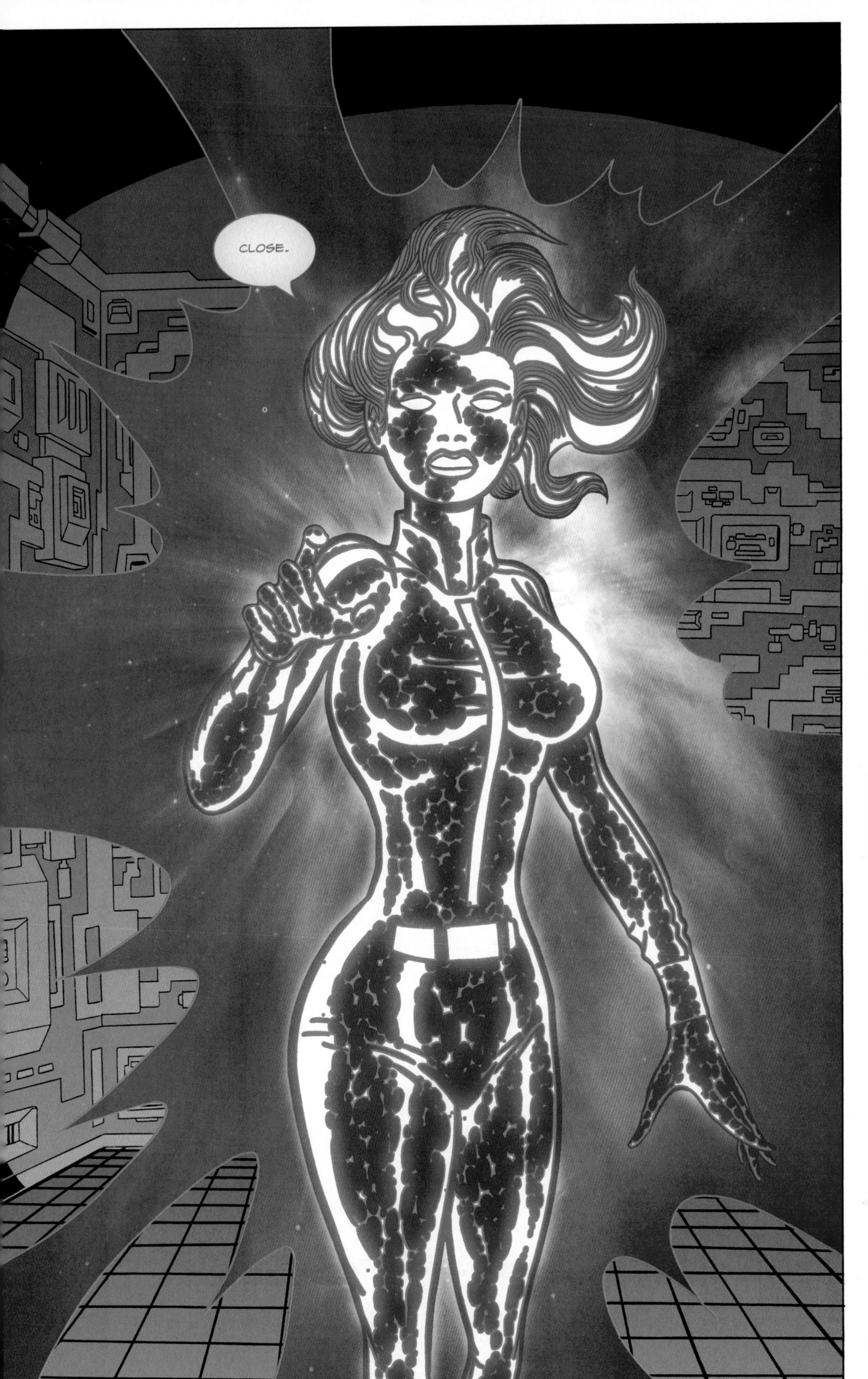
CLOSE.

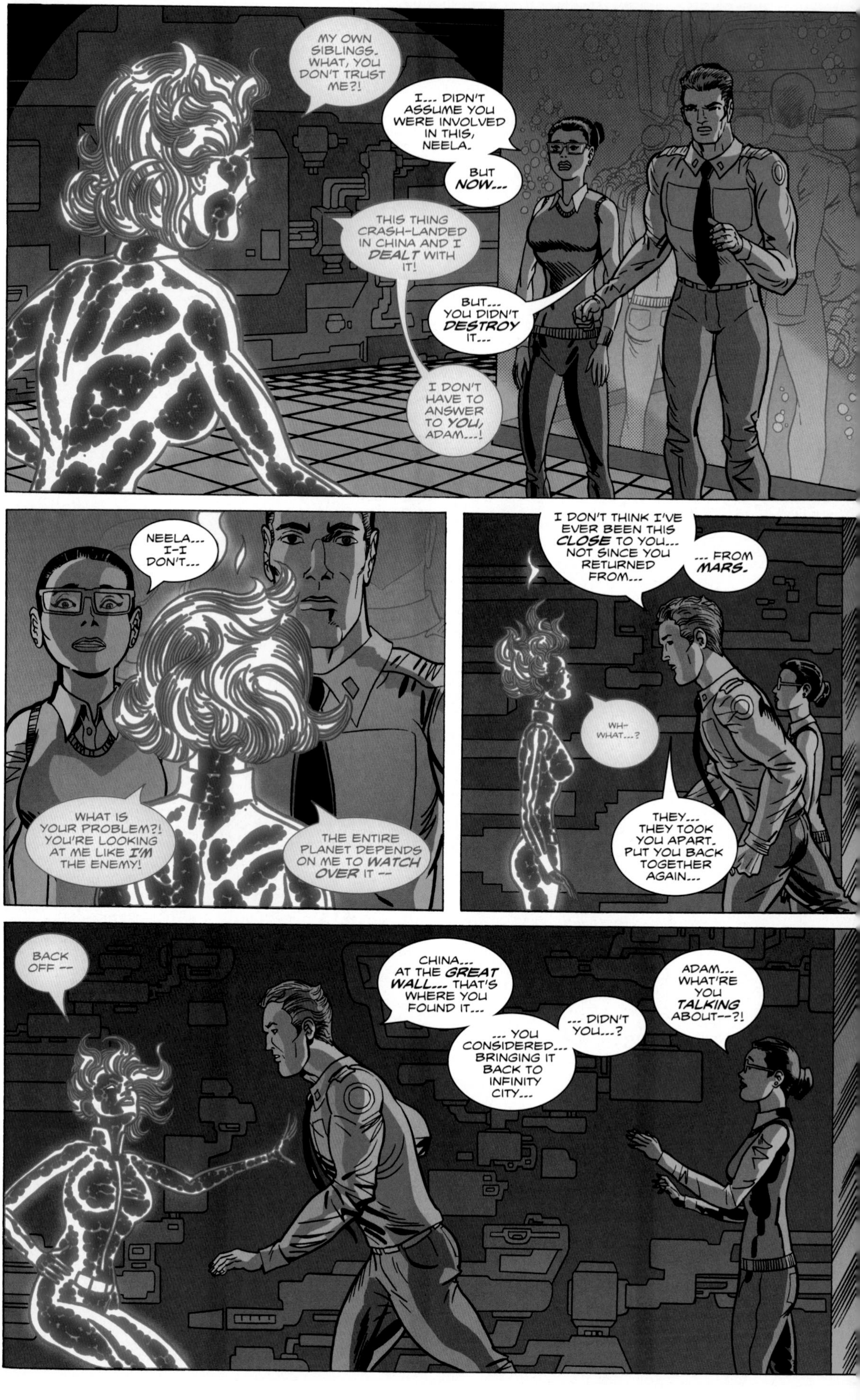
MY OWN SIBLINGS. WHAT, YOU DON'T TRUST ME?!
I... DIDN'T ASSUME YOU WERE INVOLVED IN THIS, NEELA.
BUT NOW...
THIS THING CRASH-LANDED IN CHINA AND I DEALT WITH IT!
BUT... YOU DIDN'T DESTROY IT...
I DON'T HAVE TO ANSWER TO YOU, ADAM...!
NEELA... I-I DON'T...
WHAT IS YOUR PROBLEM?! YOU'RE LOOKING AT ME LIKE I'M THE ENEMY!
THE ENTIRE PLANET DEPENDS ON ME TO WATCH OVER IT --
I DON'T THINK I'VE EVER BEEN THIS CLOSE TO YOU... NOT SINCE YOU RETURNED FROM...
... FROM MARS.
WH-WHAT...?
THEY... THEY TOOK YOU APART. PUT YOU BACK TOGETHER AGAIN...
BACK OFF --
CHINA... AT THE GREAT WALL... THAT'S WHERE YOU FOUND IT...
... YOU CONSIDERED... BRINGING IT BACK TO INFINITY CITY...
... DIDN'T YOU...?
ADAM... WHAT'RE YOU TALKING ABOUT--?!

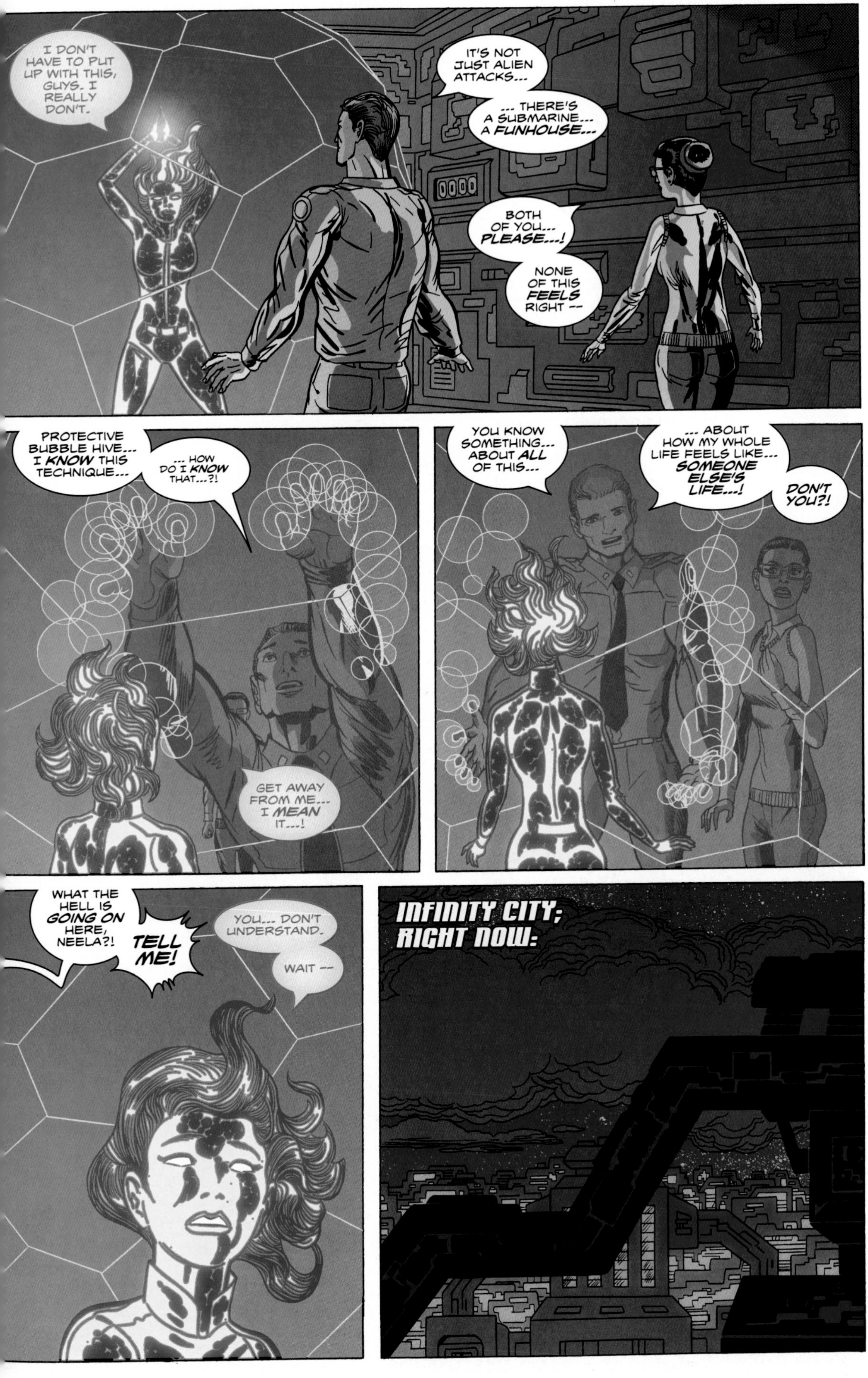
I DON'T HAVE TO PUT UP WITH THIS, GUYS. I REALLY DON'T.
IT'S NOT JUST ALIEN ATTACKS...
... THERE'S A SUBMARINE... A FUNHOUSE...
BOTH OF YOU... PLEASE...!
NONE OF THIS FEELS RIGHT --
PROTECTIVE BUBBLE HIVE... I KNOW THIS TECHNIQUE...
... HOW DO I KNOW THAT...?!
GET AWAY FROM ME... I MEAN IT...!
YOU KNOW SOMETHING... ABOUT ALL OF THIS...
... ABOUT HOW MY WHOLE LIFE FEELS LIKE... SOMEONE ELSE'S LIFE...!
DON'T YOU?!
WHAT THE HELL IS GOING ON HERE, NEELA?!
TELL ME!
YOU... DON'T UNDERSTAND.
WAIT --
INFINITY CITY; RIGHT NOW:

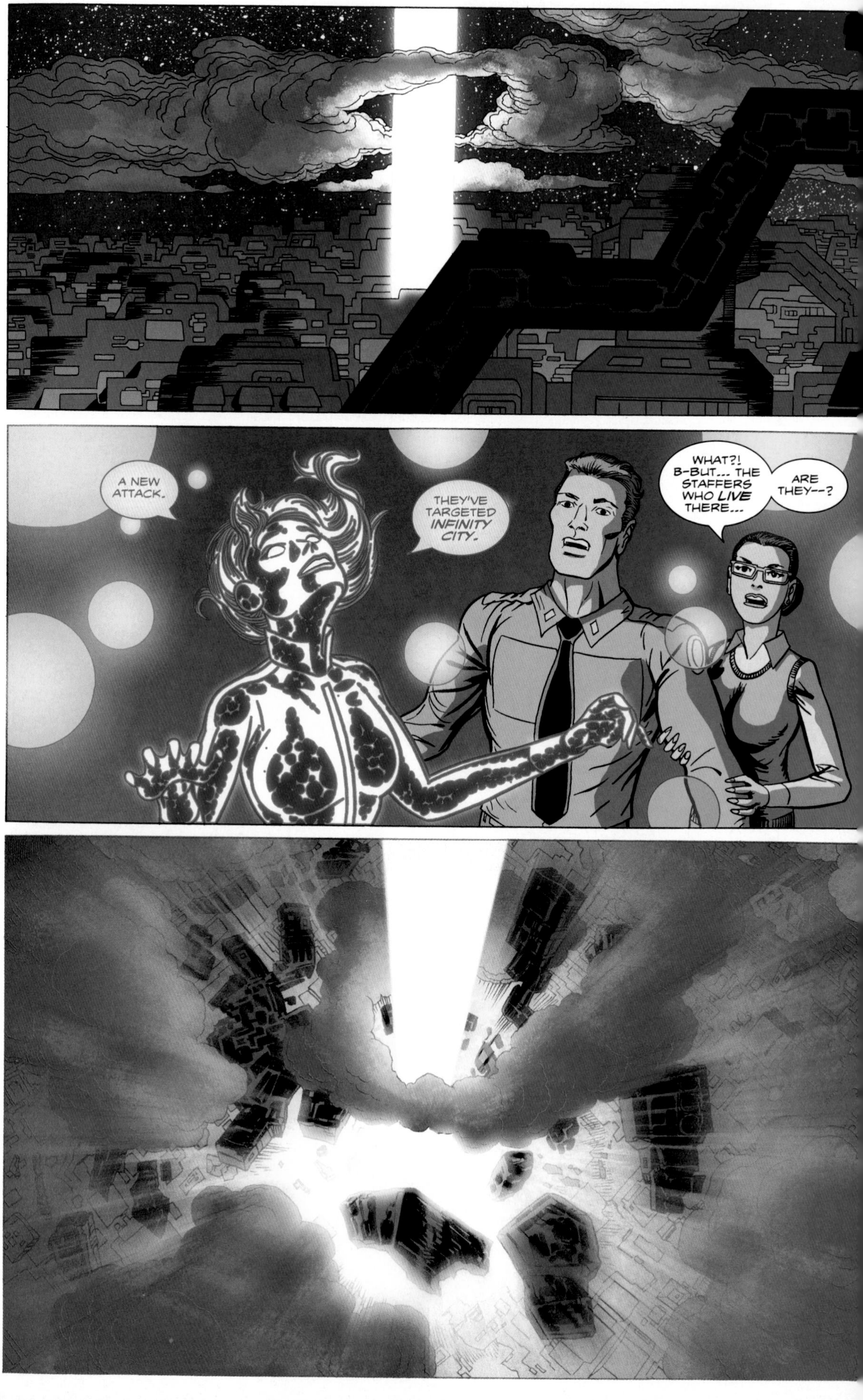
A NEW ATTACK.
THEY'VE TARGETED INFINITY CITY.
WHAT?! B-BUT... THE STAFFERS WHO LIVE THERE...
ARE THEY--?

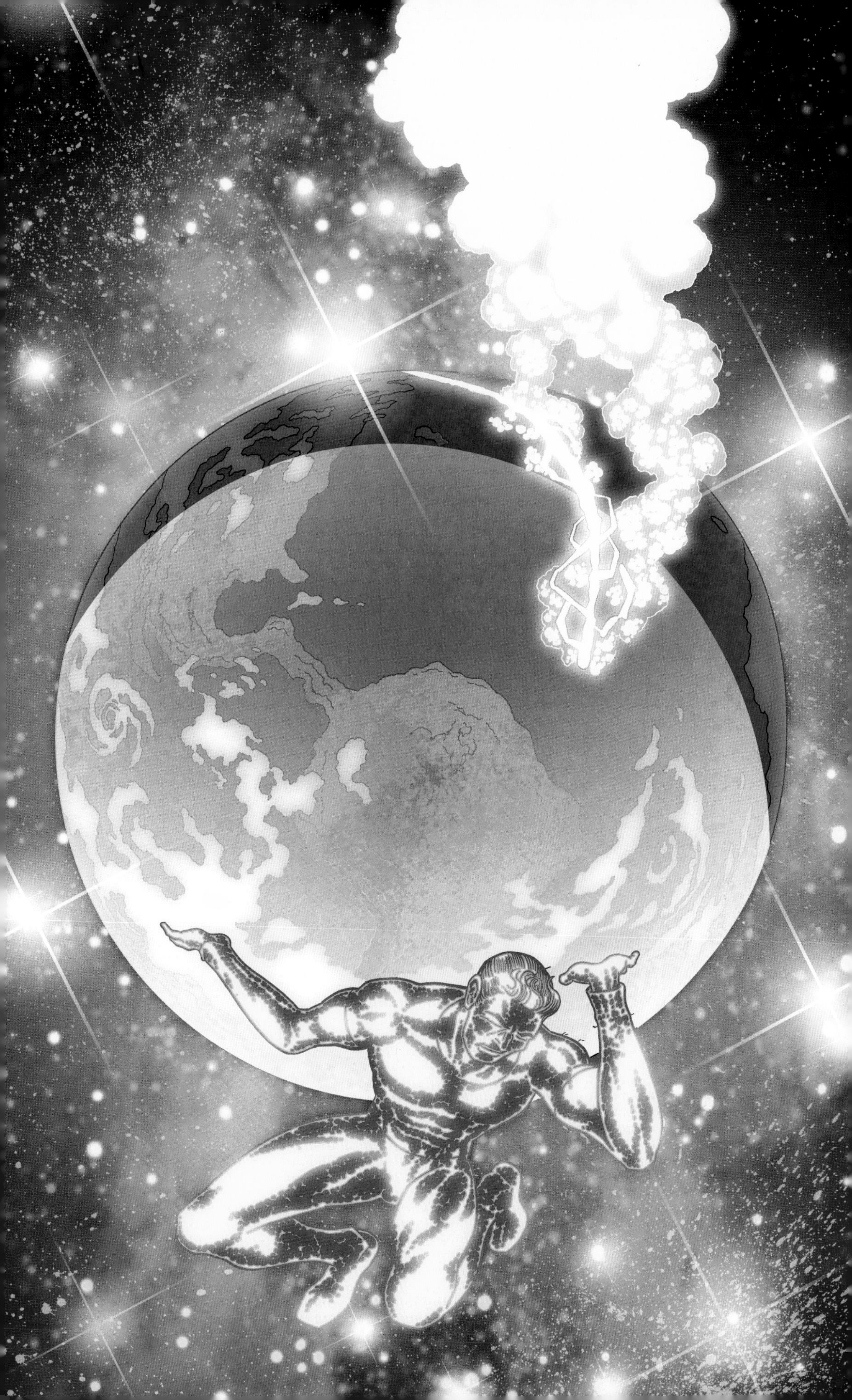

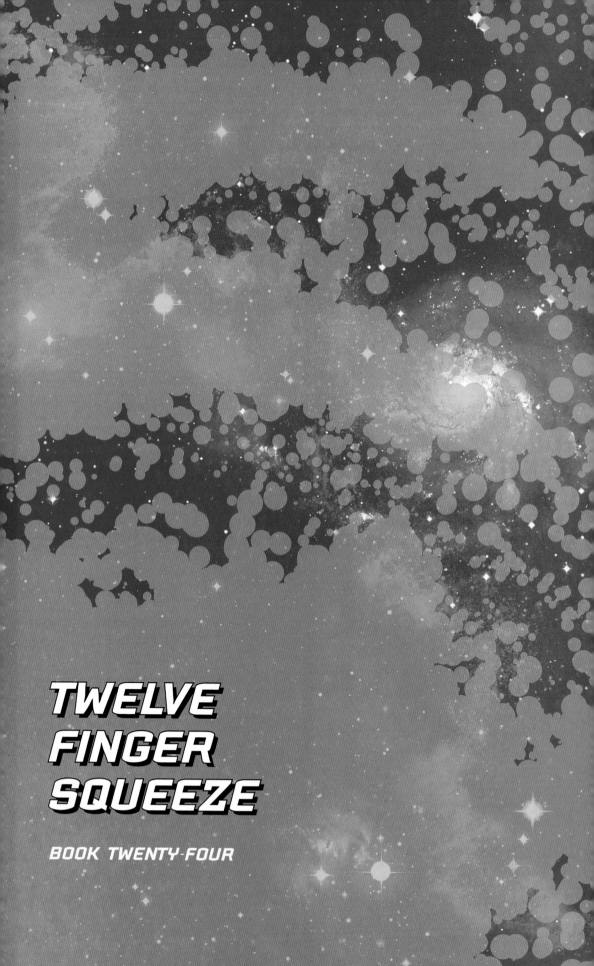

TWELVE FINGER SQUEEZE

BOOK TWENTY-FOUR

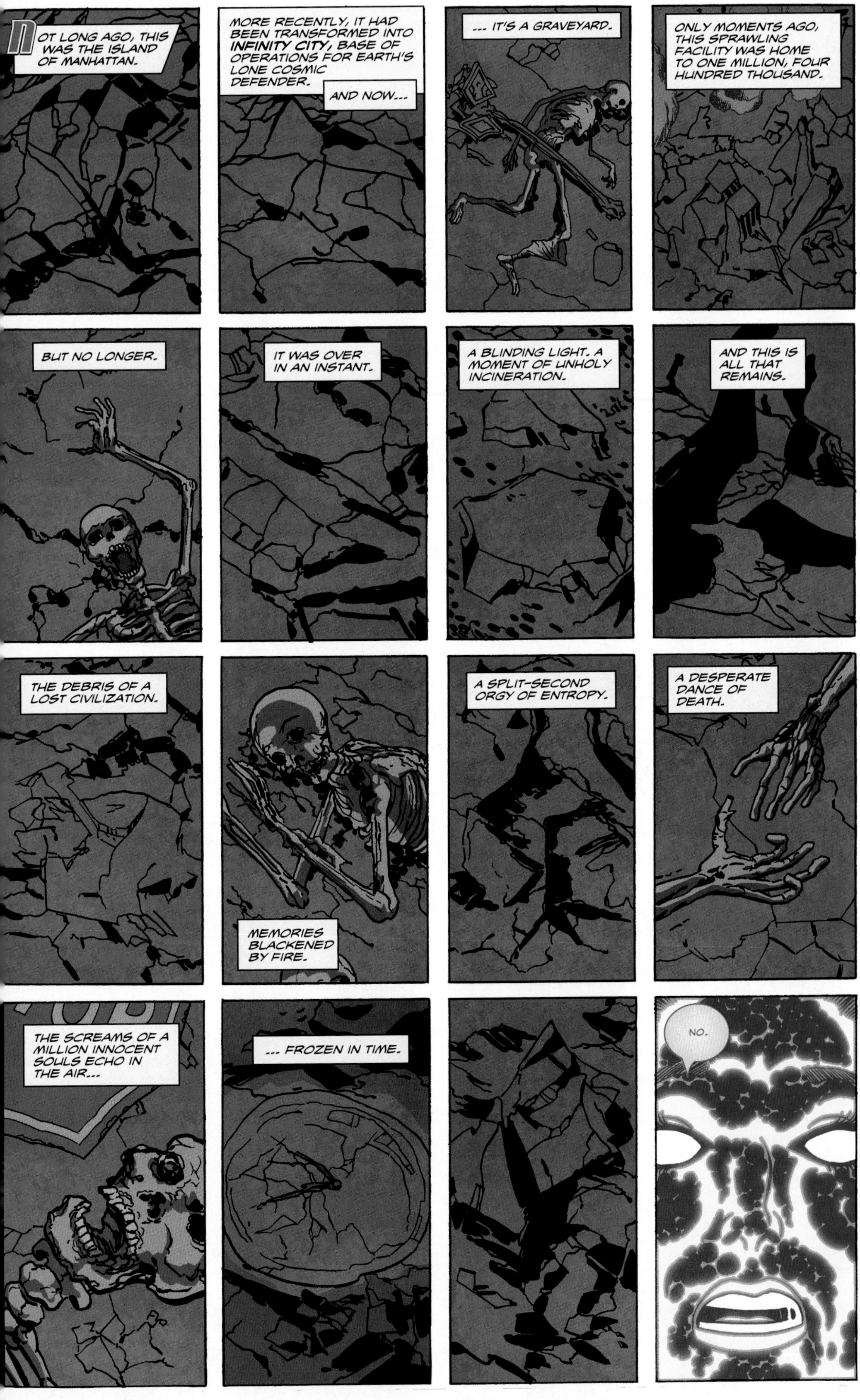
NOT LONG AGO, THIS WAS THE ISLAND OF MANHATTAN.
MORE RECENTLY, IT HAD BEEN TRANSFORMED INTO INFINITY CITY, BASE OF OPERATIONS FOR EARTH'S LONE COSMIC DEFENDER.
AND NOW...
... IT'S A GRAVEYARD.
ONLY MOMENTS AGO, THIS SPRAWLING FACILITY WAS HOME TO ONE MILLION, FOUR HUNDRED THOUSAND.
BUT NO LONGER.
IT WAS OVER IN AN INSTANT.
A BLINDING LIGHT. A MOMENT OF UNHOLY INCINERATION.
AND THIS IS ALL THAT REMAINS.
THE DEBRIS OF A LOST CIVILIZATION.
MEMORIES BLACKENED BY FIRE.
A SPLIT-SECOND ORGY OF ENTROPY.
A DESPERATE DANCE OF DEATH.
THE SCREAMS OF A MILLION INNOCENT SOULS ECHO IN THE AIR...
... FROZEN IN TIME.
NO.

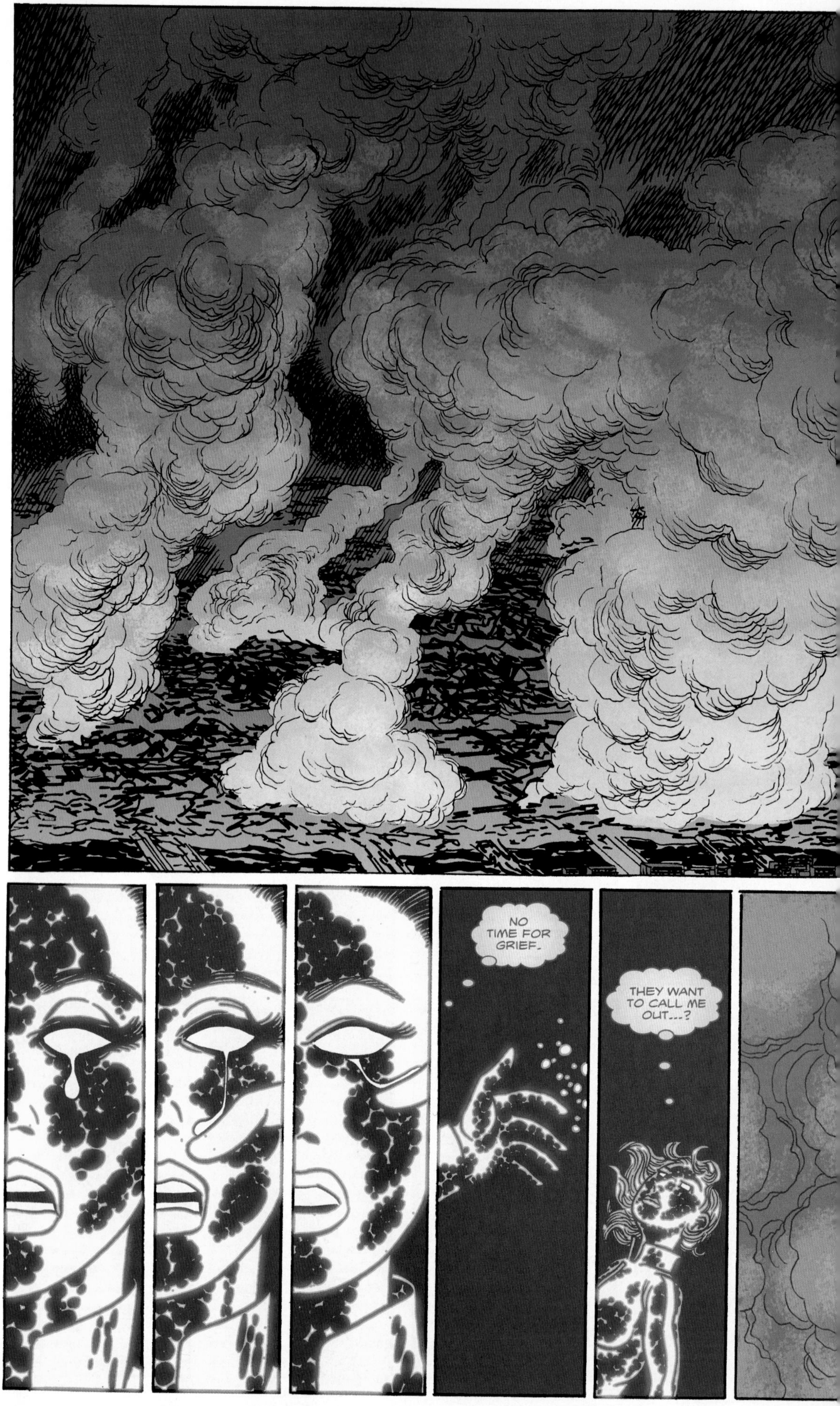

NO TIME FOR GRIEF.
THEY WANT TO CALL ME OUT...?

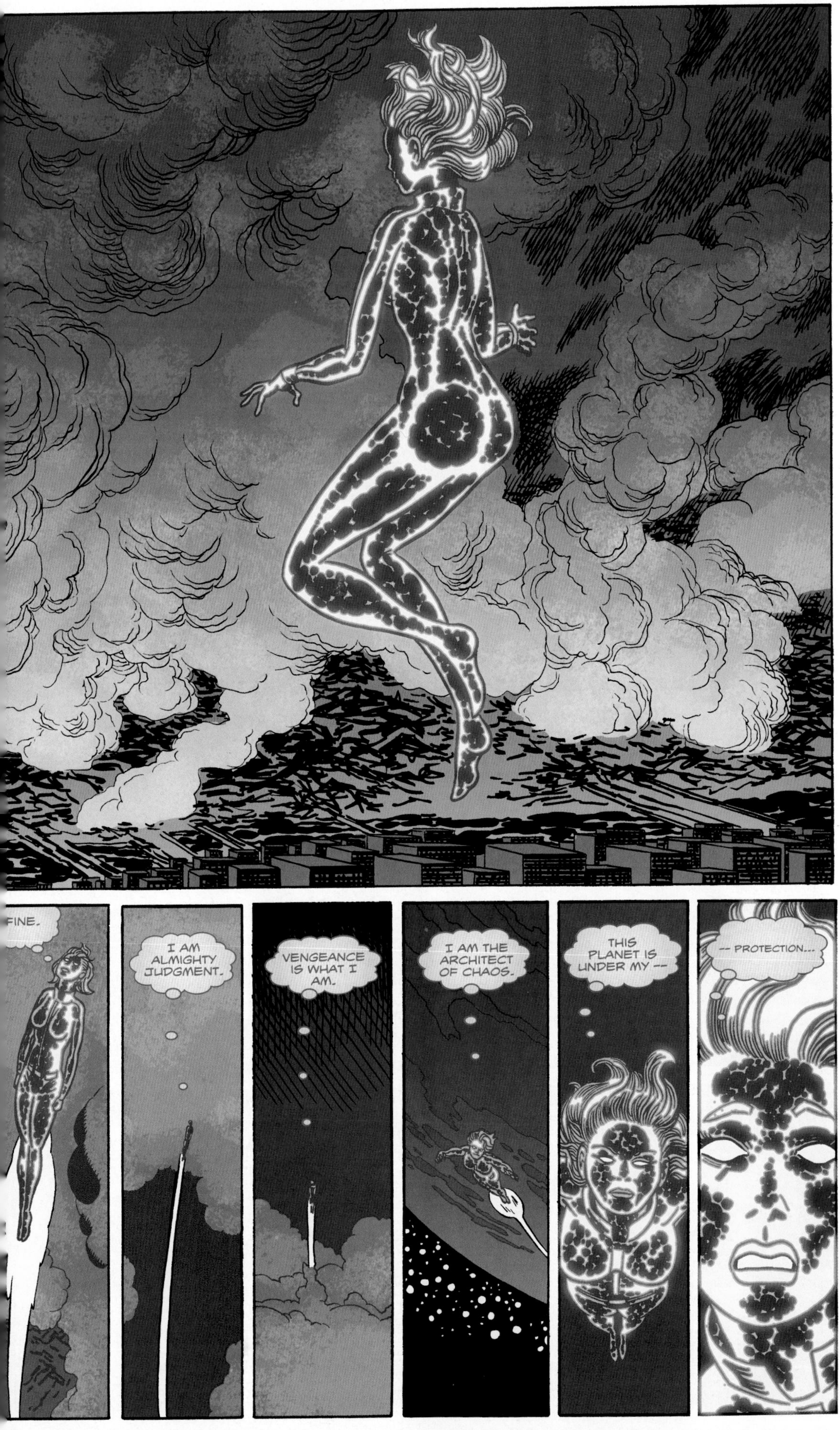
FINE.
I AM ALMIGHTY JUDGMENT.
VENGEANCE IS WHAT I AM.
I AM THE ARCHITECT OF CHAOS.
THIS PLANET IS UNDER MY --
-- PROTECTION...

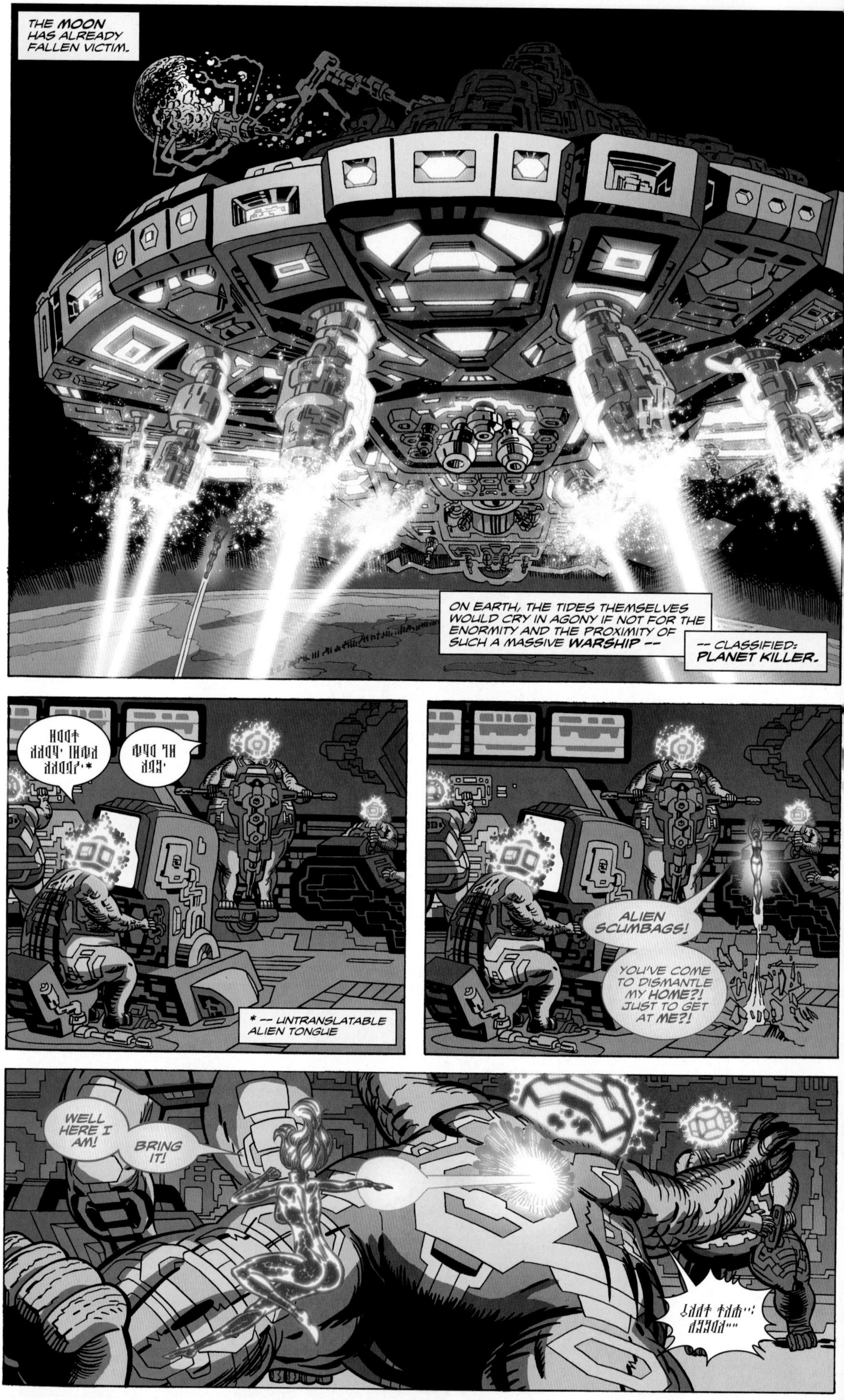
THE MOON HAS ALREADY FALLEN VICTIM.
ON EARTH, THE TIDES THEMSELVES WOULD CRY IN AGONY IF NOT FOR THE ENORMITY AND THE PROXIMITY OF SUCH A MASSIVE WARSHIP --
-- CLASSIFIED: PLANET KILLER.
* -- UNTRANSLATABLE ALIEN TONGUE
ALIEN SCUMBAGS!
YOU'VE COME TO DISMANTLE MY HOME?! JUST TO GET AT ME?!
WELL HERE I AM!
BRING IT!

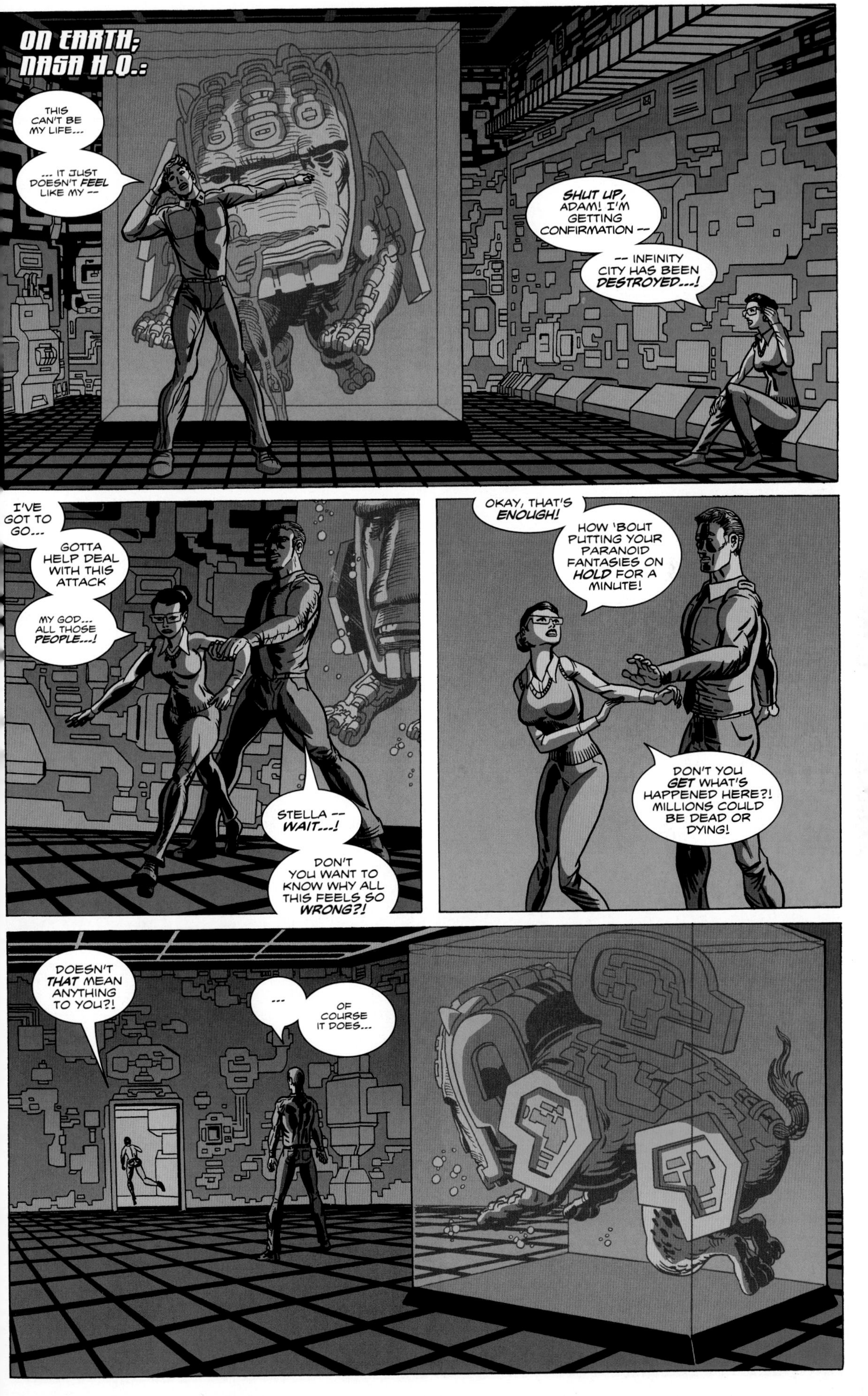

ON EARTH; NASA H.Q.:
THIS CAN'T BE MY LIFE...
... IT JUST DOESN'T FEEL LIKE MY --
SHUT UP, ADAM! I'M GETTING CONFIRMATION --
-- INFINITY CITY HAS BEEN DESTROYED...!
I'VE GOT TO GO...
GOTTA HELP DEAL WITH THIS ATTACK
MY GOD... ALL THOSE PEOPLE...!
STELLA -- WAIT...!
DON'T YOU WANT TO KNOW WHY ALL THIS FEELS SO WRONG?!
OKAY, THAT'S ENOUGH!
HOW 'BOUT PUTTING YOUR PARANOID FANTASIES ON HOLD FOR A MINUTE!
DON'T YOU GET WHAT'S HAPPENED HERE?! MILLIONS COULD BE DEAD OR DYING!
DOESN'T THAT MEAN ANYTHING TO YOU?!
...
OF COURSE IT DOES...

AM I GOING *INSANE*--?!

ALL FLESH AND DEPRESSION...

WHA--?!

ARE YOU SO QUICK TO FORGET THE GALACTIC TRUMP?

SO MUCH TIME AND EFFORT... FOR A MIND SO *WEAK*!

THE FATE OF STARS WEEPS TRUE TEARS TODAY!

OMIGOD--!

WAIT...

STAY AWAY FROM ME--!

... DO I *KNOW* YOU...?

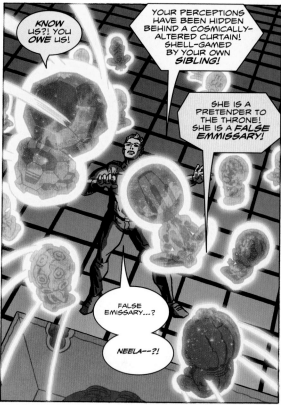

KNOW US?! YOU *OWE* US!

YOUR PERCEPTIONS HAVE BEEN HIDDEN BEHIND A COSMICALLY-ALTERED CURTAIN! SHELL-GAMED BY YOUR OWN *SIBLING*!

SHE IS A PRETENDER TO THE THRONE! SHE IS A *FALSE EMMISSARY*!

FALSE EMISSARY...?

NEELA--?!

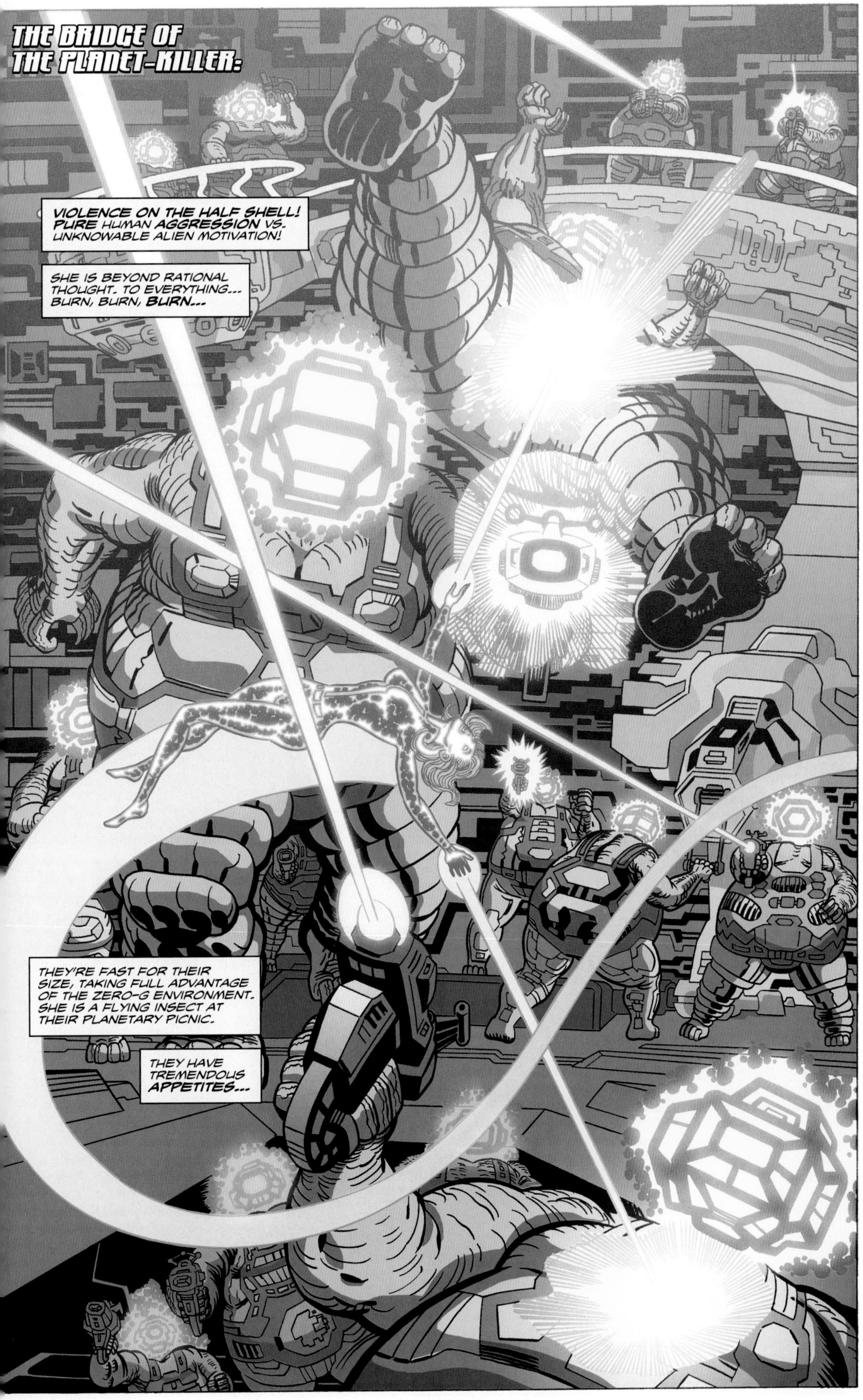
THE BRIDGE OF THE PLANET-KILLER:
VIOLENCE ON THE HALF SHELL! PURE HUMAN AGGRESSION VS. UNKNOWABLE ALIEN MOTIVATION!
SHE IS BEYOND RATIONAL THOUGHT. TO EVERYTHING... BURN, BURN, BURN...
THEY'RE FAST FOR THEIR SIZE, TAKING FULL ADVANTAGE OF THE ZERO-G ENVIRONMENT. SHE IS A FLYING INSECT AT THEIR PLANETARY PICNIC.
THEY HAVE TREMENDOUS APPETITES...

... AND THEIR APOCALYPSE CONTINUES UNABATED!

MASSIVE BANKS OF TURBO TERROR CANNONS SWIVEL AND FIND THEIR NEXT TARGET --

-- AUSTRALIA!

TWENTY-ONE MILLION AUSSIES *SCREAM* AS INHUMAN FIRE RAINS DOWN UPON THEM. AND IN A MATTER OF MERE *MINUTES* --

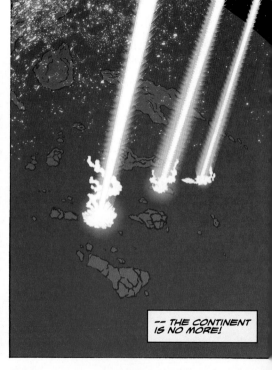

-- THE CONTINENT IS NO MORE!

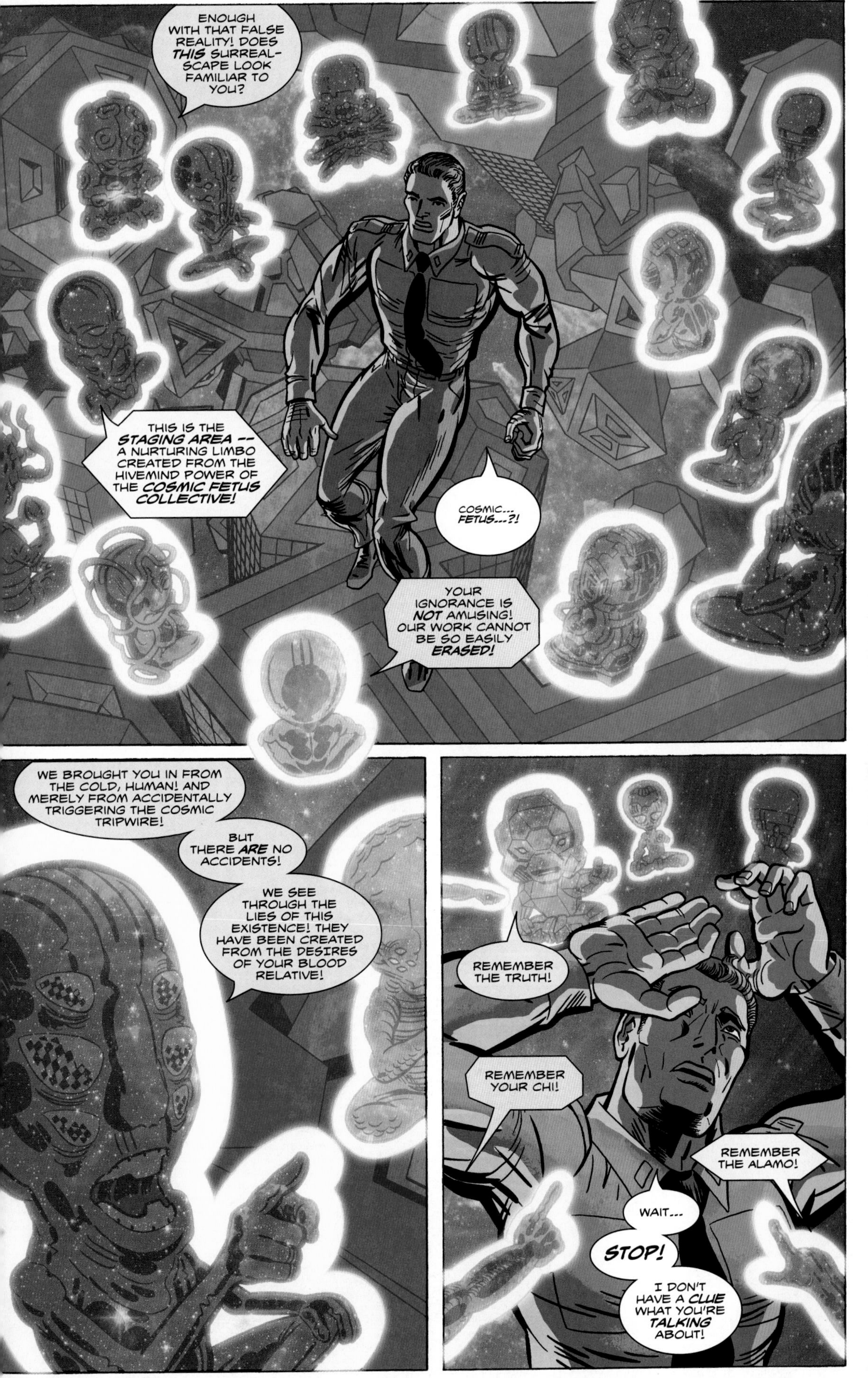
ENOUGH WITH THAT FALSE REALITY! DOES THIS SURREAL-SCAPE LOOK FAMILIAR TO YOU?
THIS IS THE STAGING AREA -- A NURTURING LIMBO CREATED FROM THE HIVEMIND POWER OF THE COSMIC FETUS COLLECTIVE!
COSMIC... FETUS...?!
YOUR IGNORANCE IS NOT AMUSING! OUR WORK CANNOT BE SO EASILY ERASED!
WE BROUGHT YOU IN FROM THE COLD, HUMAN! AND MERELY FROM ACCIDENTALLY TRIGGERING THE COSMIC TRIPWIRE!
BUT THERE ARE NO ACCIDENTS!
WE SEE THROUGH THE LIES OF THIS EXISTENCE! THEY HAVE BEEN CREATED FROM THE DESIRES OF YOUR BLOOD RELATIVE!
REMEMBER THE TRUTH!
REMEMBER YOUR CHI!
REMEMBER THE ALAMO!
WAIT...
STOP!
I DON'T HAVE A CLUE WHAT YOU'RE TALKING ABOUT!

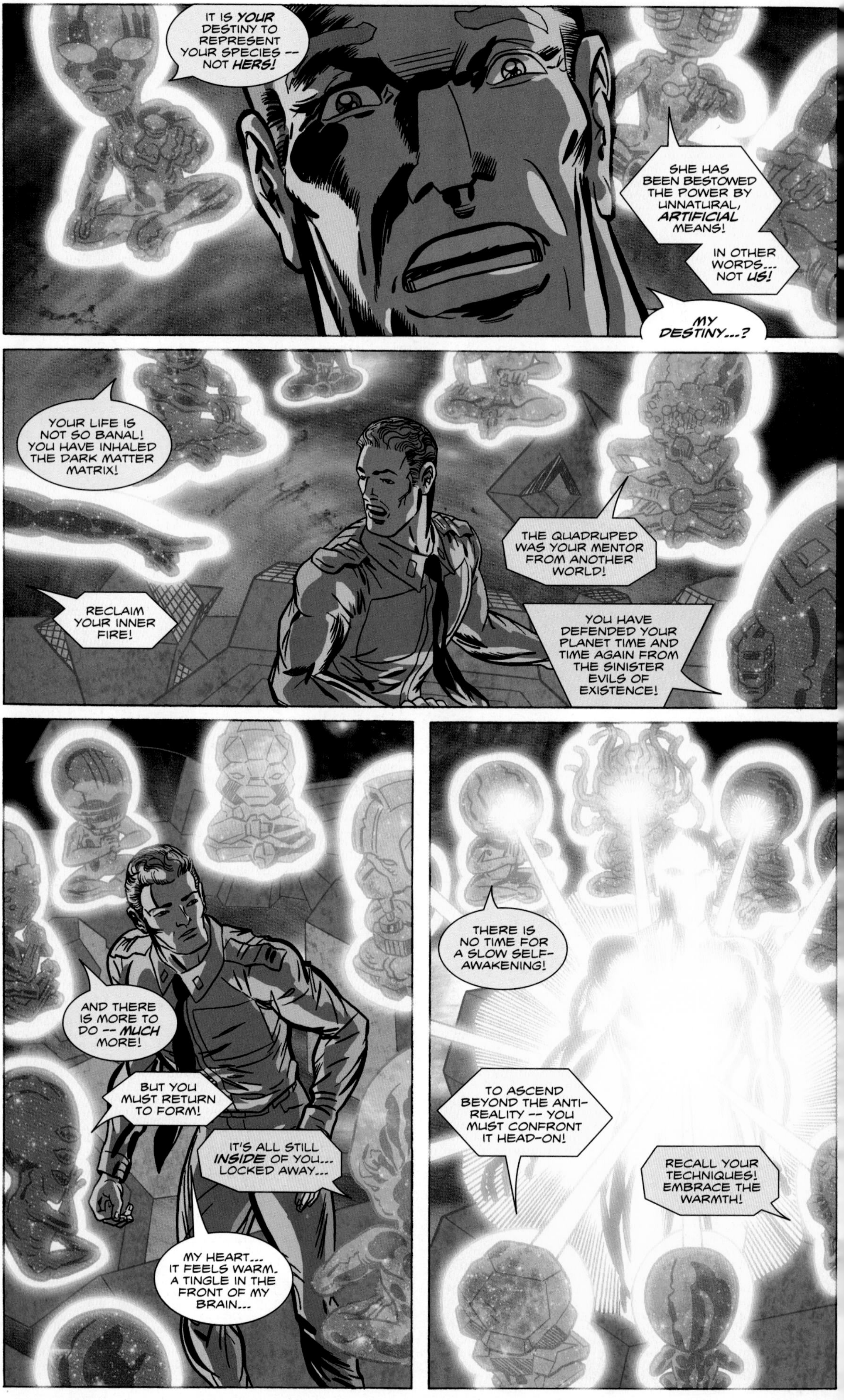
IT IS YOUR DESTINY TO REPRESENT YOUR SPECIES -- NOT HERS!
SHE HAS BEEN BESTOWED THE POWER BY UNNATURAL, ARTIFICIAL MEANS!
IN OTHER WORDS... NOT US!
MY DESTINY...?
YOUR LIFE IS NOT SO BANAL! YOU HAVE INHALED THE DARK MATTER MATRIX!
THE QUADRUPED WAS YOUR MENTOR FROM ANOTHER WORLD!
RECLAIM YOUR INNER FIRE!
YOU HAVE DEFENDED YOUR PLANET TIME AND TIME AGAIN FROM THE SINISTER EVILS OF EXISTENCE!
AND THERE IS MORE TO DO -- MUCH MORE!
BUT YOU MUST RETURN TO FORM!
IT'S ALL STILL INSIDE OF YOU... LOCKED AWAY...
MY HEART... IT FEELS WARM. A TINGLE IN THE FRONT OF MY BRAIN...
THERE IS NO TIME FOR A SLOW SELF-AWAKENING!
TO ASCEND BEYOND THE ANTI-REALITY -- YOU MUST CONFRONT IT HEAD-ON!
RECALL YOUR TECHNIQUES! EMBRACE THE WARMTH!

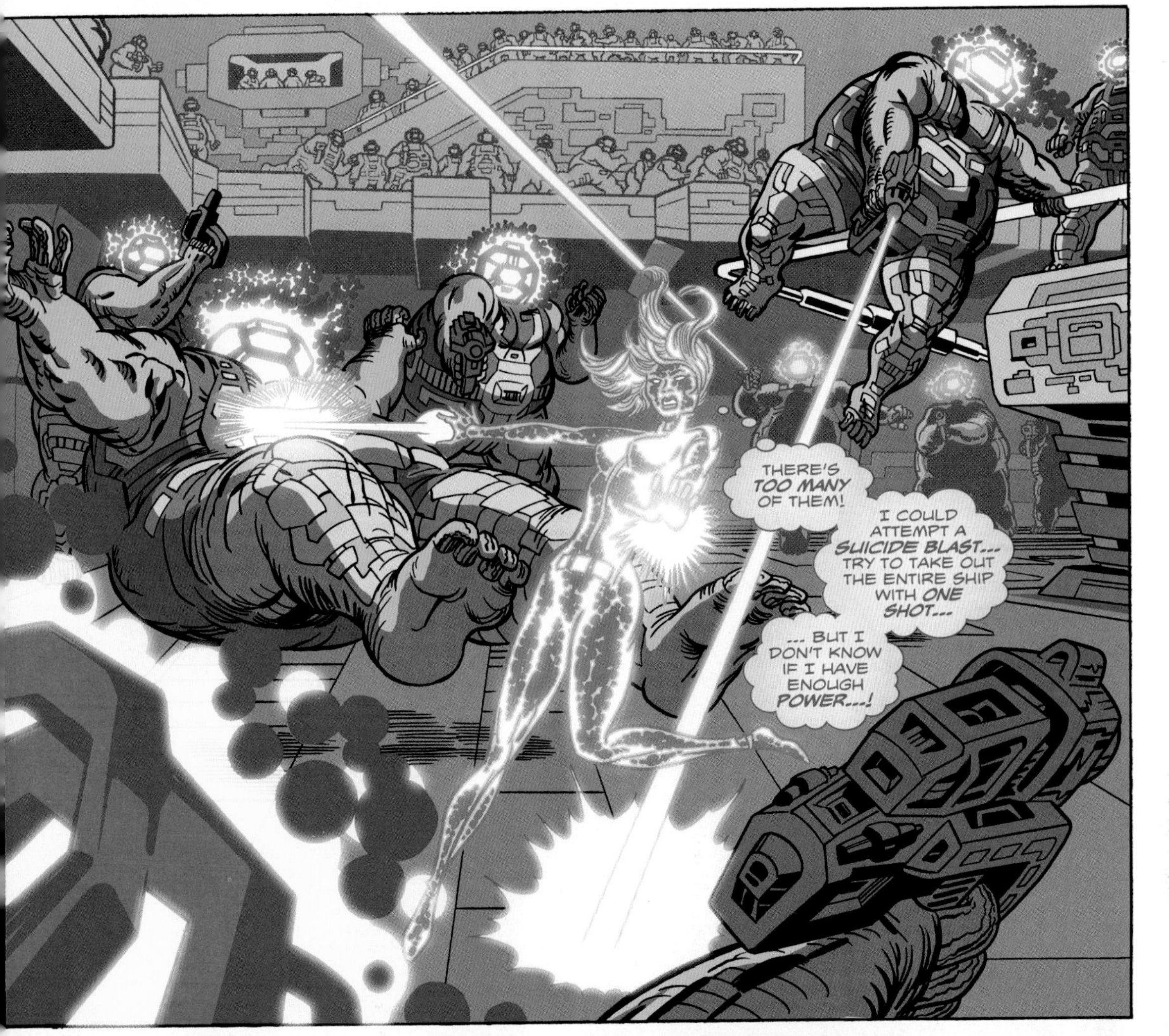
THERE'S TOO MANY OF THEM!
I COULD ATTEMPT A SUICIDE BLAST... TRY TO TAKE OUT THE ENTIRE SHIP WITH ONE SHOT...
... BUT I DON'T KNOW IF I HAVE ENOUGH POWER...!

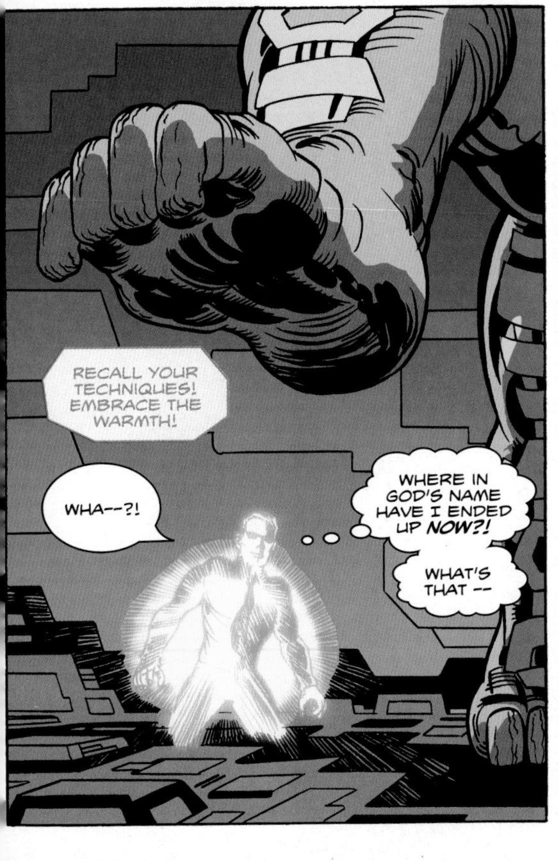
RECALL YOUR TECHNIQUES! EMBRACE THE WARMTH!
WHA--?!
WHERE IN GOD'S NAME HAVE I ENDED UP NOW?!
WHAT'S THAT --

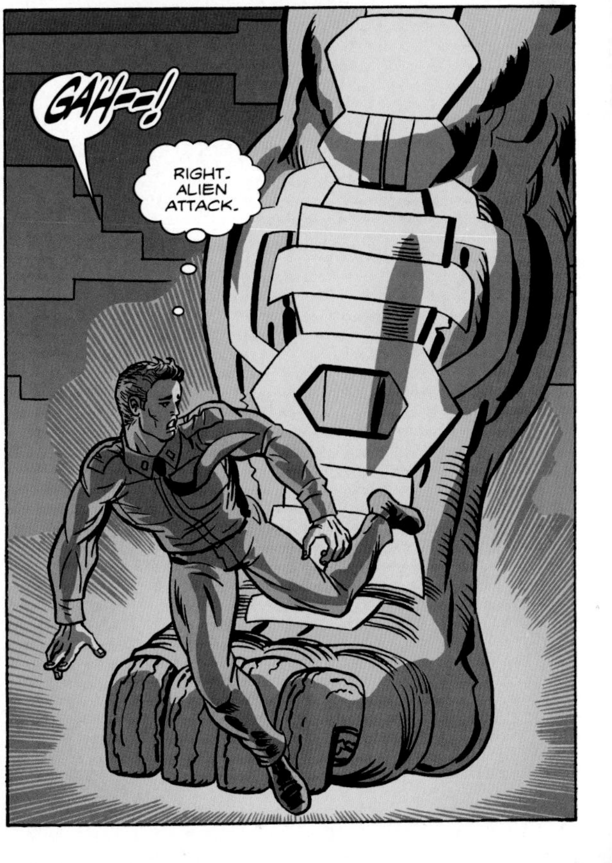
GAH--!
RIGHT. ALIEN ATTACK.

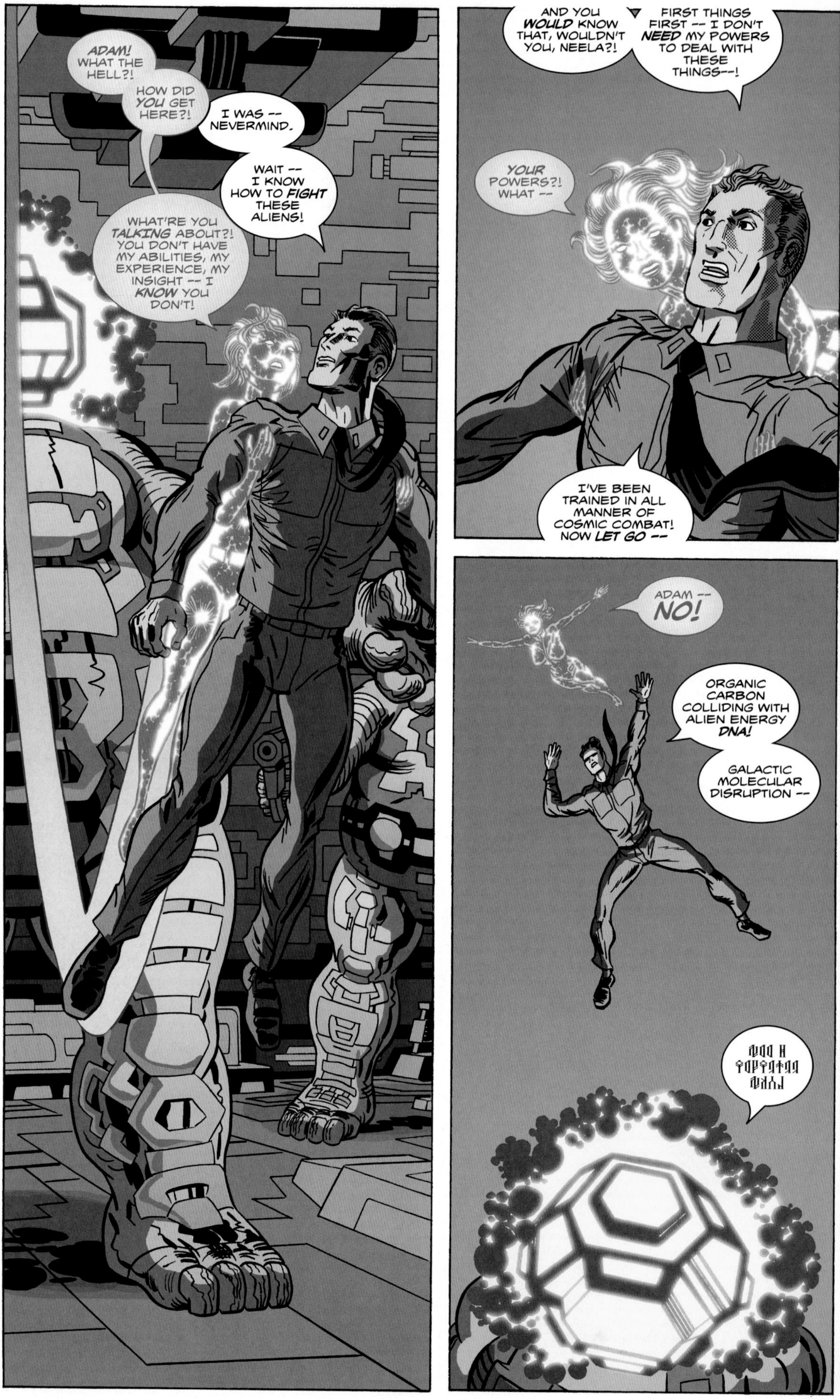
ADAM! WHAT THE HELL?!
HOW DID YOU GET HERE?!
I WAS -- NEVERMIND.
WAIT -- I KNOW HOW TO FIGHT THESE ALIENS!
WHAT'RE YOU TALKING ABOUT?! YOU DON'T HAVE MY ABILITIES, MY EXPERIENCE, MY INSIGHT -- I KNOW YOU DON'T!
AND YOU WOULD KNOW THAT, WOULDN'T YOU, NEELA?!
FIRST THINGS FIRST -- I DON'T NEED MY POWERS TO DEAL WITH THESE THINGS--!
YOUR POWERS?! WHAT --
I'VE BEEN TRAINED IN ALL MANNER OF COSMIC COMBAT! NOW LET GO --
ADAM -- NO!
ORGANIC CARBON COLLIDING WITH ALIEN ENERGY DNA!
GALACTIC MOLECULAR DISRUPTION --

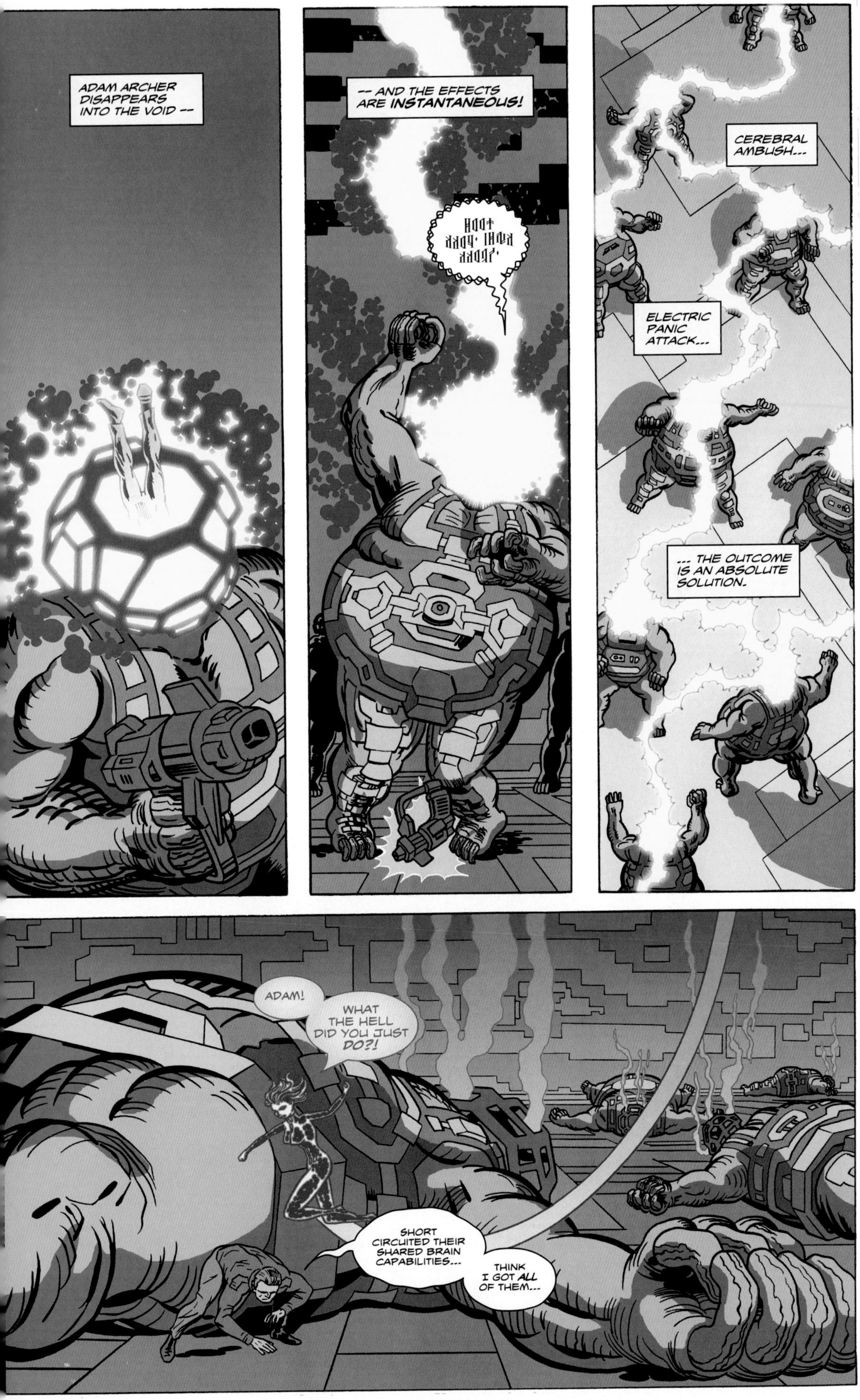
ADAM ARCHER DISAPPEARS INTO THE VOID --
-- AND THE EFFECTS ARE INSTANTANEOUS!
CEREBRAL AMBUSH...
ELECTRIC PANIC ATTACK...
... THE OUTCOME IS AN ABSOLUTE SOLUTION.
ADAM!
WHAT THE HELL DID YOU JUST DO?!
SHORT CIRCUITED THEIR SHARED BRAIN CAPABILITIES...
THINK I GOT ALL OF THEM...

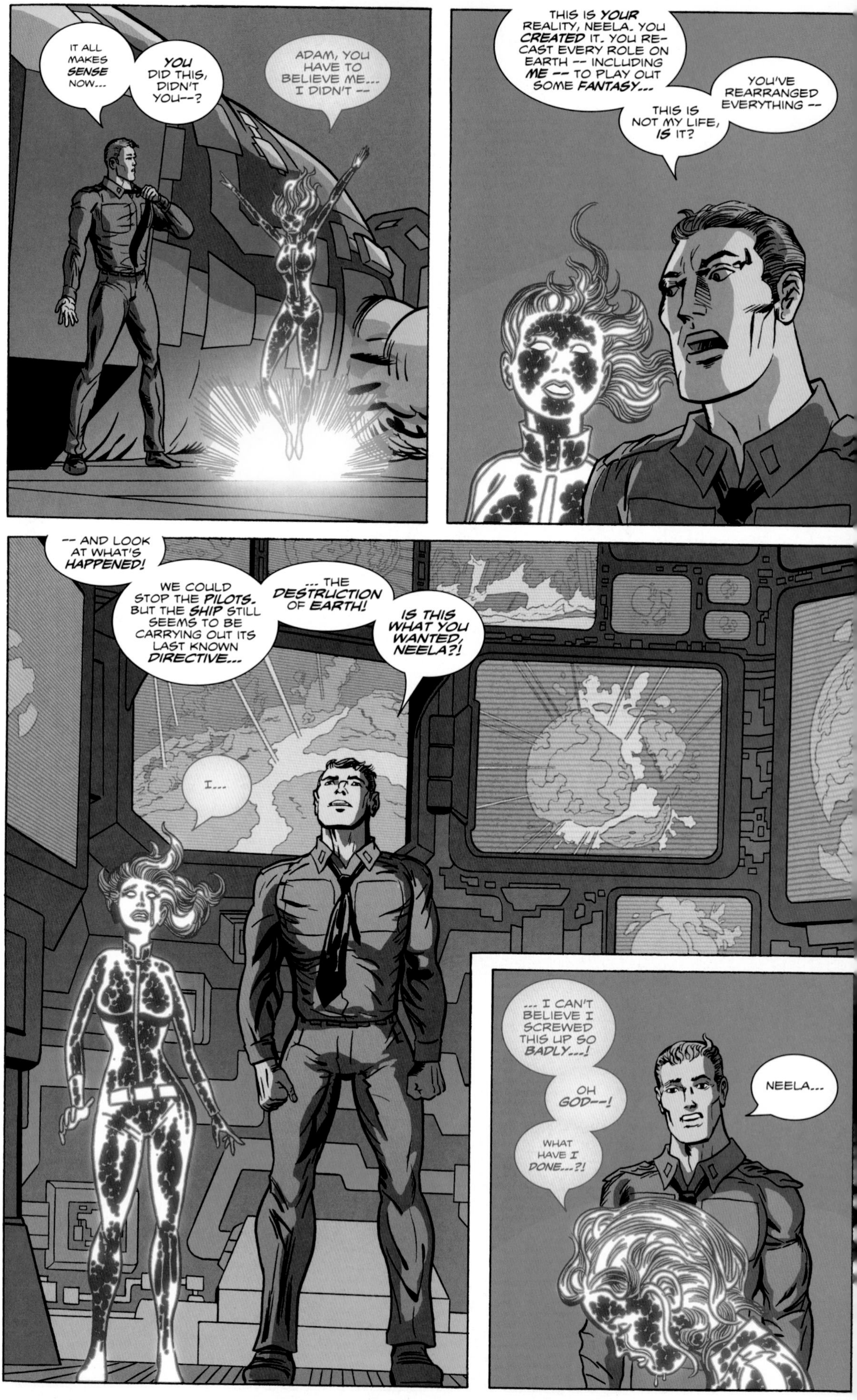
IT ALL MAKES SENSE NOW...
YOU DID THIS, DIDN'T YOU--?
ADAM, YOU HAVE TO BELIEVE ME... I DIDN'T --
THIS IS YOUR REALITY, NEELA. YOU CREATED IT. YOU RECAST EVERY ROLE ON EARTH -- INCLUDING ME -- TO PLAY OUT SOME FANTASY...
THIS IS NOT MY LIFE, IS IT?
YOU'VE REARRANGED EVERYTHING --
-- AND LOOK AT WHAT'S HAPPENED!
WE COULD STOP THE PILOTS. BUT THE SHIP STILL SEEMS TO BE CARRYING OUT ITS LAST KNOWN DIRECTIVE...
... THE DESTRUCTION OF EARTH!
IS THIS WHAT YOU WANTED, NEELA?!
I...
... I CAN'T BELIEVE I SCREWED THIS UP SO BADLY...!
OH GOD--!
WHAT HAVE I DONE...?!
NEELA...

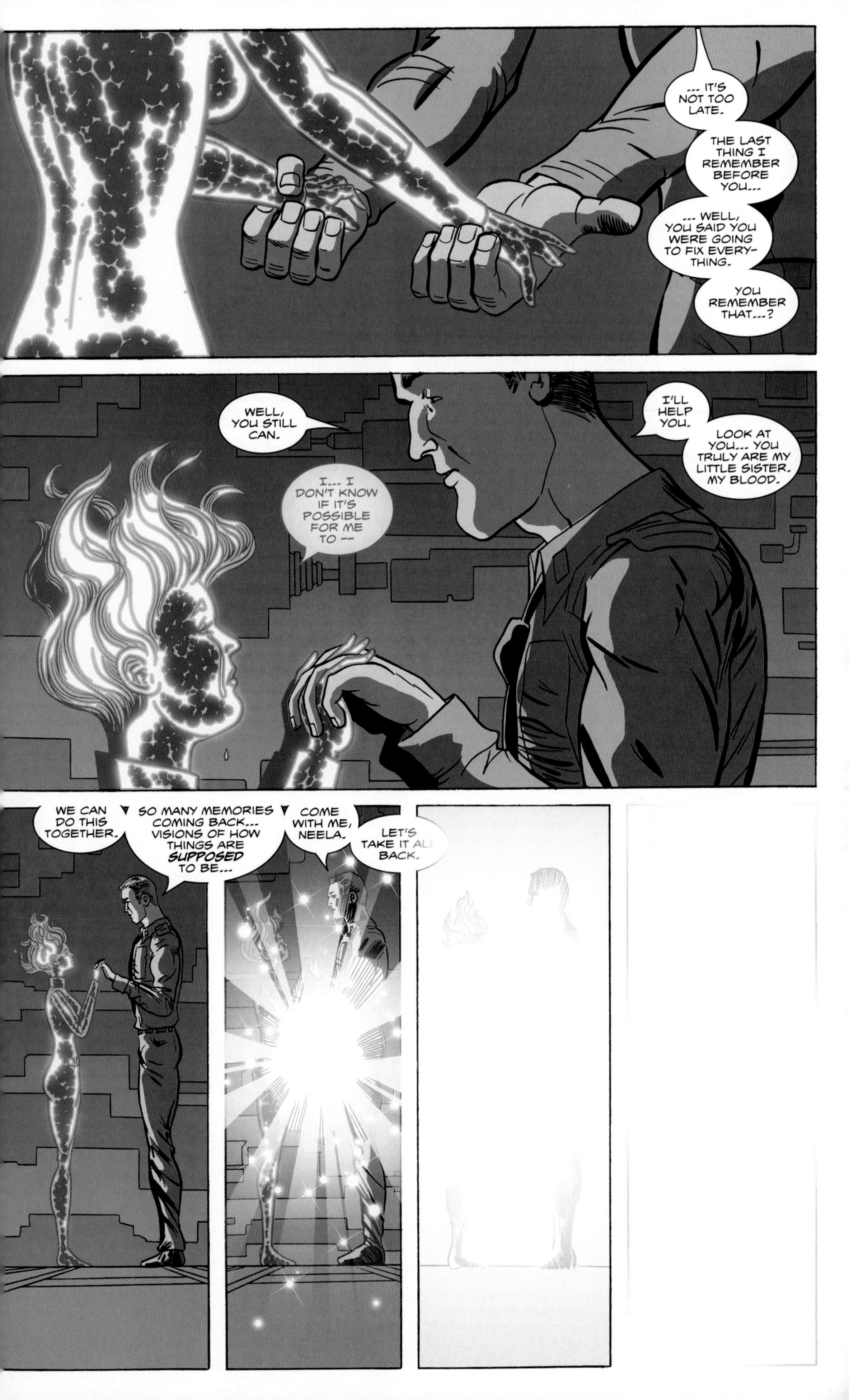
... IT'S NOT TOO LATE.
THE LAST THING I REMEMBER BEFORE YOU...
... WELL, YOU SAID YOU WERE GOING TO FIX EVERY-THING.
YOU REMEMBER THAT...?
WELL, YOU STILL CAN.
I... I DON'T KNOW IF IT'S POSSIBLE FOR ME TO --
I'LL HELP YOU.
LOOK AT YOU... YOU TRULY ARE MY LITTLE SISTER. MY BLOOD.
WE CAN DO THIS TOGETHER.
SO MANY MEMORIES COMING BACK... VISIONS OF HOW THINGS ARE SUPPOSED TO BE...
COME WITH ME, NEELA.
LET'S TAKE IT ALL BACK.

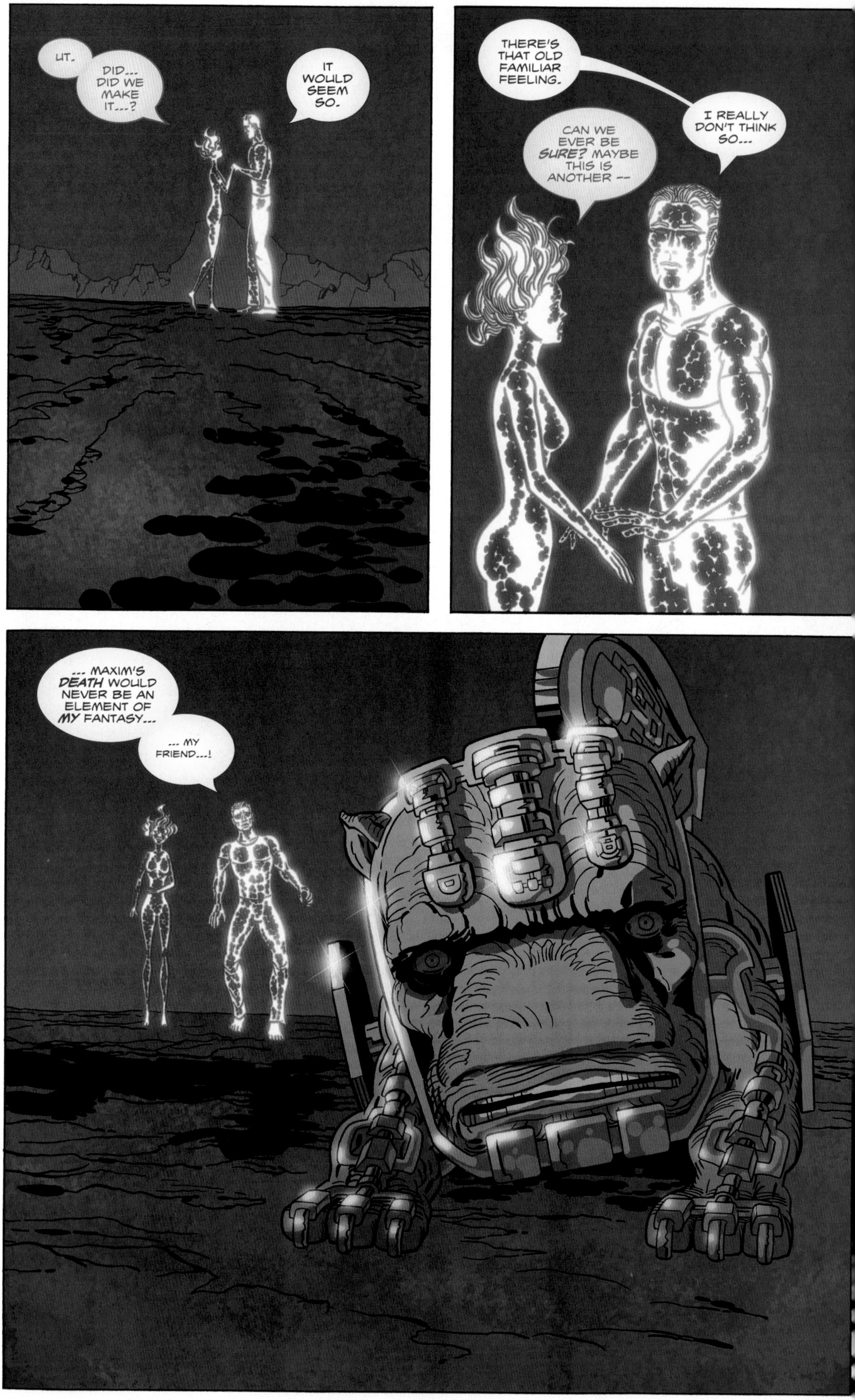
UT.
DID... DID WE MAKE IT...?
IT WOULD SEEM SO.
THERE'S THAT OLD FAMILIAR FEELING.
CAN WE EVER BE *SURE?* MAYBE THIS IS ANOTHER --
I REALLY DON'T THINK SO...
... MAXIM'S *DEATH* WOULD NEVER BE AN ELEMENT OF *MY* FANTASY...
... MY FRIEND...!

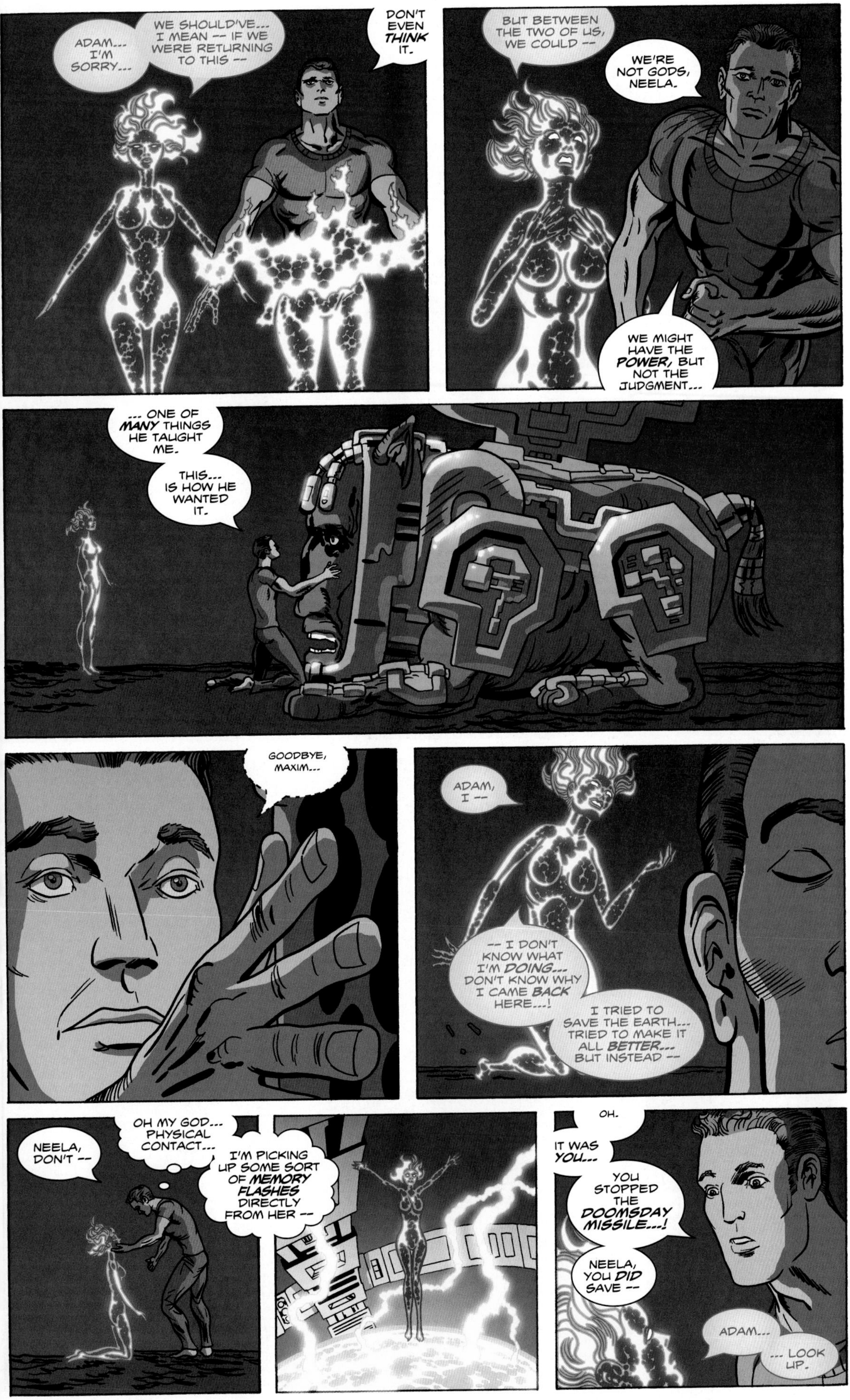
ADAM... I'M SORRY...
WE SHOULD'VE... I MEAN -- IF WE WERE RETURNING TO THIS --
DON'T EVEN THINK IT.
BUT BETWEEN THE TWO OF US, WE COULD --
WE'RE NOT GODS, NEELA.
WE MIGHT HAVE THE POWER, BUT NOT THE JUDGMENT...
... ONE OF MANY THINGS HE TAUGHT ME.
THIS... IS HOW HE WANTED IT.
GOODBYE, MAXIM...
ADAM, I --
-- I DON'T KNOW WHAT I'M DOING... DON'T KNOW WHY I CAME BACK HERE...!
I TRIED TO SAVE THE EARTH... TRIED TO MAKE IT ALL BETTER... BUT INSTEAD --
NEELA, DON'T --
OH MY GOD... PHYSICAL CONTACT...
I'M PICKING UP SOME SORT OF MEMORY FLASHES DIRECTLY FROM HER --
OH.
IT WAS YOU...
YOU STOPPED THE DOOMSDAY MISSILE...!
NEELA, YOU DID SAVE --
ADAM...
... LOOK UP.

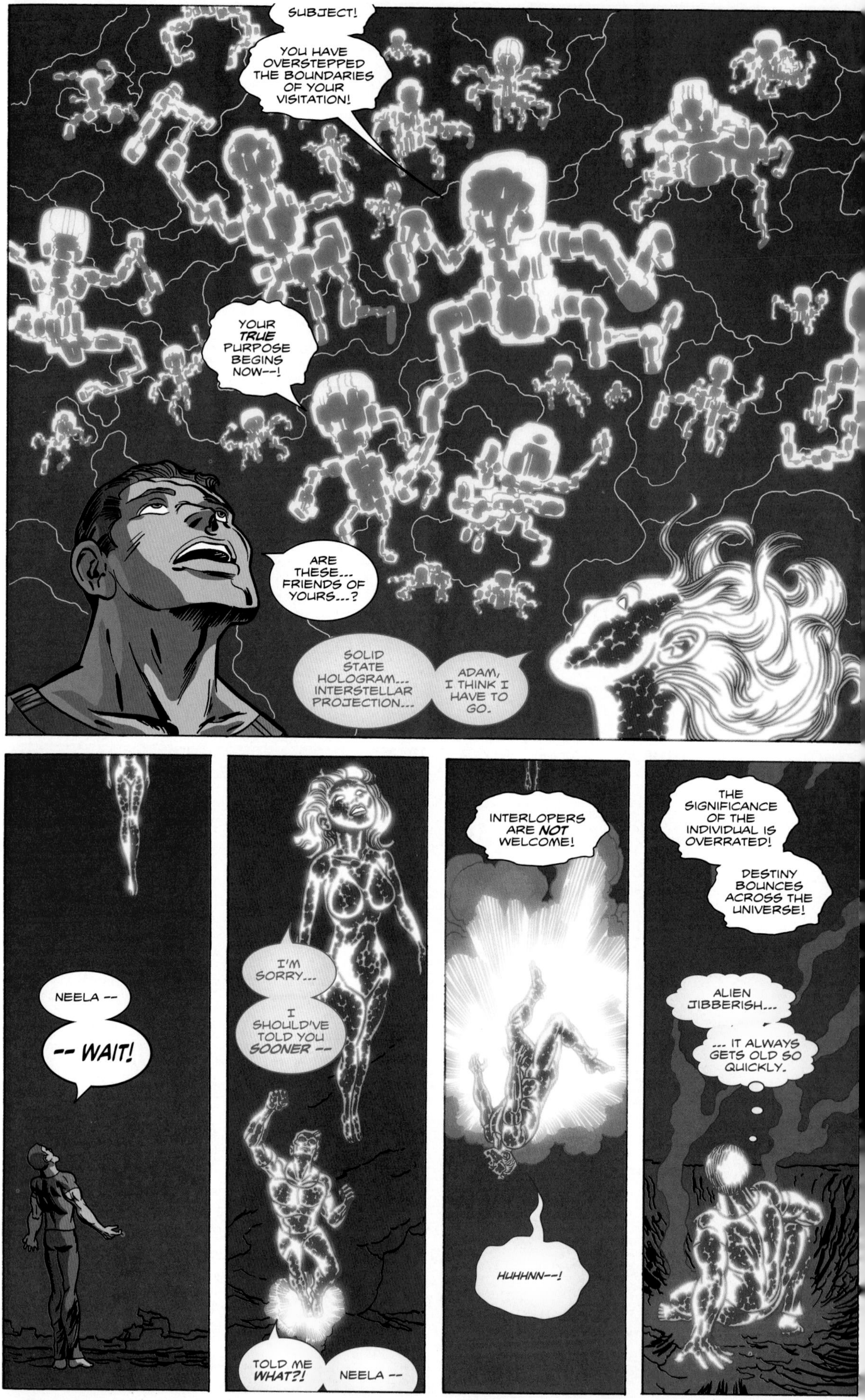
SUBJECT!
YOU HAVE OVERSTEPPED THE BOUNDARIES OF YOUR VISITATION!
YOUR TRUE PURPOSE BEGINS NOW--!
ARE THESE... FRIENDS OF YOURS...?
SOLID STATE HOLOGRAM... INTERSTELLAR PROJECTION...
ADAM, I THINK I HAVE TO GO.
NEELA --
-- WAIT!
I'M SORRY...
I SHOULD'VE TOLD YOU SOONER --
TOLD ME WHAT?!
NEELA --
INTERLOPERS ARE NOT WELCOME!
HUHHNN--!
THE SIGNIFICANCE OF THE INDIVIDUAL IS OVERRATED!
DESTINY BOUNCES ACROSS THE UNIVERSE!
ALIEN JIBBERISH...
... IT ALWAYS GETS OLD SO QUICKLY.

NOW AND FOREVER MORE... THIS ONE IS OURS.

IBOGA IS A LIE. *THIS* IS THE REAL TRUTH.

ADAM.

TELL MY *SISTERS*...

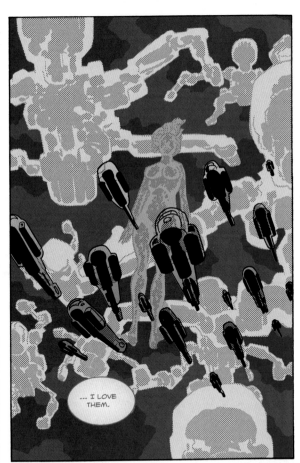

... I LOVE THEM.

BY FEDERAL AUTHORITY -- ALL GROUND COMBATANTS ARE ORDERED TO STAND DOWN!

REPEAT: BY FEDERAL AUTHORITY...

PERFECT TIMING, AS ALWAYS...

... THEY HONESTLY THINK I STILL RECOGNIZE THEIR *"AUTHORITY"*?

IF THAT'S WHAT THEY WANT TO BELIEVE...

... BUT I *KNOW* WHAT I HAVE TO DO NOW.

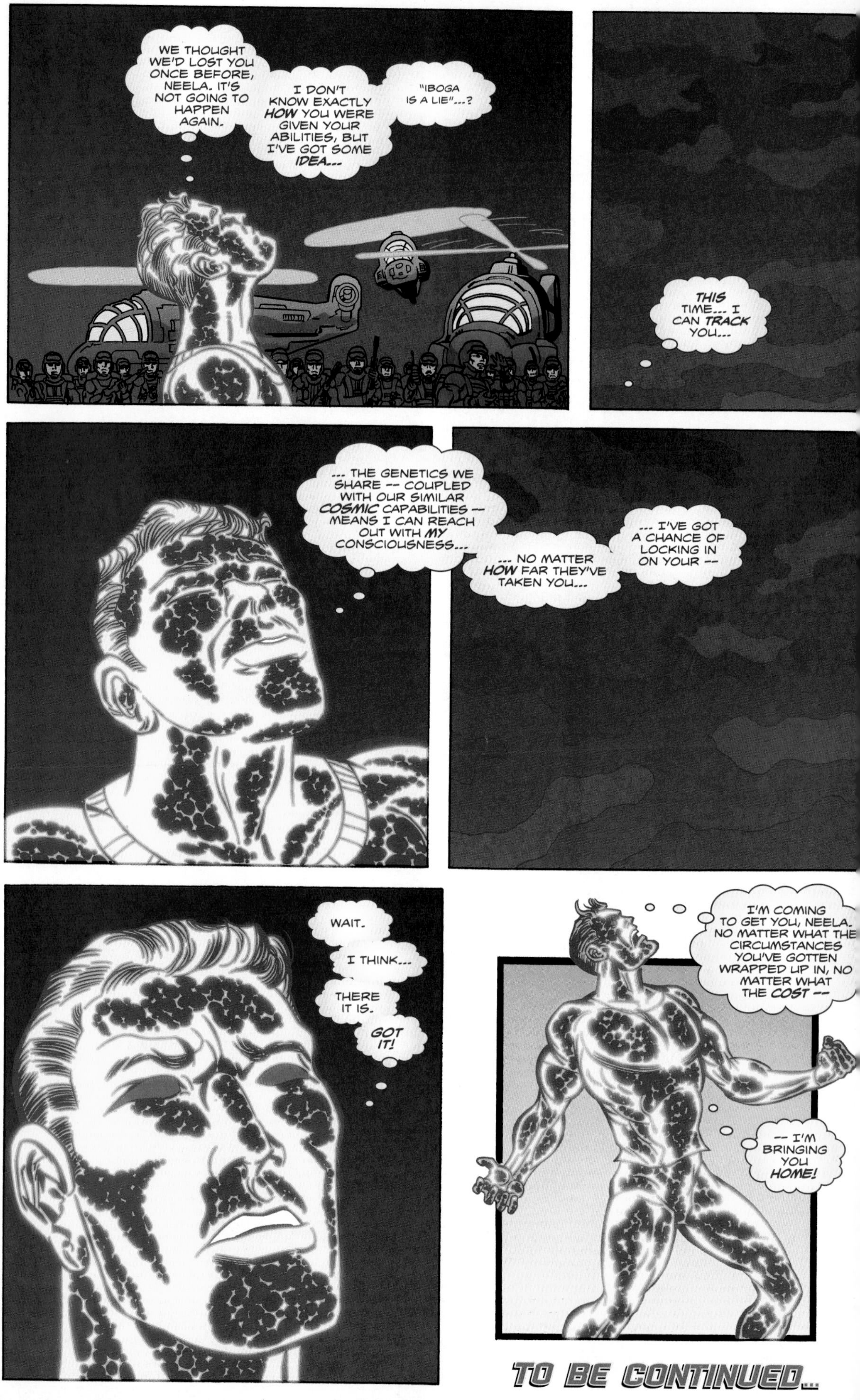
WE THOUGHT WE'D LOST YOU ONCE BEFORE, NEELA. IT'S NOT GOING TO HAPPEN AGAIN.
I DON'T KNOW EXACTLY HOW YOU WERE GIVEN YOUR ABILITIES, BUT I'VE GOT SOME IDEA...
"IBOGA IS A LIE"...?
THIS TIME... I CAN TRACK YOU...
... THE GENETICS WE SHARE -- COUPLED WITH OUR SIMILAR COSMIC CAPABILITIES -- MEANS I CAN REACH OUT WITH MY CONSCIOUSNESS...
... NO MATTER HOW FAR THEY'VE TAKEN YOU...
... I'VE GOT A CHANCE OF LOCKING IN ON YOUR --
WAIT.
I THINK...
THERE IT IS.
GOT IT!
I'M COMING TO GET YOU, NEELA. NO MATTER WHAT THE CIRCUMSTANCES YOU'VE GOTTEN WRAPPED UP IN, NO MATTER WHAT THE COST --
-- I'M BRINGING YOU HOME!
TO BE CONTINUED...

TOM SCIOLI (ARTIST/CO-CREATOR) GREW UP ON THE MEAN STREETS OF PHILADELPHIA. HE WENT TO COLLEGE TO STUDY ENGINEERING, BUT SWITCHED TO A SAFER BET BY PURSUING A CAREER IN ART. HE CURRENTLY LIVES IN PITTSBURGH WITH HIS WIFE, ERIN.

JOE CASEY (WRITER/CO-CREATOR) ESCAPED A CHILDHOOD FILLED WITH NOTHING BUT COMICBOOKS, MOVIES AND ROCK 'N' ROLL... ONLY TO CRASH HEADLONG INTO AN ADULTHOOD FILLED WITH NOTHING BUT COMICBOOKS, MOVIES AND ROCK 'N' ROLL. FINDING A WAY TO GET PAID FOR HIS INTERESTS IN ALL OF THESE WAS HIS GREATEST PERSONAL ACHIEVEMENT. HE LIVES, WORKS, WRITES, ROCKS OUT AND TAKES CARE OF HIS FAMILY IN HOLLYWOOD, CALIFORNIA.

NICK FILARDI (COLORIST) GREW UP IN NEW LONDON, CONNECTICUT WATCHING BATMAN THE ANIMATED SERIES, READING *SCUD: THE DISPOSABLE ASSASSIN*, AND HIDING IN THE EL 'N' GEE CLUB LISTENING TO SMALL TOWN HERO. AFTER GRADUATING FROM SAVANNAH COLLEGE OF ART AND DESIGN IN 2004, HE COLORED FOR ZYLONOL STUDIOS UNDER LEE LOUGHRIDGE IN SAVANNAH, GA. CURRENTLY LIVING IN PHILADELPHIA WITH HIS THREE-LEGGED DOG, DENIRO, HE ALSO COLORS *POWERS*, *PIRATES OF CONEY ISLAND*, AND *THE CROSS BRONX*.

RUS WOOTON (LETTERER) HAS BEEN A LETTERER SINCE 2003, CURRENTLY HUNKERED DOWN IN SOUTH FLORIDA. HE SPENDS MOST OF HIS TIME SITTING AT HIS MAC LETTERING FOR THE LIKES OF JOE CASEY... AS WELL AS FOR IMAGE, MARVEL AND DARK HORSE. DRAWING AND WRITING KEEP HIM SANE WHILE DR. PEPPER, ITUNES AND NETFLIX ARE LARGELY RESPONSIBLE FOR KEEPING HIM IN A STATE OF SEMI-CONSCIOUSNESS. HE'S AVAILABLE FOR PAID ENDORSEMENT OF THE AFOREMENTIONED PRODUCTS AND/OR SERVICE.

THE DEFINITIVE HARDCOVER

written by
JOE CASEY

art by
CHARLIE ADLARD

A cult hit is back, the way it was always meant to be seen, from co-creators Joe Casey (GØDLAND) and Charlie Adlard (THE WALKING DEAD). Cameron Daltrey is an L.A. bail bondsman. His specialty is criminals of the superhuman persuasion. They're the type that rarely make their court dates. And so Cameron leads an interesting double life: bail bondsman by day, masked bounty hunter by night.

Packed with extra features, INCLUDING AN ALL-NEW CODEFLESH STORY BY CASEY AND ADLARD—THE FIRST IN SEVEN YEARS!

FULL-COLOR • 128 PAGES • $34.99

FEBRUARY 2009

BACK AT IMAGE IN A FINAL, ALL-NEW, FULL-COLOR COLLECTION!

RE-EXPERIENCE THE CLASSIC CRIME NOIR COMIC FOR THE VERY FIRST TIME!

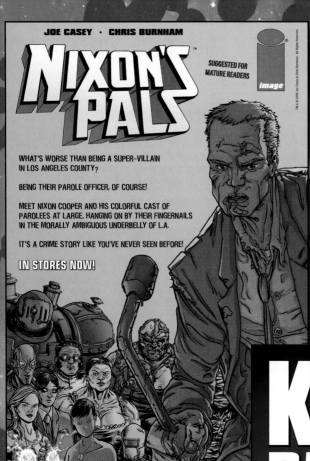
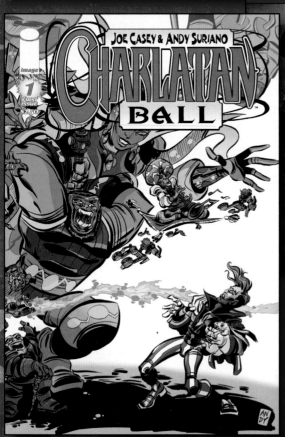